A Field in Flux

A Field in Flux

Sixty Years of Industrial Relations

Robert B. McKersie

Foreword by Thomas A. Kochan

Published in association with
Cornell University Press
Ithaca and London

First published 2019 by Cornell University Press

Library of Congress Cataloging-in-Publication Data

Names: McKersie, Robert B., author.
Title: A field in flux : sixty years of industrial relations / Robert B.
    McKersie.
Description: Ithaca : Cornell Publishing in association with Cornell
    University Press, 2019. | Includes bibliographical references.
Identifiers: LCCN 2018060443 (print) | LCCN 2019001429 (ebook) |
    ISBN 9781501740022 (pdf) | ISBN 9781501740039 (ret) |
    ISBN 9781501740015 (cloth)
Subjects: LCSH: Industrial relations—Study and teaching (Higher)—
    United States. | McKersie, Robert B. | Industrial sociologists—United
    States—Biography.
Classification: LCC HD6960.5.U5 (ebook) | LCC HD6960.5.U5 M45 2019
    (print) | DDC 331.092 [B]—dc23
LC record available at https://lccn.loc.gov/2018060443

My wife and four children have been with me on this journey,
and I dedicate this book to them

Journeying is an art. . . . If we stop, we don't go forward and we also miss the goal.

—Pope Francis

Contents

FOREWORD

The history and evolution of a field of inquiry can be written by reviewing key historical events or by highlighting the people who shaped those events. This book combines these two methods to produce a creative, engaging, and insightful commentary on the last sixty years of industrial relations. In fact, it goes even further, because the author is himself one of those people who has shaped the field, and because he is at the center of so much of the field of inquiry the history is also a personal journey.

A Field in Flux serves two important functions: it demonstrates how people have influenced past employment policies and practices when called to action in critical situations, and it seeks to instill confidence in those who will be called on to address the big challenges facing the future of work now and in the years to come.

We live in a very troubled time, one in which so many of the basic values and principles of industrial relations are being challenged and, in some cases, downright violated. The moral of the story covered in this book is that as we adapt to a changing world of work we must not forget about the value we place on efficiency, equity, and inclusive employment policies and practices. Norms that come through loud and clear in this book are worth carrying forward: showing respect for all who work, championing the cause for voice and worker representation in a democratic society, and engaging professionals both to learn from their experiences and to foster innovations. Nothing could be more energizing to those who will take this field of study and practice into the future.

This book could be written only by one remarkable individual, Robert B. McKersie. Bob chronicles the unique and personal journey through his career and, in doing so, provides a window into the life and work of one of the most important industrial relations scholars and leaders of our time—if not *the* most important. I've been privileged to work with Bob for a good part of his sixty-year career, and I am pleased to offer a few words about how he has helped shape the events discussed in this book and our field of study.

In a piece commenting on Bob's lifetime achievement award from the International Conflict Management Association, Joel Cutcher-Gershenfeld and I described Bob as "an integrative scholar." It was an obvious play on one of the central concepts in his 1965 book with Richard Walton, *A Behavioral Theory of Labor Negotiations*, about which you will learn more in the pages that follow. But it was also a statement about McKersie the friend, mentor, and colleague to the legions of people he has influenced over his career. As we wrote, "'Say hello to Bob McKersie for me.' How many times have either of us heard someone at a professional meeting ask us to say this to Bob next time we see him? It is more than a perfunctory request. Bob's warmth and friendship and his impact on those he has interacted with over the last sixty years far surpasses the surface memories people have of each other, many of which fade over time. Not with Bob."

The McKersie most people know is one who always reads what students and colleagues send his way. No one ever comes back empty-handed. His suggestions are always preceded by encouraging comments. He takes a genuine interest in what those around him are doing and presses them to dig a bit deeper, to go back into the field to learn more about how things actually work. When the work is completed, he celebrates and promotes the author.

Bob has probably opened more doors to useful contacts for students and young scholars than anyone else in our profession. He did just that for me when I was an entry-level faculty member at Cornell University. I remember when he took me by the arm at a reception at a professional meeting. "You have to meet my friend Jack Sheinkman," he said. "He will be interested in what you are doing." It was the beginning of a lifelong friendship and partnership in several key efforts with Jack, who was president of the Amalgamated Clothing and Textile Workers Union. Just about everyone Bob knows has one or more stories like mine.

There is a side of Bob that only those who have seen him up close in action can fully appreciate. He is one of the most persistent advocates for fairness I've ever met. He can't let an injustice go unaddressed. You will read in chapter 3 about his work on civil rights in Chicago during the 1960s and get a flavor of that part of his personality. How many junior faculty members today would have the gumption to get involved in what was then the most profound social movement of the day at such a level of intensity that the Reverend Jesse Jackson was compelled to do a video on Bob's work fifty years later? (For his remarks, see Jesse Jackson, "Making Sense of the Senseless: Fifty Years after Selma and *A Behavioral Theory of Labor Negotiations*," *Negotiation Journal* 51, no. 4 (2015): 459–60, https://onlinelibrary.wiley.com/doi /full/10.1111/nejo.12128.)

Another side of Bob is his modesty. Several of us who read early drafts of this book had to push him to overcome his reluctance to give himself credit for his own contributions to our field. The best example comes from our first reading of chapter 3, about his time at the University of Chicago. The early draft detailed the accomplishments of giants such as George Shultz and others, for page after page, followed by a single paragraph that essentially said (I'm paraphrasing), "Oh, by the way, Dick Walton and I wrote a book during those years."

Well, that book—*The Behavioral Theory of Labor Negotiations*—became a fifty-year classic. Several of us who read that draft of this volume's chapter 3 had to insist that Bob expand on what was written to discuss the important role the book played and continues to play in the study, teaching, and practice of negotiations. And we went further, constituting a kind of "kitchen cabinet" to make sure Bob didn't get away with any more omissions of that sort.

Here, in their own brief words, are why these colleagues were eager to do so. Fred K. Foulkes, professor of organizational behavior and director of the Human Resource Policy Institute at Boston University, comments, "Bob excels in giving back. His great questions and wise perspectives always make a difference, whether it is with respect to a labor-management matter or a personal career issue." David B. Lipsky, Anne Evans Estabrook Professor of Dispute Resolution at Cornell University's ILR School, notes that "Bob's illustrious career coincides with many of the most significant changes that have occurred in the field of industrial relations. While his characteristic humility keeps him from taking credit, he exercised leadership through many of these changes—and also transformed the ILR School at Cornell, as dean, into one of the nation's foremost research centers on labor and employment relations." Mary Rowe, an adjunct professor in work and organization studies at the MIT Sloan School of Management comments, "The precepts of negotiation theory that Bob helped develop are simple, elegant, and of extraordinary power in helping to understand all interactions of two or more points of view. They are taught around the world and are on track to endure, quite possibly, forever. I use them as an ombudsperson, as a family member, in consulting, in seeking to understand world events—and even, wryly, in negotiating with myself when I have two or more points of view about something." And Joel Cutcher-Gershenfeld, a professor at the Heller School for Social Policy and Management at Brandeis University notes that "Bob McKersie's career has not only tracked but also shaped the evolution of industrial relations. He has helped me appreciate, among other things, the centrality of the internal bargaining needed for lateral alignment, the integrative potential in what others may view as intransient conflicts, and the importance of tackling big issues."

Let me end with a little vignette that encapsulates pretty much all you need to know about McKersie before you join him on his journey through time in our field.

On a Friday evening in 1988, at about 6:00 p.m., Bob and I were returning from a conference we had attended together. We were both living in the Boston suburb of Arlington and had driven to Logan Airport together in Bob's 1964 Chevy Nova, which he had inherited from an uncle who could no longer drive. I can best describe the car as a small tank largely held together in various places by bits of duct tape.

When we got in the car at Logan to head home, Bob said in his own cautionary voice, "This vehicle hasn't been running well lately, but it should be okay." True to his warning, it started hard, but with Bob's expert coaxing it got going, and off we went.

Traffic was very heavy coming out of the airport during that Friday rush hour, so Bob proceeded to get on what was then a narrow but heavily jammed Route 1A to get to one of the "shortcuts" he likes to find around Boston. No sooner did we get out in the middle of the road than the old Nova stalled—and, despite Bob's best efforts, would not start again. Meanwhile, the traffic was quickly piling up, unable to get around us. What to do?

I noticed a couple of young fellows, two vehicles behind us, in an old pickup truck, and the driver was blowing his horn in obvious agitation over the gridlock. Bob and I had a thought. Since we were only about two hundred feet from an exit, perhaps they could push us down the off-ramp and we could coast to some safe spot so the traffic could move on.

I got out of the Nova, went to the pickup, and described the dilemma. "If you guys would push the car to the exit," I said, "we can probably coast down and you and everyone else can move on."

Their initial response was "no way."

I thought about what Bob would have said next, appealing to our common interests: "We're all stuck here until the Nova can be moved." That didn't work. So then I appealed to another interest they might have. "Look," I said. "I'll pay you something for doing this. How about ten dollars?"

They looked at each other, and one responded, "Fifty."

"No way," I said. "That's too much. Look, it's only about two hundred feet, and you'll be on your way." Then I took a risk and made a "final" counteroffer, pulling out a twenty-dollar bill from my wallet and handing it to them. "This is what I have."

"Okay," they said, "we'll do it."

And they did! We managed to maneuver their truck behind the car and they pushed Bob's small tank of a vehicle to the ramp with enough momentum that it could coast down the exit. And off they went. This was what Bob describes in chapter 5 as "integrative bargaining"—a win-win solution. They got out of a traffic jam and made twenty dollars in the process, and we got off the highway.

In true McKersie fashion, though, the best part of the story was yet to come. As we coasted down the ramp, Bob spied a parking lot where we could safely get off the road. He pulled in and noticed some fellows gathered around a trash barrel fire for warmth. They were wearing picket signs.

Bob instantly recognized them as Teamsters from Local 25 and said that he knew George Cashman, the local president. So he went over to them and asked what they were striking about. It was some sort of grievance with management of the terminal across the street.

Bob struck up a conversation about his work with Cashman and they all began to bond. Then he told them that his car wasn't working and that he might have to leave it in the lot overnight until he could get it towed. No problem, they said. They were going to be there and promised to take care of it, which they did.

Over the years, I've watched and admired the various ways in which Bob McKersie's personal values and lifestyle—including his well-known frugality when it comes to family vehicles—have interacted and intersected with his professional skills and experiences. I learned to apply the lessons he taught us all in negotiations, and then I watched the master at work, building trusting relationships that would pay dividends down the road—like the willingness of a group of workers, strangers only a few minutes earlier, to guard his vehicle that night in East Boston because of his prior work with their union leader.

This tells you a bit about the man and about the field he has studied, practiced, and led for longer than just about any other scholar in our field. His sixty-year journey, recounted in this book, is full of stories that introduce you to people he worked with and the impact they had on the evolving field of industrial relations. Enjoy.

Thomas A. Kochan
Cambridge, Massachusetts
July 31, 2018

ACKNOWLEDGMENTS

As Pope Francis has observed, keep going and good things will happen. That certainly has been my experience. This entire book has been an acknowledgment for the counseling and collegiality that has come my way from many, many students and faculty who I have encountered in my journey over the past six decades. So, in one sense, I could stop here and urge you to read the chapters to identify the individuals who have shared their wisdom and passion for understanding the complexities inherent in industrial relations.

Beyond my academic associates, I owe much to the practitioners who have been willing to go the extra mile in helping me understand the ever-evolving territory of our field. Industrial relations has to be studied where it takes place, and I thank the many workers and labor and corporate leaders who have opened their doors for me.

There is one set of individuals who need a special shout-out: the members of the "kitchen cabinet" Tom Kochan assembled to urge me to get going on this project, and who along the way have provided invaluable feedback and augmentation of the stories that needed to be told. The following colleagues have provided this counsel: Joel Cutcher-Gershenfeld of Brandeis

University; Fred Foulkes of Boston University; Dave Lipsky of the ILR School at Cornell University; and Mary Rowe of MIT.

Academics like to think their prose is precise and elegant and needs no editing. If I ever held that view, this project has demonstrated the value and importance of a good editor. Scott Cooper has been outstanding in so many ways, making sense when the text was obscure and sharing his insights about many subjects (he is a student of labor history). Most important, he's been fun to have on the other end of the phone line.

While most of us old-timers try to use modern-day word processing, Cherie Potts has provided a big assist. And Jackie Martelli has been invaluable in helping gather photos (and the permission to use them) for the center section, thus bringing life to many of the individuals who appear in this chronicle.

I have dedicated this book to my wife Nancy and to our children William, Elizabeth, Robert, and Alison, who have been with me on this journey in so many important ways. Their support has given me the time and space to pursue a career focused on identifying the lessons that this amazing field of industrial relations has to offer.

A Field in Flux

Chapter 1

An Industrial Relations Journey

I spent the fall semester of the 1979–80 academic year at the Sloan School of Management at the Massachusetts Institute of Technology (MIT). At the time, I was on leave from the ILR School at Cornell University. I was already scheduled to spend the following spring on sabbatical in England. My time at Sloan was aimed at determining whether there was a potential fit between its courses in industrial relations and my interests. I was considering a move.

The following fall, in 1980, I joined Sloan's industrial relations group, as did Thomas Kochan—my colleague from Cornell whom I had brought to the ILR School and with whom I had worked closely on research projects. Little did I know that the first decade at MIT would be one of tectonic shifts in labor relations in both the public and private sectors, as well as in the academic field of industrial relations. And I could not have foreseen that the transformation that was happening would prompt a multiyear faculty and student collaborative effort to understand what was unfolding before our eyes.

That work required taking a new look in new ways at a field that had long been doing the same things in the same ways. The success of what we called the transformation project can be traced in part to a combination of factors: our own fresh start, the fresh eyes of collaborating faculty colleagues and tremendously talented graduate students, and the MIT culture, characterized by a problem-solving focus coupled with innovative ways of addressing those problems. The result was to breathe new life into our field, which had become somewhat staid. And while the ILR School continued to flourish at Cornell, a succession of large-scale research projects involving collaborative teams of MIT faculty and doctoral students leveraged the MIT culture in ways that introduced new areas of research and transformed our understanding of the field.

This book tells the story of industrial relations from my personal perspective over more than sixty years, a period during which I have been fortunate to observe the field as a student, a newly appointed professor, a dean, and a senior faculty member. In these chapters, I explore the evolution of industrial relations, drawing on my personal journey and recounting interactions with a large number of the field's leading figures from my graduate school days at Harvard University to my current emeritus faculty role at MIT, with stops along the way at the University of Chicago and Cornell. I also draw on my encounters with business and union leaders as I did fieldwork and when these leaders came to campus. And I introduce and discuss some of the major events and dramatic changes to the field over six decades.

I can think of no better way to chronicle this story than through what I have learned from and admired in the people who are part of my story while at the same time observing events as they unfolded. What we can learn from my own history in this field of study, and what can help guide industrial relations into the future, are the major topics of this book.

My First Encounters with an Evolving Field of Study and Practice

My first formal encounters with industrial relations occurred at Harvard Business School (HBS) in the late 1950s, both in courses and in encounters with a group of distinguished scholars authoring what turned out to be one of the landmark studies of collective bargaining.[1] It was a decade during which labor-management relations were front and center in the business world. There were no clues then about the future decline of unions.

At the University of Chicago in the next decade, the 1960s, I was a new faculty member in an industrial relations group headed by George Shultz. As unionization in the public sector was growing among school teachers and other public-sector workers, it was beginning to decline in the private sector, although not in a way that was especially visible—at least not yet. Our attention shifted to technological change and worker displacement, as well as to how to fashion more effective equal employment opportunity and related labor market policies.

The 1970s took me to Cornell University to be dean of the ILR School. That placed me in a position to foster research on a variety of topics, especially worker alienation and the quality of work life. The ILR School had a mandate from the state, and research on collective bargaining in the public sector was a particular concentration. The decline in private-sector union membership that had by then been underway for two decades was not on the agenda of many faculty in the ILR School. Gradually, as we recruited a new generation of faculty trained more deeply in the mother disciplines of economics and the behavioral sciences and more skilled in state-of-the-art research methods, the faculty expertise diversified and deepened in labor economics, human resource management, and organizational behavior. At the same time, new faculty in collective bargaining and labor history—the areas that had been and continue to be central to the ILR School's core identity—also adopted theory and methods from these allied disciplines. As a result, the school evolved with the changing nature of work and employment relations.

I have been based at the Sloan School at MIT since 1980, participating in studies that have tracked the fundamental changes occurring in labor and management relations throughout our economy. In my earliest years at MIT, even if President Ronald Reagan had not fired the air traffic controllers in 1981 and thus sent a powerful message to employers that they could take on their unions, it still would have been clear that something substantially different was occurring in industrial relations. Recognizing this fundamental shift opened up the MIT program to a steady diversification of interests by faculty and PhD students alike.

My Personal History

My particular take on industrial relations, though, has to be contextualized with how I came to be involved with the discipline at all. When I was a boy, my Uncle Jim was a conductor on the Erie Railroad. That was a union job. My Uncle Lester was a housepainter; my Uncle David was a letter carrier; my mother was a schoolteacher; and my father worked at the post office and was in the clerks' union—all close relatives working in jobs typically represented by unions. Still, I don't recall any talk about unions at family gatherings when I was young.

A piece of my father's history, however, is relevant—and it was only after I became interested in labor-management relations at HBS that I learned much about it. It turns out my father had participated in a large general strike in Paterson, New Jersey, in 1914 called by the Industrial Workers of the World (IWW) under the leadership of Elizabeth Gurley Flynn and "Big Bill" Haywood (in his later years my father remembered their names and even commented on Haywood's height).[2] The strike sought to improve conditions in the textile mill where my father then worked. The union headquarters was my hometown of Haledon, New Jersey, in a house owned by Italian immigrants. The strikers couldn't meet in Paterson but were afforded a hospitable environment by Haledon's socialist mayor.

Perhaps these family connections opened me up to the possibility of pursuing industrial relations as a career. But there is also my fascination with an industry—specifically, the transportation industry—that grew from my fascination with its "product."

I have always loved transportation, and especially public transportation. It's not that I dislike getting behind the wheel of a car; it's just that early on I developed a preference for leaving the driving to someone else.

The enjoyments of travel by bus were imprinted on me during the four years I commuted from my home in Haledon to Central High School in Paterson, some six miles away. I doubt whether I did much homework during the twenty to thirty minutes of transit time, but the interlude gave me an opportunity to observe the passing scene—and daydream.

I also liked trains as a youngster, my brother and I owned a model train set, and, as mentioned, my Uncle Jim worked as a conductor on the Erie Railroad. My father would take us to the train station that adjoined the Paterson post office, where he worked at the time, so we could see the real thing. Big steam locomotives would pass through town; the highlight for me was watching the exchange of mailbags that happened without the train even stopping in the station. Later, when I attended the University of Pennsylvania as an undergraduate, actual travel by train became familiar to me; it was the best means for getting to and from Philadelphia during those four years. I would board the train in Newark and, about ninety minutes later, arrive at Thirtieth Street Station in the City of Brotherly Love.

Railroading holds many memories and is still my favorite mode of travel. While my colleagues at the Cornell ILR School would drive from Ithaca to Albany—a distance of about 170 miles—to conduct business with state agencies, I would instead drive the roughly sixty miles to Syracuse, park the car, and take the train. Doing so would take about twice as much time as driving directly, but the train from Syracuse followed the Erie Canal and afforded many fine views of small (former) manufacturing towns such as Amsterdam and Canajoharie.

For me, air travel came earlier than expected. In June 1948, I was a member of the freshman crew team at Penn as the end-of-season Poughkeepsie Regatta approached. I wanted to participate, but it would mean missing the start of summer training for the Naval Reserve Officers Training Corps (NROTC) and the West Coast departure of my assigned ship. Fortunately, my unit's commanding officer solved that dilemma by booking a seat for me on the Nonstop Hotshot—the Naval Air Transport Service's famous overnight flight between Washington, D.C., and Moffett Field in San Francisco. We were in the air for something like ten or twelve hours.

Between NROTC training and three years of active duty in the U.S. Navy, I traveled long distances on water and visited many parts of the world. Being on the water is always special for me, whether in a shell rowing crew or as a sailor on a battleship.

Then there's trucking. I confess to a strong desire to get behind the wheel of a large eighteen-wheeler. So far in my love affair with transportation, though, that dream remains unrealized; at best, I have enjoyed getting behind the wheel of a small rental truck on a few occasions.

While I cannot say so for certain, this fascination with transportation could have greased the wheels for the trajectory my career would take. While a graduate student at HBS, I took a very satisfying course titled "Problems in Labor Relations" that led me to sign up for a more focused course on labor negotiations. I found the subject fascinating, and wondered what had predisposed me to be so interested in the discipline. My studies in electrical engineering certainly had not primed me in any way to understand or provide insight into union-management relations.

In the end, whatever it was that impelled me into industrial relations as an academic discipline—fascination with an industry, my family history, compelling graduate courses, or a combination of all three—it became my life's work.

What Came before My Time?

Although in this book I focus on the evolution of industrial relations as an academic field of study from the 1950s onward, a few words about its origins and earlier history are needed to set the stage for the chapters that follow. Most scholars point to the work of John R. Commons and his students at the University of Wisconsin in the first three decades of the twentieth century as the beginning of the study of industrial relations in the United States. Indeed, Commons is generally regarded as the father of U.S. industrial relations, as Sidney and Beatrice Webb are viewed as the parents of the discipline in Britain.[3] The key insights of these pioneering scholars, which have endured over the years, are well documented elsewhere and thus need only brief mention here.[4]

First, labor, unlike other factors of production, is more than a "commodity" that responds passively to the economic forces of supply and demand. Labor— that is, *workers*—have specific interests and aspirations that lead them to assert their interests independent of or in response to economic or technological forces. Workers often take these actions collectively. So, we need to understand what interests workers bring to employment relationships and build specific theories that don't ignore, but also are not totally determined by, economic or technological forces.

Second, worker and employer interests are mostly in conflict on some employment matters (often, for example, on the appropriate wage and benefits for a given job) and are mostly common or shared on others (such as building and maintaining a safe workplace). The art and science of industrial relations has historically focused on policies, institutions, practices, and processes for resolving these inherent conflicts and promoting cooperation in those areas of common concern. Over the course of the twentieth century, collective bargaining emerged as the central process favored by industrial relations researchers and U.S. policymakers for resolving these conflicts and promoting cooperation.

Commons and his students did such a good job of developing these basic ideas and principles that they (actually, Commons's students, since Commons himself was in failing health by the early 1930s) became key architects of the labor legislation enacted in the 1930s as part of President Franklin D. Roosevelt's New Deal. They helped draft the National Labor Relations Act, the Unemployment Insurance Act, and the Social Security Act, and then went on to take up key roles in the administrative agencies that enforced these new laws. This illustrates another imprint Commons and his students made on the industrial relations field that has been carried over ever since— namely, the high esteem afforded to scholars who apply their theories and research evidence in public service or by working directly as "neutrals" (mediators or arbitrators) with labor and management professionals.

These foundational features of industrial relations were all well in place before I entered graduate school. The faculty members I encountered were deeply ensconced in these traditions and carried the values, theoretical perspectives, and—as my interactions with them described in chapters 2 through 5 demonstrate—a commitment to engagement with private-sector labor and management practitioners and public officials. This was the world of industrial relations I discovered as I entered the field.

Big Changes in Academia and Union Density

As I have aged, the labor movement in the United States—in terms of the size and importance of unions—has declined, presenting what I think is the central challenge to the industrial relations field of study. This is one backstory to the book: when I signed on to study industrial relations in the mid-1950s, the extent of unionization had peaked at 35 percent; in the second decade of the twenty-first century it stands at 7 percent of the U.S workforce.

Over this period of declining unionization, academic programs such as those at Cornell and MIT adapted and continue to thrive; those that did not—as at Chicago, Harvard, Wisconsin, and elsewhere—have faded away.

Against this decline is another backstory: the broadening out of the field as it has attempted to deal with greater workforce diversity, variation in the nature of employment relationships (e.g., "fissurization" and growth of contract work[5]), globalization, and a shift from a production-centered economy to one more centered on "knowledge industries." In other words, while we may find the labor movement per se in decline, the field of study itself persists because workers still work, employers still employ, and the relationships inherent in these facts are eminently worthy of study and even of pragmatic interventions.

Why did some academic programs change while others did not? Although there is no definitive answer to this question, the decline of some programs reflected the lack of interest some universities had in replacing retiring faculty who focused on union-management relations with younger scholars who would undertake research on the industrial relations field of study's newer topics of interest. Essentially, this lack of interest could be summed up as, absent strong unions, who cares? Let other groups in business, sociology, or economics cover the changing nature of work and employment relations.

Being in a business school can sometimes be uncomfortable for industrial relations scholars. They are often places of antipathy, and in some cases downright hostility, to unions. To MIT's credit, any antipathy has been at worst a minor nuisance. More often it has challenged those of us in industrial relations to be rigorous and relevant, reinforced by the slow but steady diversification of student and faculty interests, research, and teaching. Even at MIT, however, the number of faculty members associated with industrial relations and related studies has shrunk over the years—despite no letup in the broadened arena of study.

My own work has evolved over the past sixty years, reflecting the changes that have taken place in the labor movement and in the basic character of labor-management relations in the United States. My teaching in the various academic homes I've had over time has shifted away from the traditional union-management relations courses toward more generic courses on negotiations and eventually to teaching courses on the great works of literature—in the latter case using classic stories and plays to illuminate leadership issues. Throughout all these years, however, I have remained heavily involved in industrial relations as a researcher, labor educator, and third-party neutral.

The same *why* question about academic programs changing or not changing can be asked about unions declining in density. But it is not my purpose in this book to analyze all the reasons for this decline. I do, in the chapters that follow, offer examples of employer opposition to unions and missteps by union leaders that shed some light on the forces at work.

Even with the decline, though, collective bargaining is still alive in many sectors, especially in an industry that has always fascinated me: transportation— just as industrial relations persists as a field of study in universities. Much can be said about efforts to keep collective bargaining in place. I chronicle some examples of labor-management cooperation and initiatives that attest to the premise that collective bargaining at its best can be a very constructive and beneficial institution. These accomplishments teach us many lessons for improving employment relations going forward—and point to areas of focus for the future of industrial relations as a field of study.

Why Bother with a Retrospective?

But, one might ask, why bother with a retrospective look at the last sixty years given all the changes in this field? Aside from George Santayana's famous caution that failure to learn from history risks repeating that failure (not his exact words), there is one reason that gets to the heart of the contribution that industrial relations makes to social science research and policymaking. Industrial relations—historically, currently, and, I hope, well into the future—is uniquely positioned in the social sciences as a problem-oriented and problem-solving field of study. It focuses *directly* on how people work; how organizations, labor market institutions, and public policies structure and govern employment relations; and the consequences of these arrangements for the workforce, employers, and society. Scholars of economics, law, history, and other social sciences generally see work-related phenomena as laboratories for building theory that advance their specific disciplines. Industrial relations is focused directly on work and employment relations. It draws on these other disciplines as they might help to understand employment dynamics and to improve employment relations. The goal is to have a positive impact first and then, secondarily, to advance the field or discipline.

The issues have changed over the years, but the need to address and improve employment matters is not going away—and that fact speaks precisely to why it is so important that industrial relations persists as a field of study. Indeed, if anything, current employment problems loom as large as perhaps at any time in the sixty-year span of this book. For example, how are we to bridge the divides in society laid bare by the 2016 election between those thriving in our changing economy and those individuals, families, and communities left behind? Can our level of income inequality, which has grown so sizably over the past several decades, be sustained without threatening our democracy? How can advancing technologies be harnessed to improve (*augment* is the term many use) work rather than simply eliminating jobs and displacing workers? And given that change will continue, how do its beneficiaries compensate those who bear the costs of a dynamic economy and advancing technologies?

This list of big problems and questions could go on, but there is one question that is just as relevant now as it was before the dawn of the New Deal: Which future systems of worker voice and representation fit the needs of the present and future workforce and economy? If industrial relations has a most notable and enduring calling card, it is the deep-seated belief—one I share fully—that a democratic society needs to hear and heed the voice of the workforce in economic and political affairs. It is those of us in this field that stand ready to help bring that voice once again to the fore.

As I provide in the chapters that follow a historical context for the challenges of the present, you will see the various centers of activity in industrial relations through a combination of two distinct lenses. First, my perspectives on the advances in the field that were made at HBS, Chicago, Cornell, and MIT are shaped by my own career progress and different roles at different times. While this is in part a limitation, it is also a feature. Many of the matters I encountered in the past—those facing doctoral students, newly appointed professors, deans, and senior faculty—are still challenges and opportunities at the turn of the twenty-first century. Second, all of the narrative is presented with the benefit of hindsight. While looking back carries with it the risk of "rose-colored glasses," it also offers the advantage of being able to review the trajectory as a whole. It turns out that understanding how the historic shifts in the field have shaped my own career path provides the clearest lessons looking ahead.

So I hope the chapters that follow are not read as just a set of historical artifacts dragged out of my notes and memories. They are intended to provide a platform for thinking about how to build on our legacy by those who will shape the future of our field of study—with a sharp focus on the contemporary and future challenges in the world of work.

Chapter 2

APPRENTICESHIP

Harvard Business School, 1954–1959

It is seductive in writing about my studies at Harvard Business School (HBS) to put my time there into a very logical sequence of leaving the U.S. Navy with an eye on starting an academic career. That, though, would be very far from the way the journey unfolded. The idea of pursuing an academic career was not something I had given much thought.

On leaving the navy, I debated whether to apply to law or business schools. I did not know any lawyers, however, and the thought of mastering detailed knowledge of statutes was not attractive. At the University of Pennsylvania's Moore School of Electrical Engineering, where I had earned my undergraduate degree, the curriculum had involved a problem-solving approach, with an emphasis on principles coupled with open-book exams. When I visited Harvard Business School and observed the case method in action, I felt comfortable with that method of study.

Like its parent institution, Harvard University, HBS has a venerable history. It began in 1908, launched by the humanities faculty as a place to study diplomacy and government service, and was modeled somewhat after the

École libre des sciences politiques in France. By 1913, it was a separate, independent administrative unit within the university. The curriculum was focused on specific business topics, and the faculty saw its role as training public administrators who would be so well qualified that governments would have to hire them, which would lead to better public administration in the United States.

The corporate world came running to the new school, however, and the focus shifted. Within a few years of its founding, the business leaders who had already graduated from HBS were filling starting positions with newer alumni.

Eventually, the original master of arts degree in business the humanities faculty had structured was replaced by the master's and doctorates in business administration.

I left the navy and entered the MBA program at HBS in September 1954. I entertained a somewhat fuzzy idea that upon graduation I would enter industry and put my engineering and soon-to-be-acquired management know-how to the service of a career that might eventually get me to a top management position.

Ending up in academia as a career evolved over many steps. In the first semester of my second year at HBS, I enrolled in Stephen H. Fuller's course "Problems in Labor Relations," which many of us referred to as the "hour of charm." Our other instructors generally just called on people and occasionally summarized the discussions, but Steve—which is what we called him—took an active role. We loved his course, which was filled with comments, "lecturettes," and humor.

Some years later Fuller left academia to join General Motors (GM) as a vice president for personnel. The move demonstrated his interest in understanding and shaping the applied side of business, which became evident as he championed programs to improve the quality of work life within GM. The strike at GM's Lordstown, Ohio, facility (which will come up again in chapter 4) had dramatized that the company could no longer get away with dumb, dull jobs. Fuller provided the intellectual leadership GM needed to begin engaging workers and their unions in efforts to expand and enrich these jobs.

Fuller's impact on industrial relations echoed similar influences scholars have had over the years. In chapter 3, I describe how Clark Kerr and George Shultz established a model for labor-management partnerships with the creation of Armour and Company's Automation Fund Committee, which they chaired for many years. Many other examples could be cited of arbitrators stepping out of roles in deciding specific cases and entering into mediation/consulting roles, helping parties solve systemic problems.

My satisfaction with Fuller's class led me to sign up for a more focused course on labor negotiations taught by Benjamin M. Selekman. I found myself fascinated by the subject, and wondered what had predisposed me to be so interested in the field. My studies in electrical engineering certainly had not primed me in any way to understand or provided any insight into union-management relations. Could it have been that the predisposition to involve myself in labor-management relations as an academic pursuit was somehow in my DNA?

As I had no basis for comparison, I did not realize then that my choice of Harvard for graduate studies placed me at an institution that at that time employed the most distinguished collection of industrial relations scholars in the country. These faculty members respected one another and worked together very well. Their commitment to field research and case studies, as well as their penchant for understanding industrial relations in all of its complexity, certainly rubbed off on someone new to the field.

I also didn't realize at the time that I was entering the industrial relations field just as labor unions were at the pinnacle of their membership numbers and power. The ascendance of unions had begun with passage of the 1935 National Labor Relations Act, more popularly known as the Wagner Act, after Democratic senator Robert Wagner of New York, who was its primary sponsor. It laid the foundation for workers to join unions and for collective bargaining to grow across private-sector industries. The National War Labor Board (NWLB), a tripartite government, labor, and business body created by the administration of President Franklin D. Roosevelt, oversaw collective bargaining during World War II and helped institutionalize many labor relations and personnel management principles that carry forward to the present, such as grievance arbitration, industry and occupational wage comparisons, and employer provided health insurance.

In the first decade following the war, many of those academics that had staffed the NWLB moved into key academic positions at Harvard and other universities that had either expanded or created new industrial relations programs. Among the Harvard faculty, Sumner Slichter had helped draft the Wagner Act; along with John T. Dunlop and James Healy, he had also served as a mediator for the NWLB. Dunlop and Healy were instrumental in launching the Harvard Trade Union Program in 1942. Selekman had worked for the Russell Sage Foundation and with his wife, Sylvia Kopald Selekman, had authored important studies on early unionization and programs for dealing with labor unrest. E. Robert Livernash had served on a regional wage stabilization board and then guided industrial relations for a large shoe company.

These academics were part of a growing number around the country who were active in helping collective bargaining evolve and work effectively, and they often helped resolve disputes as they arose. So it is not surprising that labor-management relations, collective bargaining, and management's response to unionization played such an important role in the HBS curriculum and faculty research.

Little did anyone realize, however, that unionization had reached its peak in the private sector. Dramatic events were taking place in the 1950s. I will discuss two of them in a bit more depth later in this chapter: the so-called Treaty of Detroit in the auto industry in 1950 that introduced the "annual improvement factor," and the great strike in 1955 against Westinghouse Electric Corporation by the International Union of Electrical Workers (IUE), then the major electrical workers union in the United States.

As our MBA studies ended, my classmates—who had spent their summers during the program working in industry—were getting ready to begin their careers in business. I had spent my summers as the director of the University Camp for Boys, which served Philadelphia's underprivileged population and where I had been a counselor while an undergraduate at Penn—when I wasn't on cruises with the navy. There I developed a deep affection for Dana How, a Quaker who had been, in effect, the godfather of the camp for many decades.

My work at the camp served a social purpose, and I saw unions serving a social purpose, too. This helped put the exposure to unions in my first year of study in perspective and help motivate me to learn more about them when I returned to Harvard that fall.

I decided to sign on for another year at HBS as a case writer under the guidance of Selekman. After writing cases for almost two years, several faculty suggested I enroll in the doctoral program. "All you have to do is take a few courses and write a dissertation," I was told. "You can be finished in just over another year."

In the remainder of this chapter, I describe the next steps in my journey toward an academic career—beginning with a kind of apprenticeship. The subject of industrial relations during the three years after I received my MBA was hot: there were major strikes, and companies were struggling to normalize labor relations. A major research project documenting the changes taking place was underway at HBS. These and other markers for the late 1950s are amplified in the pages that follow.

What Makes for a Good Apprenticeship?

Initially I had envisioned a two-year stay at Harvard Business School to complete the MBA program. Instead, as I worked toward a doctorate, I spent five years in what could be called an apprenticeship, a notion familiar to anyone who studies or is involved in employment relations. Formal apprenticeship programs emphasize both theory and practice, and my studies followed this model quite closely. Mentors play an important role in apprenticeship, and in mine at HBS several faculty members were particularly influential as I began an academic career.

One part of my HBS apprenticeship involved observing faculty teamwork. The experience imprinted on me an understanding of the value of collaborative inquiry, and this explains why, with one exception (my memoir about the Chicago civil rights movement), all my previous books have been co-authored. Topics such as productivity bargaining, labor negotiations, and partnerships are exceedingly complex, and I have found it essential to work with colleagues. The discovery process is much more efficient and satisfying when multiple perspectives are brought to bear.

It was a heady time to be in the field. Many companies, especially in manufacturing, had only recently been organized in the postwar years, and their procedures and relationships were being regularized. Healy, Livernash, and Slichter were involved in a massive study of industrial relations in the United States. Although Slichter's appointment was in Harvard's Department of Economics, he was still a strong presence in our lives at HBS. In 1941, earlier in his career, he had authored an important book that described the evolution of collective bargaining after World War I—especially during the late 1930s, when unionism in manufacturing surged as a result of the procedures for gaining recognition outlined in the Wagner Act.[1]

With a grant from the Brookings Institution and the goal of updating Slichter's earlier 1941 study, Healy, Livernash, and Slichter, along with three research assistants, spent several years collecting voluminous data and organizing them into a large volume with the title *The Impact of Collective Bargaining on Management.*[2] The book was so large that people sometimes referred to it in jest as *ICBM*: like an intercontinental ballistic missile, it would be dangerous were it ever to get loose!

Slichter had a notable approach to research: "The factors involved in industrial relations are so numerous, and occur in so many combinations and permutations, that worthwhile theories are difficult to formulate. What is important is to know what is going on, and to see that every industrial relations situation is more or less unique and must be explained as a whole."[3]

Unfortunately, Slichter died before the magnum opus was published, spending his last days in a hospital bed pouring over the final draft.

My HBS apprenticeship, and the approach articulated by Slichter, also taught me that industrial relations can be understood only by engaging the actors and what Selekman called their "territory." Industrial relations has always been a field with an array of problems and issues, and learning about them firsthand by interviewing participants (now called stakeholders) is the style of research I learned to appreciate and execute. Going into the field, or having the field come to the academy, is a powerful way to understand the nature of challenges and solutions. This emphasis on primary sources has been my modus operandi throughout my career.

Sumner Slichter modeled this approach for us in the weekly seminar he chaired. It took place in a large meeting room in Littauer Hall and featured a procession of visiting management and labor leaders who came to share their experiences. For young graduate students eager to learn about the current state of labor relations, it was the place to be.

Among the labor leaders who spoke in the seminar, two stand out. Harold Gibbons, who headed the Teamsters in St. Louis, represented the best in progressive leadership—and as part of a larger international union that had a lot of bad associated with it. In his local, he had pioneered health care centers, vacation lodges in the Ozark Mountains, good pension plans, and support for public housing. Much later, he publicly opposed the Vietnam War and even visited Hanoi, which surely kept him from moving up in a union led by Jimmy Hoffa and others who supported that war. Although Gibbons never made it to the top of the Teamsters, his pioneering work set an example that a union should serve all the needs of its members. He helped create for the Teamsters an alternative to the union's all-to-frequent image as coercive and dominated by unsavory elements.

Richard Gosser also came to the Slichter seminar. Leader of a large United Auto Workers (UAW) local in Toledo, Ohio, he was lauded for his progressive initiatives, which included helping organize the Toledo Industrial Development Council and being the prime mover for the Labor-Management Cooperation Council. (Later he was swept up in the investigation of the U.S. Senate Select Committee on Improper Activities in Labor and Management, spent some time in federal prison for conspiracy and jury tampering, and came home to Toledo, where two thousand people feted him at a "welcome home dinner."). During the 1950s the opportunity for labor and management to work together rather than just facing each other down in opposition gained in Gosser a very influential advocate. He epitomizes both the best and worst aspects of union leadership: sometimes a labor leader who makes a very constructive mark may also be involved in some very bad stuff.

There was also the Trade Union Program, which brought leaders to the HBS campus for eight to nine weeks every January and February. On a few occasions I led case discussions for these leaders. The sponsorship of the program by HBS underscored the school's commitment to the labor movement. This commitment changed over time, and eventually—as part of the emasculation of all things related to labor at HBS (including research, teaching, and extension work; I turn to this topic in chapter 6)—the program was moved first to the Kennedy School of Government and then to Harvard Law School.

One can only wonder whether HBS would have maintained a reasonable, if not leading, presence in research and for mentoring future industrial relations scholars had the school held on to the Trade Union Program and recruited top-quality faculty to support it. Indeed, sixty years later three MBA students at the Massachusetts Institute of Technology published an op-ed piece in the *Boston Globe* that reminded Harvard (and other business schools) of the labor heritage it had allowed to disappear at the expense of the course content MBA students badly need.[4]

A Professor Sets My Path

Harvard Business School made an important statement when it hired Benjamin Morris Selekman, who came to the school as a professor of labor relations after serving as executive director of the Associated Jewish Philanthropies of Boston from 1929 to 1945. He enjoyed a fine office in Morgan Hall, second only to that occupied by Dean Stanley Teale. A native of Bethlehem, Pennsylvania, Selekman was noted for his view that social conflict in labor relations was largely unavoidable but was also as part of a process of economic development and building social stability.

One can only speculate about the negotiations that must have taken place to get him to come to Harvard. In the years immediately following World War II, strikes were occurring in many industries as workers and their newly organized unions were seeking to catch up economically after the stringent war years. HBS needed someone on the faculty who could help students understand this turmoil in industrial relations. The solution: hire someone like Selekman, who had conducted a range of studies for the Russell Sage Foundation during the 1920s and 1930s, many focusing on the causes of industrial conflict.

Selekman's prior work on labor unrest was pioneering, but his appointment was significant in another respect: he was the first Jewish professor at HBS. Many leaders of the early unions in garments and textiles were Jews, reflecting the common bond between nascent unions struggling against employer opposition and the discrimination Jews historically faced. Selekman occupied a new chair, the Louis E. Kirstein professorship, named for the prominent Jewish philanthropist and president of the Boston-based Filene's department store chain.

Selekman used cases to illustrate powerful concepts, and the casebook co-authored with Sylvia Kopald Selekman and Stephen H. Fuller reveals their approach to labor-management relations.[5] In it they outline their conceptual framework—a spectrum of possible relationships ranging from conflict to cooperation. At the midpoint is *balance of power*. At one end, in the constructive direction, are *accommodation* and *cooperation*; at the other are *containment* and *conflict*. An interesting category—not easily positioned—is *collusion*, a relationship that involves the parties (here, labor and management) using their power to the detriment of third parties—usually consumers and the public. The text includes case studies of negotiations in a variety of industries, including those of automobiles, steel, and consumer goods.

In many ways Selekman was the right person at the right time to be at a business school. Conflict and disorganization characterized relations between management and unions in many plants and industries, and into this world came the voice of Selekman, urging management to accept unions and share power and arguing that the parties needed to regularize procedures for dealing with grievances and resolving conflict. He called this a form of "constitutionalism": the codification of such rules and protocols into a jointly administered contract. The collective bargaining process would develop a body of rules governing the workplace and its accompanying procedures of due process, giving workers voice through their union representation and enhancing the interests of all stakeholders, including management.

Selekman challenged management to accept unions and to reject what is known as Boulwarism. This negotiating tactic, named after Lemuel Boulwar, once a vice president of General Electric, involves issuing an offer to labor unions in the form of an ultimatum, after which no revisions will be accepted. Instead Selekman emphasized the moral ground on which labor-management relations should stand. In fact, among his several books, his best-known volume was titled *Power and Morality*.[6]

I observed closely Selekman's penchant for reminding management about its responsibility to act ethically. This came into focus in a case written about the Gardner Board and Carton Company, a firm that practiced Boulwarism. Selekman criticized the company for its "take it or leave it" philosophy and very aggressive approach to labor negotiations. Stated simply, Gardner would conduct considerable research before presenting its proposal to the union, in which the company would state that it was their final position unless it could be demonstrated that the company had made an error in its analysis. Gardner's management was proud of this approach: "We know what is best for our employees and this is contained in our first and final offer."

I attended a meeting with Selekman and several Gardner executives who had been invited to campus expecting to be congratulated for their "innovative approach" to negotiations. Instead, Selekman chastised them, stating that their approach represented a cynical view of unions and their role.

Selekman's passion was the study of power—a major theme that differentiated him from the human relations group at HBS. Niccolò Machiavelli had famously advised leaders to amass and deploy power; Selekman preached the need to tame it, regardless of who exercised that power. For instance, he saw a wildcat strike as a form of raw power that needed to be dealt with firmly by management. Although he was no longer alive when U.S. air traffic controllers struck (illegally) in 1982, he certainly would have endorsed President Ronald Reagan's action to fire all the strikers.

In other ways, Selekman's voice and perspective are needed now. He emphasized the constructive use of power, and he would be quite critical of corporate executives who operated in a very self-serving fashion and thwarted workers raising their own voices in so many employment situations.

Selekman's presence at HBS helped me choose a path between two sometimes competing disciplines: labor and industrial relations and what in the early twenty-first century would be called organizational behavior (then human relations). During the 1930s Fritz J. Roethlisberger studied workers at Western Electric's Hawthorne Works in Cicero, Illinois, and, together with the plant's manager, had written a book about management and workers. The book fundamentally increased our understanding of human relations, teams, and group dynamics. The yield from those authors' pioneering work was very much evident in our courses. Subjects such as administrative practices, human relations, and personnel administration dealt with the important topics of work groups, absenteeism, and training—what in the navy we had called "matters of morale."

Although there was no formal "firewall" between the Roethlisberger and Selekman groups, each viewed the workplace quite differently. Selekman spoke dismissively about the HBS human relations group's coursework in administrative practices and its research focus on the behavior of small groups. He viewed his work as realistic, dealing with conflict (which he saw as inevitable) and the consequences of coercive power. To Selekman, the best approach was to draw conflict out into the open through negotiations and the use of procedures such as mediation and arbitration to resolve differences, which compelled him to serve as a permanent arbitrator in several industries to settle labor-management disputes. Roethlisberger and his disciples believed that wise management could unleash human motivation in ways that would eliminate conflict in employment relations. Unions and collective bargaining, they believed, could get in the way of this process. This became a defining feature of the difference between these two schools of thought for many years to come and, to a large extent, it still is.

I never heard any members of the Roethlisberger group openly disparage unions; they probably viewed them as an inconvenience. Nor did they lend their know-how about the dynamics of human behavior to any programs seeking to help companies remain free of unions. Such a connection would come later, and from other quarters. Nevertheless, I found myself drawn to labor and industrial relations and not to organizational behavior. Had I not had an association with Selekman, I would not have become attracted to the study of negotiations.

Benjamin Selekman continued to teach beyond normal retirement age, still finding a receptive audience among participants enrolled in HBS's Advanced Management Program. Although students may not always have accepted his moralizing about management's obligations to use its power responsibly, they were nevertheless intrigued by this "rabbi" holding forth at the "West Point of Capitalism."

Selekman died in a way that many academics revere—with chalk dust on his hands, teaching a Saturday morning class on April 9, 1962. A few years later, as Richard Walton and I were finishing our book *A Behavioral Theory of Labor Negotiations*,[7] we decided to dedicate the book to Selekman in recognition of his influence as the first person to expose us to the rich field of negotiations. An important part of our book drew on his spectrum of possible relationships between labor and management.

Case Writing

Linked to understanding industrial relations by engaging the actors is the part of my apprenticeship that involved writing case studies. Harvard Business School thrives on the case method. Developing cases requires visits to companies to collect primary data, something I experienced even while pursuing my MBA degree.

For some academics in industrial relations, field research is rarely if ever a part of their studies; instead, they rely on analyzing what I would call secondary data. But for most of us, the only way to relate to the actors in the field is to be knowledgeable about the big events in history and to gain firsthand knowledge of other events as they unfold. This was made apparent by my experiences writing cases, a process that continued throughout my career.

For me the study of industrial relations is very much inductive. The subject is so complex that making predictions (which is the deductive approach) is risky and difficult. Developments in the field—such as quality of work life, the civil rights movement, and equal pay—create a focus and energy for our research. If researchers rely only on secondary data and do not engage the parties directly, they miss the opportunity to develop an understanding of how problems develop and how those problems might be addressed. The "pull" of research for me has been the puzzles to be explained in the ever-evolving relations between labor and management and the satisfaction that comes from being able to conceptualize and fashion frameworks that the parties find helpful.

Toward the end of my second-year negotiations course, Selekman asked me whether I would be willing to write a case on the Gardner Board and Carton Company that would serve as the final exam for the students in the course. This came about because I had spoken with him about possibly staying on at HBS beyond graduating with my MBA and writing cases in labor relations. So I traveled to Middletown, Ohio, gathered documents, interviewed key officials, and wrote a case that I still find very relevant. Later, I sat in on the final exam, observing and writing what would become a guide for grading the case while my fellow students were wrestling with the case I had written. They assumed I was taking the exam myself. I remember my mixed feelings of intrigue and power.

Case writing became my central focus after receiving my MBA in 1956 and accepting an appointment as a research associate—continuing my apprenticeship. My first assignment was to follow the proceedings and investigations of the McClellan Committee in the U.S. Senate and develop a case study for use in the classroom. This committee—whose official name was the U.S. Senate Select Committee on Improper Activities in Labor and Management—soon turned its attention to the Teamsters Union and its two leaders, David Beck and Jimmy Hoffa. The committee's chief counsel, Robert F. Kennedy (whom history has largely judged to have been a rather inept interrogator), garnered national attention with his aggressive questioning of the union leaders that led Beck and Hoffa both to resort to the Fifth Amendment countless times.

The investigation of the Teamsters had been spurred by the many newspaper accounts about payoffs from large shippers, with money going to people at the highest levels in the union. Many of these deals hurt the interests of rank-and-file truck drivers. Suffice it to say that Beck was eventually cited for contempt and sent to prison. The committee's work set the stage for the Labor Management Reporting Disclosure Act of 1959, which established comprehensive standards and reporting requirements aimed at ensuring that unions would be democratic and their leaders would be responsive to members and not to their own monetary interests.

The AFL-CIO eventually expelled the Teamsters in 1957. Considerable attention was also placed on the Communist Party–dominated unions, such as the Farm Equipment Workers and the United Electrical Workers (UE)— both of which also severed ties with the CIO before its merger with the AFL in 1955. Covering these developments led me to see that despite the positive features of unions and union-management relations, there had also been a dark side. Being able to look at unions (and employers) with an objective and analytical lens is critical for anyone who wants to be taken seriously as a scholar in the field.

Another case writing project took me to Providence, Rhode Island, to capture the story of machine tool manufacturer Brown & Sharpe. Livernash knew the managers at the company and paved the way for me to write a case about the positive changes the company was implementing. Viewed in hindsight many decades later, this case illustrates the fragile nature of constructive labor-management relations.[8]

Thanks to my apprenticeship, I was learning about both the inspiring and the problematic aspects of industrial relations. I was also learning a lot about the dynamics of the workplace.

One of the most interesting field visits was an interview I had with the industrial relations staff at Lever Brothers.[9] My notes from this 1957 interview reveal several themes that characterized the state of labor relations in the country at that time.

Prior to unionization of the company in the mid-1950s, Lever Brothers followed the philosophy of many companies: "production at any cost." But after unionization, the tendency was to bend over backward to accommodate the union: plant management was instructed to settle all disputes as quickly as possible. Over the years, the company came to pride itself on its "fairness," and its president, Charles Luckman, even made public statements about his deep interest in employee welfare. Eventually, though, management at many locations had essentially "given the plant away" in the sense that workers were pretty much in control.

In response, Lever Brothers continued to emphasize fairness but added firmness as an ingredient. Then came a wake-up call: an unauthorized strike at the Cambridge, Massachusetts, plant. The company discharged the strike leaders, and the international union agreed to place the local union in a trusteeship and also mandated that the local union president could not hold office for another year.

While I was at HBS, the field was pulsating with other dramatic events requiring analysis and discussion. For example, even before I finished my MBA, the big strike broke out in 1955 between the IUE and Westinghouse.[10] It garnered considerable national attention, lasting five months, with management and labor at an impasse over the use of time studies (continuous observation of a task being performed, using a timekeeping device) as part of an efficiency drive.[11] Management insisted on its right to monitor the pace of work, but the union opposed the practice, fearing layoffs would result from the speeding up of operations. The bad relationship and long strike did not surprise observers, since work stoppages were common and a rivalry between the IUE and the United Electrical Workers had created an atmosphere of contention.

Although the bitter strike at Westinghouse and a subsequent strike in the steel industry in 1959 did not surprise the "experts" in industrial relations, these disruptions certainly caught the attention of top management and strengthened their resolve to avoid unionization.

The 1950 negotiations in the auto industry had introduced the concept of adjusting wages for inflation and added an annual improvement factor (linked to the national rate for productivity gains). It was an example of an innovative concept the parties had fashioned to solve the contentious issue of wage adjustments. Little did we know then that the so-called Treaty of Detroit would in the future be viewed as an important piece of industrial relations history and would establish the standard for wage negotiations for decades.[12] The agreement initiated wage-setting norms that were then spread across the economy through what came to be known as pattern bargaining. Later this historic agreement and the patterns it helped create would come to be credited as being the underlying process for sustaining the postwar social contract.[13] That is, from the 1950s to about 1980, overall wage growth in the economy moved up in tandem with increases in productivity and the cost of living and thereby moved many workers and their families into the middle class. Only by looking back now, after thirty years of rising income inequality, can we appreciate how important that Detroit accord and subsequent collective bargaining was to our economy and society until 1980.[14]

While writing cases, Selekman made sure that his research associates, including John Baitsell, Richard Walton, and myself, were exposed to what he considered the "territory" of the field. Walton became my coauthor and a lifelong friend; he figures prominently in many later parts of this book. Baitsell, after completing his doctoral studies, taught at HBS for a number of years and subsequently served for many decades as Mobil Oil's manager of labor relations.

Selekman's "territory" imperative fit perfectly with keeping abreast of the big events and gaining firsthand knowledge. For instance, he suggested that we attend the 1957 Atlantic City convention of the AFL-CIO.

On one occasion Selekman had been invited by management to give a talk at Corning Glass Works, and wanted Baitsell, Walton, and me to come along for the experience. The company sent a private plane, making transportation to central New York State very easy.

As the visit ended, Selekman turned to our host and said, "Well, aren't you going to have us go away with something?" Managers scurried around and, within a few minutes, each of us was presented with a beautiful piece of Steuben glass.

Selekman also took us to a Christmas party held at Southwick Clothiers, a large textile company in Lawrence, Massachusetts. He was serving as umpire (a type of arbitrator) between the textile workers union and the company, and he wanted us to get to know the workers in person. Even then, quite a few of the workers—most of whom were Italian—did not speak English. (In the early twenty-first century the ethnic makeup of Lawrence is very much Latino.) Selekman's commitment to understanding the people affected by the institutions of collective bargaining and decisions he and other arbitrators would make was not lost on those of us he brought to that party, and it again reinforced the importance in my apprenticeship of fieldwork. This event again makes the point that to understand what is happening it is necessary to "rub shoulders" with participants. In all these various ways, Selekman became a model for how a mentor opens doors for young people and showed us how to build and sustain relationships with practitioners on different sides of the labor-management equation.

Before leaving the subject of acquiring primary data, I want to make several observations. There is no end to the details that can be absorbed. An observer can "drown" trying to master all the information available about unions, companies, and the labor contract. Some might argue that from the viewpoint of the need to develop theory, time spent on acquiring this institutional knowledge may not be wise. But as I learned later, you can often draw on accumulated institutional knowledge and examples to test the face validity of some theoretical point or argument you are either trying to develop or that you read about in someone else's work. Rich details can enrich theory and make it better. Moreover, it is also good to have information available for ready recall when in seminars or classroom settings to illustrate a theoretical point, despite that such "anecdotes" may be discounted as lacking rigor by some fellow academics who simply don't "get it."

My Dissertation Mentor

One other important thing I learned at HBS is that apprentices often need more than one good mentor. I was privileged to have Bob Livernash as an amazing mentor for my dissertation. He was the ideal HBS faculty member, someone with both academic credentials and considerable business experience, having worked for McElwain Shoe Company for many years before joining the HBS faculty.

I don't remember just how I came to Livernash's door. I was looking for a dissertation advisor as I ended my case writing stint and was gearing up for the final leg of the doctoral program. Perhaps it was a process of elimination: Jim Healy had several other students; Steve Fuller had barely finished his own dissertation, and thus was not the best person to guide someone through the difficult research phase of graduate work. Ben Selekman, the professor for whom I had written cases, wanted me to undertake a study of power in the corporation for my dissertation—a topic so vague and complex that I was extremely reluctant to work with him.

I chose Livernash, working with him for eighteen months on my research project. The phrase "working with" is appropriate: he treated me as a partner from the beginning to the end of my work on the dissertation. It is another characteristic of a great mentor, and one I tried to emulate in later years when I found myself in that role.

One episode in particular, at the beginning of the research journey, stands out clearly and is worth summarizing. I had gone to Livernash's office, and we spoke for a while about some ideas for the dissertation. When I remarked that I needed to be home soon, we headed to the parking lot. We then stood by his car for the next half hour while he outlined a design for the study.

Most faculty, especially these days, would not think of being so helpful with their protégés. "Let them struggle, and we will react to their proposals," goes the unspoken norm.

I raced home and jotted down his ideas. And so the framework for my dissertation fell into place—a framework, I might add, that served as a fine compass and needed very little refinement.

As an important footnote to Livernash's career, I should draw attention to a volume he edited on the subject of comparable worth.[15] Although he took a rather dim view about whether legislation could correct social habits, such as the persistent differential between women's and men's wages, at the same time he firmly believed in getting such social habits to change. So he vigorously advocated for more serious career opportunities for women in business and, to help put that belief into practice, taught and supported the management training program for women at Radcliffe College. He did so at a time when most of the faculty at Harvard Business School did not put that teaching opportunity on their priority list.

Livernash guided my research interests into a comparison study of piecework versus measured day work in three industries. As a result of the Brookings study, he had become interested in the different role wage payment systems played in what could be considered relatively similar production environments. Output incentives have the advantage that the system runs itself with minimal supervision required, whereas measured day work often required disciplinary measures for failure to meet production standards. In any event, the form of wage payment was bound to have an impact on productivity, pay, job satisfaction, and labor relations.

Bob was also very helpful in opening doors to several companies. I spent many weeks in the field at Alcoa, the Ford Motor Company, International Harvester, Jones & Laughlin Steel, and Westinghouse. The matched comparisons were: an automobile manufacturer operating on measured day work versus a manufacturer of agricultural machinery, construction equipment, and trucks operating on piecework incentives; the steel industry using traditional incentives versus the aluminum industry on hourly compensation; and the cohort of Westinghouse plants themselves, since some used incentives and others operated on measured day work.

Clearly I learned the importance of mentoring, especially as the recipient of Livernash's incredibly helpful role in suggesting a dissertation topic and orchestrating many of the contacts needed to do productive field research for my doctorate. Although not all may rank his contribution to industrial relations on a par with that of Slichter, Livernash's ability to study complex processes in the field (e.g., job evaluation and wage payment systems), and to identify the important issues, qualify him in my mind as one who knew the practical side of the field and could at the same time place practices into a theoretical framework.

The Unasked Question

Another part of fulfilling Ben Selekman's admonition to get out into the "territory" found me attending the 1958 UAW convention in Detroit, where Walter Reuther asked the membership to ratify a bargaining demand seeking to reduce the number of weekly work hours to thirty-six. Ultimately this goal was modified when the Soviet Union put Sputnik in space and all attention and priorities in the country turned to working longer, not shorter, hours to "catch up" with the Russians.

Reuther became a hero of mine in large part because of what I saw and heard at that convention. He opened the discussion on economic bargaining with an impassioned speech, which I paraphrase:

> We are going to run into people who will say, "Let us cut the standard of living so we can get on with the defense effort." These people are going to say that the only way we can match the Russian Sputnik challenge is by working longer hours for the same amount of money. But the little men of big business do not have the right answer. Our problem today is not an economic one; it's the problem of complacency, of half-hearted attitudes. We need to get our values in sharper focus. We need to have values that will replace complacency with hard work, and incompetent administration with leadership. As a labor movement, we must have an answer. The wage freeze is not economic. We won the war without abolishing the forty-hour week, and there is no need to up it now. Let the politicians in Washington work harder. Our problem has been that a small group of businessmen make prices. We do not have a situation of excess demand; we have a situation of excess capacity. Capital

expansion, which business talks about, will only be possible with expansion of consumption.

Many people listened to Reuther in polite silence. The reaction of the rank-and-file delegates was not enthusiastic, and there was only moderate applause at the end. As one leader observed, "We have heard Reuther say all these things before."

Reuther and his speech impressed me. He spoke eloquently from just a few notes, at times moving through long sentences dealing with economic theory and buttressed with plenty of statistical data. Often his pitch would rise in fervor until he sounded like the Reverend Billy Graham. The speech illustrated why Reuther is generally viewed as one of the most visionary and socially progressive labor leaders of his time. It is unfortunate that his life and impact were cut short by his untimely death in an airplane crash in 1970.

Thinking back on Reuther, I realize that while a graduate student I never asked HBS faculty the following question: In the face of a union organizing campaign, would you advise management to remain neutral, mount opposition, or provide encouragement? It is worth asking why this never came up in discussions with or among prominent labor relations scholars at that time.

Clearly, among the industrial relations faculty, Selekman was the one who came close to viewing unions as beneficial; he spoke quite openly about how they should be encouraged, and it would be in the public interest and certainly in the workers' interest to have unions. His critique of Gardner management's "We know what is best for our employees" showed a clear ideological preference for unions and collective bargaining. As for my fellow students, I am sure my colleagues in the doctoral program who were majoring in industrial relations never entertained the thought that our esteemed faculty believed superior employee relations could be achieved solely with enlightened management. We thought unions were essential.

In all of my associations with Livernash I assumed that he, too, was in favor of collective bargaining. After all, he (along with Jim Healy and Sumner Slichter) had studied collective bargaining in practice and written the definitive book on it. Now, many years later, I realize I may have been wrong. Just because Bob and his colleagues documented the constructive activities taking place in many industries with strong unions, I should not have concluded what he would have advised management had there been a choice. Indeed, thinking back, it may be that Livernash was actually wondering how managers in unorganized settings thought about unionization. Given his involvement in the Harvard Trade Union Program and his need for union cooperation to do fieldwork on labor-management relations, Bob could not undertake a study himself that focused on how nonunion companies avoided union organization. He did, however, urge Fred Foulkes (then a doctoral student at HBS and presently on the faculty at Boston University) to do such a study. Foulkes's study was one of the first and perhaps still the most comprehensive analysis of the personnel practices large nonunion firms used to ensure they remained nonunion.[16]

How Livernash felt about all this was never discussed. Unions had a right to organize vigorously, and it was fine if workers wanted a union. At the same time, he may have felt that employers were wise if they countered the union organizing campaigns with their own communication programs. It was the last proposition that could not be openly embraced, at least not in the presence of union leaders and their advocates. What was discussed were the various programs and policies being implemented by management to regularize relations with unions and to deal with the challenges of wildcat strikes and overloaded grievance procedures.

It is instructive to think back about why I never asked the HBS faculty about their views on unions. Perhaps it was because it was taken for granted in the 1950s that unions were here to stay; management's essential task, therefore, was more to figure out how to manage *with* unions rather than to manage to avoid them or escape them. There certainly were firms that opposed union organizing, but most did so quietly, without making public statements about a "union-free" environment or expressing opposition to "third-party interference" in their workforce relationships. Those public statements would await the 1970s and 1980s.

The key intellectual mistake many—perhaps most—industrial relations scholars of the 1950s made was to believe that management attitudes had changed to accept unions. What had actually changed was the power relationship: management accepted unions because unions were powerful enough to discipline management's behavior, if not to change management's underlying attitudes.

A former classmate, George Chandler, gave me a glimpse into how a practicing manager had to adjust to dealing with a union regardless of his private feelings. I was serving as secretary for my MBA class of 1956, which kept me in touch with many of my classmates as I prepared several reports for the alumni bulletin each year. George and I interacted often. He had graduated from Princeton University, entered the U.S. Army, and later entered HBS. At Princeton he captained the football team, and was viewed as a leader with great potential. After graduation from HBS, he took a position with the Olin Mathieson Chemical Corporation in manufacturing.

George's first assignment put him in charge of operations at a brass mill in Winchester, Connecticut, just outside of New Haven. The International Association of Machinists (IAM) had unionized the plant a few years before Chandler's arrival. In the first labor agreement, the union had won a change in work schedules, from rotating shifts to a standard three-shift schedule. In voting for a union, it was clear the senior workers anticipated that a major benefit would be to exercise their seniority and work day shifts rather than the more disruptive life of rotating shifts.

It turned out that the schedule of nonrotating shifts proved quite troublesome for the company. The salaried staff who worked the day shifts never came in contact with staff from the other two shifts, and junior workers (who all ended up on the night shifts) did not possess as much experience as their senior coworkers on the day shift. Consequently, management decided to revert back to rotating shifts. They felt they were on firm ground, since the contract stipulated a thirteen-cent pay premium for rotating shifts. The union, though, objected, and when the reversion went into effect immediately called a strike.

My view was that management was in error and had no right to make a unilateral change—which is how I thought any arbitrator would have ruled. The union's mistake, though, was bigger: it conducted an illegal strike, since the contract gave the union the right to strike only at the termination of the old contract.

George reported that, although there was some nervousness among his management colleagues about what they were doing, he was determined to make the change and see it through; indeed, Olin Mathieson was prepared for a long strike. I suggested to George that he get in touch with the IAM's national office. This proved to be a good suggestion: the national leaders recognized the local union leadership was in a tough spot, having engaged in an illegal strike, and ordered the workers back to work. They complied, and George thought I was a genius.

As I reflect on my interactions with George Chandler, I wonder why I never questioned him about his attitude toward unions and collective bargaining. After all, I strongly believed then (and still do now) that when workers are represented by a union, good things happen: workers can get a hearing for their issues, production problems can be addressed on a joint basis, and management will be much more on its toes given the presence of union eyes and ears.

My guess is that George would have viewed such arguments as overly idealistic and not in line with the behavior and reality of the union relations he encountered on a day-to-day basis in the plant. Instead of my list of good outcomes, he could counter by pointing to work slowdowns, lengthy grievance discussions, and senior union officials often more absent than present. I could point to the many examples of positive labor-management relations we studied in class, and he could point to just as many examples of labor-management relations falling far short of the ideal.

George is now deceased, so I cannot ask him what he thinks about the loss of many manufacturing jobs to imports. In his later years he worked as executive director for the American Productivity & Quality Center in Houston, Texas. George was a hands-on manager and knew how to improve productivity on the shop floor, but running a research and education program was not his bent, and he soon retired. His career path was emblematic of that followed by many MBAs in the 1950s, who entered manufacturing and made a mark running efficient operations. Currently very few enter manufacturing upon graduation.

Reflecting back on George Chandler, I wonder whether my own view of unions has been too romantic. Like most love affairs, the infatuation has strong emotional elements. In chapter 1, I mentioned my father's participation before World War I in a textile workers' strike in Paterson, New Jersey. This piece of family history has always made me proud. Then, during my studies at HBS, I attended conventions and admired the leadership qualities of George Meany and Walter Reuther. I engaged, to some degree, in hero worship. As will be evident in chapter 3, when I discuss my involvement in the civil rights movement, I am predisposed to being swept off my feet by social action. Actually, this is the wrong metaphor, since commitment to these causes of social and racial justice often requires marching and very much being active *on* one's feet.

All this compels me to return to the big question posed earlier: In the face of a union organizing campaign, would you advise management to remain neutral, mount opposition, or provide encouragement? I wonder whether a business school is just that far away from what an actual university is supposed to do that such a theoretical question would never come up. Was its absence from the discussion willful, and thus a tacit illustration of an a priori ideological position of what to a business school is a practical question?

I think the answer is that all of us—doctoral students and faculty—were strongly focused on how this new reality of collective bargaining could be regularized and stabilized. As a result, the behavior of firms openly opposed to unions never got much attention. Yes, there was the 1954 strike at the Kohler Company in Wisconsin, but that was seen as unique.

All the centers of industrial relations around the country during the 1950s and into the 1960s had a blind spot when it came to where the hearts and minds of business executives really were. Although HBS was committed to understanding how labor-management relations were playing out and sponsored the Trade Union Program, and clearly the faculty was committed to collective bargaining where it was in place, it was only Bob Livernash who wondered about what was going on in companies that did not have unions.

As I think about all of this, there is another point to be made. In conducting field research at companies with unions, we worked with industrial relations personnel. By and large those folks accepted the legitimacy of unions, and in some cases they were former union officials themselves who had been recruited to work in management. We did not talk to top management or to finance people, where the attitudes about unions were likely to be quite different.

Consequently, I never took my discussion with George Chandler beyond addressing the issues he faced at the time to the fundamental level of assessing whether having a union on the premises was a good thing "in theory." Likewise, such a discussion never happened with Bob Livernash and his colleagues. The question was always about how management can make the *reality* of a union being in place as positive as possible, and not whether it was, in the first place, a good idea from management's point of view to have a union.

Although my studies at HBS did not fit the normal pattern for doctoral work, I gained a deep understanding of the industrial relations discipline across the economy. Mentors and role models were abundant: Bob Livernash was instrumental in my thesis; Ben Selekman instilled in me an appreciation for how essential it is to understand process and formulate conceptual categories;

Sumner Slichter emphasized the importance of understanding the details of the subject and the hard work involved; and Steve Fuller was an example of the academic-practitioner.

Perhaps above all, my training and experience at Harvard Business School instilled a lasting respect for doing fieldwork and case study research. The data and case material collected during my Harvard years would serve as much of the material my colleague Dick Walton and I would draw on in the next decade as we sought to build a stronger theoretical structure for understanding the process of negotiations. Later, particularly in the early 1980s as the field of employment relations began to change in ways none of us studying it could quite understand, it would be time once again to return to my Harvard "roots" by going back into the field to engage practitioners who could help us see the need to update our theories and received wisdom.

Some who are familiar with the lineup of talent at HBS during the 1950s might ask, where was John T. Dunlop? Well, John was there, but not often seen; he preferred to operate alone. He had his own PhD students and was busy working on what would become his seminal 1958 book *Industrial Relations Systems,*[17] which spelled out his important concept of the "web of rules" describing the understandings—both written and informal—that guided the labor-management relationship. His book provided the framework for considerable research in our field in subsequent years.

My next stop was the University of Chicago, but I actually tried to end up in Philadelphia. As I looked for a job after receiving my doctorate, I tried to convince the Wharton School of the University of Pennsylvania to hire me on as part of the industrial relations group there, so I could continue to run the University Camp for Boys, where I had worked since my undergraduate days at Penn. The Wharton School was not interested.

Chapter 3

Becoming a Journeyman

The University of Chicago, 1959–1971

As I reflect back on the 1960s—when I was on the faculty at the University of Chicago—I am amazed at how fortunate I was to be at that special institution during what were my formative years and a time of significant changes in the industrial relations field. My years in Chicago launched me on my path to journeyman status in my career as an academic. The track to tenure at the University of Chicago followed the pattern that existed at most academic institutions: two terms as an assistant professor, followed by promotion to associate with tenure and then (assuming the record met the standards) promotion to full professor after another half dozen years. I spent twelve years on the faculty of the Graduate School of Business; currently it is known as the Booth School of Business, but in my days there everyone simply called it GSB.

It was a heady time at the school and in the city of Chicago.

The University of Chicago is a "baby" compared to Harvard University. When it opened in 1892, Harvard was already 256 years old. That was only sixteen years before Harvard Business School began.

The university began with money from oil magnate John D. Rockefeller donated to the American Baptist Education Society. One of its founding principles was "scientific guidance and investigation of great economic and social matters of everyday importance." In its earliest years, its leaders advocated for a curriculum that focused on theory and general knowledge rather than direct application, and it was from the University of Chicago that the Great Books Movement to study the key works of the so-called Western canon in literature, philosophy, and other disciplines emerged.

Business education at the University of Chicago began with the College of Commerce and Politics, chartered in 1898 within the university as an extension of that founding principle. Solely undergraduate until 1916, it then transformed into the School of Commerce and Administration, offering a research-oriented master's degree. Doctoral-level degrees came later; in fact, Chicago in 1920 initiated the first PhD program in business. In 1932, it was renamed yet again, this time as the School of Business. The MBA was first offered in 1935; the undergraduate program was phased out in 1942; and in 1959 it became the Graduate School of Business—not long before I arrived—until 2008, when it took on its current name.

GSB faculty and students, thanks to their interaction with the University of Chicago Department of Economics, played a key role in the development of what is known as the Chicago school of economics, not an institution but an economic philosophy that emerged in the latter half of the twentieth century. The philosophy pushes free-market solutions for just about everything, with minimal government involvement. Its most famous proponent was Milton Friedman, a longtime professor at the university and a Nobel Prize winner.

When I arrived, the new leadership team of Dean W. Allen Wallis and Associate Dean James Lorie had recently taken charge. The Gordon-Howell Report on business education, commissioned by the Ford Foundation, had just been issued, and it became a touchstone as Wallis and Lorie moved the school in a dramatically new direction.[1] No longer would the emphasis be on preparing graduates for particular industries; instead, GSB would emphasize acquainting students with the relevant disciplines for tackling a wide range of administrative problems.

Although the GSB curriculum included courses in personnel administration taught from a practitioner perspective, the subject of industrial relations was not studied in any concentrated way before the transformation Wallis and Lorie fostered. In line with the emphasis on disciplines, the new leader-ship team decided to recruit faculty who would approach industrial relations from an economic perspective—which was not surprising, given that the De-partment of Economics was so dominant at this discipline-based university.

I wondered whether my bent for the case method and lack of formal coursework in many of the key subject areas would be a handicap. "No," they answered. "We need some individuals like you, with your practical interests to balance our more theoretically oriented faculty."

That was a good response. The University of Chicago lagged behind other universities where groups had been teaching industrial relations for some time. Chicago was, in essence, playing catch-up. Nevertheless, the economic perspective had a certain power that I came to appreciate, and later—when I became the dean of the School of Industrial and Labor Relations (ILR School) at Cornell University (described in chapter 4)—it helped guide my efforts to transform the labor economics department there.

At Chicago, I fit in and thrived. I met George Shultz, who played a key role in my development as a scholar, teacher, and administrator. I was ex-posed to new policy perspectives and an expanded research agenda that was instrumental in my development, with my colleague Richard Walton, of the behavioral theory of labor negotiations. Beyond the campus itself, on Chicago's South Side where we lived and in the city as a whole, the civil rights revo-lution was underway and it immediately pulled me into an activist role in a major way.

George Shultz: The Extraordinary Leader of a Distinguished Team

I joined the GSB faculty in 1959, two years after George P. Shultz. Until 1969, when Shultz left to become the U.S. secretary of labor in the first adminis-tration of President Richard M. Nixon, he was the reason a "hotspot" in in-dustrial relations had developed at GSB. Shultz, who was named dean of GSB in 1962, essentially created a special time in the history of our field, with a multidisciplinary and vibrant faculty group, an emphasis on field research, and the development of projects that delivered value to practitioners and in-sights for public policy. At Chicago I saw for the first time a shift from doc-umenting industrial relations practices largely for the benefit of teaching managers to formulating policy guidance for all parties, and especially government officials.

Shultz's philosophy saw industrial relations as a field that tackles important problems. "The field of industrial relations, in my view, is problem-based," he once said. "It is not a discipline in itself, but rather draws on many disciplines for theory and techniques to understand and help solve the problems arising in the workplace, the labor market, and at the bargaining table."[2]

Later, when I became the dean of the ILR School, I realized Shultz's leadership style had provided me with a wonderful model. I had internalized a number of his values and the way he approached the administrative parts of his job. One of his priorities was to get out of the office regularly, taking time to visit faculty and PhD students where they were working. I remember calling George several different times, asking for an appointment. His answer usually was, "When would you be free? I will come by and we can talk." This technique of leaving his office and going through the corridors meant that Shultz could control the time spent on a talk. When he needed to end the conversation, he could simply rise and head for the door. A dean who is out and about is perceived as being in touch with faculty and students, and is also in a position to receive considerable informal information about how things are going.

Shultz's leadership style also emphasized collegiality and support for newer faculty members and their spouses. For example, he encouraged us, if at all possible, to live close to the campus in Hyde Park. He and his wife Obi were incredibly attentive to advising young faculty members and spouses on how to navigate housing, health care, and childcare, as well as community affairs in the neighborhood. My wife Nancy and I especially appreciated their advice, as our first child was born shortly after we arrived; we took their advice on a number of things, including the choice of a doctor. The Shultzes' hospitality showed us that the human side of academic leadership might be as important in building a vibrant and engaged faculty community as the intellectual dimensions of the job—a lesson I've taken to heart ever since seeing it in practice from a master.

I was attracted to GSB in part because of its distinct contrast with my training at Harvard Business School. Even more important to me, though, was Shultz's leadership of the industrial relations group. My Harvard advisor, E. Robert Livernash, had told me that George was an outstanding scholar and recommended him as a superb mentor and colleague. No one would have guessed then that George would eventually hold four major U.S. federal appointments, including secretary of labor, director of the Office of Management and Budget, secretary of the Treasury, and even secretary of state.

By the time I arrived, Shultz had already assembled a strong interdisciplinary group of scholars at GSB that included Arnold Weber, who had finished his studies at MIT the year before, and Joel Seidman, a labor historian and sociologist whom George persuaded to move into the business school from another department of the university. Seidman was a serious researcher who had already authored several books and articles on the labor movement—including a book on the "yellow dog contract."[3]

I hate to admit it, but whereas I knew a yellow dog contract restricted a worker's freedom to join a union, for the longest time I did not know the term's origin. Why that particular image? There's nothing like Google for providing the necessary background: a worker who, as a condition of employment, signed a contract not to join a union was seen as something useless—like a mongrel or a dying dog. The Norris-LaGuardia Act of 1932 made the yellow dog contract illegal.

During the 1960s, while at GSB, Joel Seidman also conducted a study for the somewhat controversial Fund for the Republic on the subject of the Trainmen's Union and just how democratic the unions were. What we would now call a think tank, the fund sponsored several studies assessing the damage done by anticommunism and McCarthyism, for which it was roundly attacked and deemed "un-American."[4]

Seidman's study was one of several in the 1960s that examined the internal operations of unions. Given the power that unions were exercising at the time, colleagues imbued with the perspective of the Chicago school would ask whether the members were able to control their "bosses." As was mentioned in chapter 2, the McClellan Committee had already investigated a number of unions—including, quite pointedly, the Teamsters, a union that was tainted with the charge of racketeering—and this led to the 1959 passage of the Landrum-Griffin Act to regulate the internal affairs of unions and the relationships their officials had with employers.[5]

Scholars were also very interested in the International Typographical Union (ITU), which had been touted in a 1956 book—Seymour Martin Lipset, Martin Trow, and James Coleman's *Union Democracy* (which was then and remains very influential)—for its internal democracy, including having two active internal political "parties" and many worker associations.[6] The

ITU was seen by many as a model for ensuring democracy in the trade union movement. Now, more than a half century later, much less attention is paid to whether unions are "democratic." This could be due to the decline in union power and the realization that the caucus system for grooming leaders meets an acceptable standard. In many unions, only one caucus operates—in which a kind of "sorting" takes place that resembles a single party's primary election process. The presumption that those who make it to the top through this caucus system represent the interests of a majority of the members raises the question of whether there is open access to leadership positions.

The GSB curriculum also included the study of personnel administration; Thomas L. Whisler carried the flag on this subject for some time, and George Shultz made sure he felt included in the group. This was just one of what I later realized were signs of George's broad vision for our field. In too many other programs, labor relations and personnel management (later called human resource management) were beginning around this time to go their separate ways, but this was not the case at GSB. This made an impression on me that I carried forward.

There were many other distinguished team members. Bernard Meltzer taught labor law and was considered a member of our "virtual" industrial relations community. Robert Burns, who had established the Industrial Relations Center (IRC), was a force in his own right. He and his colleagues served many corporate clients and conducted surveys to identify issues that affected employee morale. All the faculty members in the industrial relations group had office space in the IRC. The opportunity to "hide" in an office and work on research was a must for getting tenure, and it was an attractive fringe benefit.

The connection between GSB and the Department of Economics was very close, as was illustrated by numerous joint workshops. As faculty, we felt the pull (interesting research was always on the agenda) as well as the push ("It's your *duty* to be there each week") to attend each of them.

I did not consider myself a labor economist, although Shultz insisted that I use this label when asked about my discipline. Shultz, along with Albert Rees and Arnie Weber, made up the core group of the industrial relations faculty, and they were economists. As I have mentioned, the discipline was dominant in other areas of the business school: economics was considered the mother discipline of industrial relations. In fact, when the Industrial Relations Research Association (IRRA) decided to hold its first annual meeting, it decided to partner with the American Economic Association.[7]

From the outset, the study of unions and collective bargaining had attracted the attention of economists, and labor economics quickly became a respected area of scholarship. As attention expanded from unions' impact in the marketplace to their internal operations and their role in the workplace, other behavioral disciplines became interested—especially sociology and political science. The group assembled at the University of Chicago in the 1960s was an early example of the value of bringing researchers from multiple disciplines together to discuss and study industrial relations issues.

H. Gregg Lewis guided the workshop in labor economics, where faculty could present their work in progress and hear scholars from other institutions. As an economist, Gregg worried about the inflationary pressure that unions could create with their demands at the bargaining table, and he orchestrated a broad study of the impact of unions and collective bargaining on wages. A cadre of PhD students analyzed data for many industries, and Gregg pulled it all together into a definitive study of the subject, concluding that, overall, unions raised wages about 10 percent higher than they would have been in the absence of unions.[8] Of course, those of us who were partial to the unions saw this as a positive outcome—after all, isn't raising wages for workers what unions should be doing?

Perhaps more important than the specific estimate of the size of the union effect, Gregg's method for generating this estimate became the standard approach that would be replicated by countless labor economists for decades to come.

Milton Friedman and George Stigler, two economists who would eventually win Nobel Prizes, played a prominent role in the intellectual atmosphere at GSB. They both believed in the free market, with minimal government regulation of the economy. Certainly their perspective on unions and collective bargaining as a hindrance to the functioning of a free economy differed from the views most of us in the industrial relations group held. Although there may have been differences, the culture remained one of cordiality and professional respect.

Nevertheless, I have often been asked how I was able to handle being closely associated with the likes of Milton Friedman while at the same time connecting with labor leaders in Chicago. Actually, the dichotomy was not sharp; my "leaders," George Shultz and Al Rees, had a remarkable ability to bridge any divide. Both men valued the positive role of unions in the economy, as their coauthored study of the labor market makes clear.[9] And during the 1960s, while I was at the university, Shultz was active in the IRRA, which for many union leaders was their professional organization of choice; he even served as its president in 1968.

These facts probably assuaged any of my union contacts' concerns. The labor leaders with whom I interacted frequently—Jesse Prosten, vice president of the Packinghouse Workers; Timuel D. Black Jr. of the Chicago Teachers Union; Seymour Kahan of the United Auto Workers (UAW); and leaders of The Independent Telephone Workers of Illinois—never challenged me about the Chicago school. They knew I offered a course in collective bargaining and union history, and they appreciated that I was able to coexist with the advocates of free markets.

Academically, Friedman was a proponent of the Chicago approach, which emphasized ideas, rigor, and empirical justification for any subject under discussion. I recall attending a meeting with him following a seminar given by a visiting faculty member. The visitor clearly felt "under the gun" as Friedman— true to his Chicago approach—pressed questions and explored issues raised by the seminar. Nevertheless, after a dinner, Friedman commented on how much he enjoyed the give-and-take, and I heard the visitor say (to himself) something about how inadequate he felt about his interaction with this giant thinker.

Politically, most of my colleagues, and certainly most faculty in the Department of Economics, were Republicans, so they favored Richard Nixon over John F. Kennedy in the 1960 presidential election. Shultz regularly invited faculty to his home for socializing, and at a party around that time I realized that professor of labor economics Al Rees and I were the only Democrats in the room.

Al Rees played a very important role for me over the years. A quote from his 1962 book on the economics of trade unions reveals why, and also shows why Shultz chose to work with him on their later Chicago Labor Market Study. Rees certainly identified with the Friedman view that unions were a restraint on the free market, and commanded respect from the free-market economists for that view, at the same time he recognized the role unions play and affirmed their valued in the marketplace. As Rees wrote in 1962,

If the union is viewed solely in terms of its effect on the economy, it must in my opinion be considered an obstacle to the optimum performance of our economic system. It alters the wage structure in a way that impedes the growth of employment in sectors of the economy where productivity and income are naturally high and that leaves too much labor in low income sectors of the economy like southern agriculture and the least skilled service trades. It benefits most those workers who would in any case be relatively well off, and though some of this gain may be at the expense of the owners of capital, most of it must be at the expense of consumers and the lower-paid workers. Unions interfere blatantly with the use of the most productive techniques in some industries, and this effect is probably not offset by the stimulus to higher productivity furnished by some other unions.

Many of my fellow economists would stop at this point and conclude that unions are harmful and that their power should be curbed. I do not agree that one can judge the value of a complex institution from so narrow a point of view. Other aspects of unions must also be considered. The protection against the abuse of managerial authority given by the seniority systems and grievance procedures seems to me to be a union accomplishment of the greatest importance. So too is the organized representation in public affairs given the worker by the political activities of unions. If, as most of us believe, American should continue to have political democracy and a free enterprise economy it is essential that the great mass of manual workers be committed to the preservation of this system and that they should not, as in many other democracies, constantly be attempting to replace it with something radically different. Yet such a commitment cannot exist if workers feel that their rights are not respected and they do not get a fair share of the rewards of the system. By giving workers protection against arbitrary treatment by employers, by acting as their representative in politics, and by reinforcing their hope of continuous future gain, unions have helped assure that the basic values of our society are widely diffused and that our disagreements on political and economic issues take place within a broad framework of agreement. If the job rights won for workers by unions are not conceded by the rest of society simply because they are just, they should be conceded because they help to protect the minimum consensus that keeps our society stable. In my judgment, the economic losses imposed by unions are not too high a price to pay for their successful performance of this role.[10]

The willingness of Al Rees not to be so doctrinaire in the way that economists might ignore *anything*—including unions—that do not accord with their theory of how the labor market *should* work revealed a pragmatism that was a breath of fresh air. It was something Shultz clearly saw in Rees, and it was an important component of my own work.

Research and Data Collection

My experiences at the University of Chicago taught me how important it is for a researcher to be close to the data, to the raw material.

During the summer of 1960, I worked with George Shultz to prepare a report for the Eastern States Standard Oil Company, or Esso, which would later become Exxon. Jerry Rosow of Esso, who would later launch the Work in America Institute, asked George to test the feasibility of installing a version of the Scanlon Plan—a gainsharing program for employees based on improved productivity generated by implementing suggestions from workers—at the company's refineries and in its marketing departments. When it came time to draft our report, I gave George all my raw notes about what we had observed.

My approach to research did not always put me in the best position with George. He expressed surprise that I had not delivered the Esso notes organized into recommendations. His own notes, which he shared with me, were in a sharply delineated framework embodying the concepts of participation, achievement, and rewards.

Being close to the data is not enough; I learned from George something else of equal importance: how important it is to formulate a structure that organizes the data into recommendations and programs that can be implemented.

I am not sure whether anything ever came of the report in terms of implementation, but it gave me the opportunity to see George in action and to appreciate how effective he was in doing field research and making presentations—in this case, to Esso's top management.

I will have more to say in chapter 5 about the role of the Scanlon Plan in bringing management and labor together to improve productivity and share the savings that resulted. The fact that companies do not implement such plans stems from the belief held by most managers that they can elicit increases in productivity without committing to a formal plan for gainsharing.

Al Rees and George Shultz, with help from several foundations, undertook a major multiyear research project—the Chicago Labor Market Study—while I was at GSB.[11] The study involved considerable interviewing and data collection from various sectors of the labor market, and was a pathbreaking analysis that provided data for several PhD dissertations. Among other findings, it added to our knowledge about the role of formal and informal intermediaries, making clear that better employment matches often occurred in informal markets rather than through employment agencies. The study is still cited by researchers using the Rees and Shultz distinction regarding the importance of workers having intensive knowledge about a prospective job (in the sense of having more inside information on actual job and working conditions) as opposed to relying simply on extensive data available from public sources.

The Chicago Labor Market Study reinforced the lessons about how to conduct research that I had learned from George Shultz earlier—lessons applicable to the entire industrial relations field.

As for my own research, I renewed my contact with International Harvester (IH), which was, in many ways, a unique resource for me. While a graduate student at Harvard Business School, I had traveled to Chicago with my mentor, Bob Livernash, to collect data for a case study on IH's history of labor relations. That research became a major example and case study in my doctoral dissertation.

The accessibility of IH and other nearby heavy manufacturing firms in the steel, meatpacking, and automobile industries ranked high on the list of reasons I chose to begin my teaching career in Chicago. Easy access to research sites is a very important part of being able to do research in a subject as applied as industrial relations. George Taylor—one of the earliest academics in the field—made his mark with his on-site study of the history and development of the hosiery industry in Pennsylvania, first as an undergraduate at the Wharton School and then as a professor; his father had been a superintendent at a hosiery mill. Scholars at the University of California—Berkeley such as Neal Hartman wrote about the longshore industry in San Francisco, to which he had easy access. The faculty at the excellent centers such as those at the University of Wisconsin and the University of Illinois needed to travel to where industry was located, whereas I was fortunate to have a site at my doorstep.

Another advantage was the ease of connecting with the practitioners at professional meetings. While I was at the University of Chicago, I attended meetings sponsored by the local chapter of the IRRA and the Industrial Relations Association (which involved management types) and took advantage of the informal contacts to arrange for other site visits.

International Harvester—a major company facing many industrial relations challenges—was only a short train ride away, and I took full advantage of the opportunity to study firsthand how labor relations there were unfolding. Shultz's model of going to the field to collect data that would deepen our understanding of important issues facing unions and companies was certainly a motivator.

The company also provided data for my first publication—always important in an academic career.[12] I analyzed a program instituted by IH and its major union, the UAW, to reduce the backlog of grievances by requiring that rather than committing positions to paper, complaints would be handled orally. This compelled the parties to deal with the issues at the lowest level and involve the individuals who best knew the circumstances of the case. It was a powerful innovation that put those with the most at stake at the center of discussions. It also eliminated any paper trail and the tendency in many grievance systems for both sides to argue the merits of the case with written briefs.

After several months, the large backlog of several thousand grievances nearly vanished as supervisors and stewards engaged in serious efforts to resolve problems rather than filling out forms. I don't think William Reilly, manager of IH's labor relations, believed even in his most hopeful moments that his idea would be so successful.

The situation IH faced—what could be termed a distressed system—characterized many grievance systems during the 1950s and 1960s. The myriad issues and inequities that had led to the rapid growth of unions during the preceding decades now could be addressed with the dispute resolution procedures outlined in the contract. The parties were learning how to regularize their relationships and to resolve problems. Now the parties in many industries employ procedures that are much more sophisticated and address a wide-ranging agenda. I should have done research to determine whether the "oral" handling of grievances took hold in other companies and served as a starting point for the much more systematic and problem-focused approach to dispute resolution currently in practice.

My rapport with IH developed to the point that I was asked to take a strategic look at the firm's overall approach to its relations with its workers. Past negotiations had often deteriorated into strikes, and the tenor of labor-management relations could fairly be termed "adversarial." I doubt my report said anything the parties had not thought about, but it did provide raw material for an article that appeared in a book on bargaining structure edited by Arnie Weber. I wrote, "By far the most important structural development has been the shift to local contract administration that the grievance prevention program had fostered. This development gave evidence of dramatically altering the climate of union-management relations at International Harvester, thereby portending significant changes in the atmosphere and outcome of future negotiations."[13]

My experience with IH provided not only data but also a lifelong friendship with Seymour Kahan, who had joined the UAW when he returned to civilian life after serving in World War II. He went to work at IH in Melrose Park, on Chicago's West Side, became a rank-and-file activist, and soon ascended through a series of union leadership positions. An idealist, Seymour was willing, when necessary, to confront and fight management. Early in his UAW career he and other officials took on the challenge of defeating a rival union, the Communist Party–dominated Farm Equipment Workers.[14]

By the time I got to know him in the early 1960s, Seymour was an international representative in the UAW's Farm Equipment Department, a role in which he served his members with passion and integrity. I had met his union boss, Pat Greathouse, while doing fieldwork at IH for my doctoral studies at Harvard Business School.

Midlevel union officials like Seymour are all too often overlooked or underappreciated for their impact and their insights on union strategies, with the limelight left to the higher-up leaders to whom they report. I found that a key to learning what they really think about important issues was to get them into the classroom, and Seymour become a regular guest years later in my classes at the MIT Sloan School of Management (as I will describe in chapter 5).

A Focus on Policy

My time at Harvard Business School had taught me the value of having deep connections to the world of practice, and I had focused during my graduate studies there on collecting cases and field data so I could bring the problems being experienced by practitioners into the classroom. My work at Harvard had had little emphasis on public policy, despite the fact that public policy has been part of the mainstream of the industrial relations field ever since the Depression-era beginnings of the National Labor Relations Board. But that changed dramatically for me soon after arriving at the University of Chicago. My years there showed the close connections between industrial relations research and involvement in public policy. That hallmark of our field traces its origins to the leadership of John R. Commons at the University of Wisconsin, whose students went on to help shape the New Deal labor, employment, and social security policies.

Colleagues in Chicago were deep in public policy. George Shultz—a skilled mediator—was one of several scholars who had been called upon to take up important university leadership positions, in part because they could work with and maintain the respect of diverse constituencies, even in the tumultuous 1960s. John Dunlop at Harvard, Robben Fleming at the University of Michigan, Clark Kerr at Berkeley, Ed Young at Wisconsin, and later Abraham Siegel at MIT and Arnie Weber at Carnegie Mellon University, the University of Colorado, and Northwestern University all illustrated this point: industrial relations scholars can make major contributions in important areas where leadership skills are essential.

After my arrival at GSB, I learned that Shultz was involved in a major effort sponsored by the Committee for Economic Development (CED) to prepare a white paper on the subject of labor policy. The CED's "independent study group" included an impressive lineup of academics: Kerr was the chair, and Shultz was director of the staff. Others included Douglass Brown, Abraham Siegel, and Robert Solow, all from MIT; Chicago's Albert Rees; and Harvard's John Dunlop. David Cole, an arbitrator, was the sole practitioner. The group was a veritable "who's who" of industrial relations and economics of that era.

In the early twenty-first century it's difficult to imagine a major study on employment being delegated to such a blue-ribbon academic group, but the fact that the CED turned to these men was a sign of the respect with which leading academics were once regarded in high-level policy circles and among practitioners. Little did we know then that Dunlop, Rees, Shultz, and Solow would each play important roles in shaping efforts to moderate or control wage and price increases for future presidents.

A number of developments prompted the creation of this independent study group in 1959. Strikes had become increasingly severe; that year, a strike in the steel industry lasted 116 days. Labor relations in the private sector in the 1960s remained unsettled, and strikes and slowdowns occurred with some frequency.

Automation was the term given at the time to the new technologies sweeping into manufacturing and causing worker displacement. Academics and government officials in the United States were concerned about what was called wage push inflation. Unions were seen as powerful actors in the domestic economy. Negotiations and negotiated contracts in major industries such as steel and in Ford, General Motors, and other large companies were watched closely for their impact on prices.

The CED-sponsored group met frequently, which ultimately led to a publication on price and wage controls in 1961.[15] The report outlined measures to make labor and product markets more competitive and more flexible, including education and training, lower minimum wages for teenagers, an improved system of information in labor markets, and an improved employment service. It noted, "The effects of wage settlements on price level and on relative wages and employment have recently caused concern." Another fear was characterized this way: "Large unions, large bargaining systems, or small groups strategically placed, have led to public fears of too great private power." On the matter of inflation, the CED report concluded, "The evidence that collective bargaining has caused inflation is far from conclusive."

Consequently, the study group opposed establishing government machinery to regulate wage determinations made through collective bargaining, characterizing such negotiations as a process that was, to use a phrase I learned in the navy, "Steady as it goes." The group was unconcerned about the size of unions or any of the outcomes, such as strikes, that it viewed as inevitable parts of the process. The report did tilt slightly toward management in two respects: the group thought employers should be able to lock out workers and, as a counter to union strike funds, that companies should be able to engage in mutual assistance and avail themselves of strike insurance.

In retrospect this study clearly influenced George Shultz's thinking. Shortly after becoming secretary of labor at the beginning of the Nixon administration, he issued a policy directive that prior administrations had been too quick to intervene in strikes by threatening or actually imposing the national security clause in labor law to force a temporary stop to a strike or lockout. He put labor and management on notice that the U.S. government would not intervene unless there was an exceptionally dire need to do so. Otherwise, the parties were on their own; they shouldn't come to him looking for help. That shift in policy has been the norm ever since.

In many ways, the CED report could be seen as a complement to *The Impact of Collective Bargaining on Management*, the 1960 Harvard study by Sumner Slichter, James Healy, and Bob Livernash that focused on the details of collective bargaining.[16] It looked back at what had happened in the postwar period and sought to answer how the management of workers in American industry was affected by trade unions and collective bargaining. By comparison, the CED study addressed policies pertinent to labor-management relations, looking ahead and answering questions about the nature of the system and what changes needed to be made by government or by the parties in the systems governing collective bargaining.

During the 1960s income policy, encompassing guidelines and in some cases controls on price and wage movements, had taken hold in many European countries. This prompted considerable attention in the United States. Against this backdrop George Shultz teamed up with Robert Aliber, then a staff economist at the CED and later a professor at the University of Chicago, to sponsor a major conference, with funding from the Rockefeller Foundation. Many economic luminaries attended.

Later, as the organizers observed,

> The spread of informal guides, designed by the Executive branch of the federal government, to affect the behavior of individual businesses and labor unions has been a major policy development of recent years. The rationale for this policy, both here and abroad, is that informal controls make it possible to achieve higher levels of employment and avoid either rising prices or the need for formal price and wage ceilings . . . .
>
> A review of these alternatives (wage-price guideposts and guidelines for foreign trade and investment) shows that guidelines are not the only policy; it also shows that all the alternatives are genuinely controversial.[17]

This work had set the stage for the 1960s, a decade that was characterized by many joint programs using collective bargaining to solve problems of mechanization—including, for example, the West Coast Mechanization and Modernization Agreement signed in 1960. It also set the stage for Armour and Company's Automation Fund Committee (whereas, technically, mechanization is a step before automation, the issues were largely intertwined). The University of Chicago in the 1960s broadened my perspectives on industrial relations as a field that had a lot to offer public policy. In retrospect, it is clear that the field was just beginning to recognize the opportunities that better theory and more systematic use of rigorous research methods would offer for both deepening traditional union-management subjects and for exploring new topics in the field—all of which became clearer when I moved to the ILR School at Cornell (the subject of chapter 4).

Delivering Value to Practitioners

The industrial relations discipline has always had a problem focus. During the 1960s, George Shultz and Clark Kerr, president of the University of California, undertook leadership of an important project, the Armour Automation Fund, to help workers being displaced from meatpacking plants shutting down across the Midwest. This involved action research, studying the impact of closing on displaced workers, and instituting a variety of remedial steps to cushion the impact and help workers continue with their careers—largely in other industries.

A 1966 summary by Shultz and Weber on the subject of the displaced workers was published at a time when many policymakers were looking for guidelines related to the extensive restructuring taking place in many industries.[18] In the space of two weeks, they dictated a draft that required little editing before being sent to the publisher.

Shultz's work with the Armour Automation Fund also provided key opportunities for faculty and PhD students to connect with major labor leaders. One was Ralph Helstein, who had become president of the Packinghouse Workers after being general counsel for the union for several years—a path Jack Sheinkman followed on his way to becoming president of the Amalgamated Clothing and Textile Workers Union. Helstein lived across the street from Shultz in Hyde Park. I remember discussions with other faculty about the pros and cons of the practice of allowing only individuals who had been "in the trenches" to stand for top union offices versus allowing professionals with expertise, such as lawyers, to guide the organization. Those of us enamored of the record of the UAW agreed with the premise in the union that unless a person seeking office had "worked on the line," that individual would never be able to convince the membership that he (exclusively male in those days) understood the important issues of the workplace.

Consequently, the members of most industrial unions, such as the UAW, would never have supported someone assuming a leadership role unless that person had come up through the ranks. The Packinghouse Workers were, however, an exception. Lawyers also are the exception because they gain knowledge about the work of a union's members by representing them in grievance proceedings and contract negotiations; if that same individual also exhibits leaderships skills, the members may be more willing to be led by an outsider who has become an insider.

Helstein compensated for his lack of packing plant experience by having a special assistant, Jesse Prosten, who knew the trade and had the confidence of the rank and file from his early days with the Packinghouse Workers Organizing Committee in Boston during the late 1930s. With his "Hey, guy!" greeting, Jesse always made his presence known in a big way. He made sure the Packinghouse Workers gave substantial support to the civil rights movement, and the union even provided free office space for the Negro American Labor Council, an organization I worked with closely during the 1960s.

Many in the union thought Jesse should have been president rather than Helstein, but there was a rumor around that he had been a member of the Communist Party—which, if true, would have resulted in his union being thrown out of the AFL-CIO if he held elected office.

Although I did not join the Armour Automation project, I learned a great deal in seminars and in conversations with George and Arnie about measures needed to cushion the impact of job losses. These insights were subsequently put to good use when I headed the Continuity of Employment Committee jointly sponsored by the State of New York and the Civil Service Employees Association (described in chapter 4).

In some respects, the use of the term *automation* for the Armour Project was a misnomer. The closing of meatpacking plants located in urban areas was due to a shift of operations closer to the supply of livestock. But the term did resonate, given how labor has always been buffeted by new technologies that lead to displacement and the need to learn new skills. Computers were just coming on the scene, and many scholars were assessing the machines' impact on labor.[19] In the early twenty-first century the question of impact now revolves around an even higher level of automation in the form of robots and artificial intelligence.

The Journey to *A Behavioral Theory of Labor Negotiations*

The biggest and perhaps most lasting research product from my Chicago years was a joint effort with my colleague and lifelong friend Richard Walton, who was teaching at Purdue University at the time. Working together over five years, we wrote *A Behavioral Theory of Labor Negotiations.*[20] It was with great pride and joy that we both participated in two symposia on the occasion of its fiftieth anniversary in 2016, which were testaments to the impact and staying power of the book that neither of us could have ever predicted. So it probably is worth a discussion here of how we came to write the book. (In chapter 5, my MIT years, I discuss how the book has been used in various ways.)

Initially we were drawn to the subject of negotiations as a result of courses taken with Benjamin M. Selekman at Harvard Business School, where we studied transcripts of actual negotiations. These became the bedrock of our analysis. These rich data, our direct exposure through interviews with negotiators, and some direct observation of negotiations in action provided the empirical basis for the theoretical framework that emerged out of this project. My approach to research has always been to dig deep into the topic, the problem, the array of parties, and the nuances of the situation in order first to understand what is going on and then to formulate a framework (or hypothesis, to be more formal) that captures the important features of the territory.

Some of the many interviews of participants in negotiations took place as a result of my contacts at International Harvester. One important opportunity came as a result of my intrusion into the negotiations between IH and the UAW. (I use the word *intrusion* because the IH manager of labor relations commented that my presence was like having an observer in the boudoir of a couple engaged in a tryst.)

The opportunity to debrief the union delegates after each bargaining session took place at the very time Dick Walton and I were developing the framework for our book. What we initially envisioned as a theory that would describe behavior at the main table was then expanded to include a similar activity at what negotiations analysts call the "second tables." It became clear as I spoke with union leaders from various locals that important negotiations were taking place within the union; presumably, the same internal bargaining was also taking place on the management side. We eventually came to identify this as a subprocess we called intraorganizational bargaining.

The considerable contact I had with economists at the University of Chicago clearly had an important effect on the development of another key subprocess in our theory, which we called distributive bargaining— that is, negotiation over the share of fixed resources. It had been the subject of formal model building for decades: the British economist John Richard Hicks, American mathematician John Nash (made famous in the film "A Beautiful Mind"), Danish economist Frederik Zeuthen and others used concepts from game theory to develop deductively propositions to predict where parties operating under the assumptions of full information might end up agreeing even when their interests were in conflict.

Similarly, Dick's exposure to some of the leading behavioral science theorists and researchers working on conflict resolution during a sabbatical he took at the University of Michigan helped us develop a deeper understanding of the social processes involved in negotiations. That led us to conceptualize two other subprocesses of negotiations that we called integrative bargaining and attitudinal structuring.

We felt our ideas could be applied to a broad range of negotiations. Two arenas outside of collective bargaining were ripe for application of the framework: international relations and civil rights. The Cuban Missile Crisis had occurred early in the decade and proved a natural episode on which to apply the theory. And I was heavily involved in the Chicago civil rights movement, providing a rich body of experience and insights.

What emerged out of our five-year joint effort—often only after spirited discussions of how all these different perspectives might be combined—built on the institutional knowledge that came from the fieldwork traditions of our Harvard training but that then conceptualized the empirical data into a theory that applied concepts from economics and behavioral science. This was initially viewed as a radical—and, for some unwelcome—departure from the institutionalist traditions of research on union-management relations. To their credit, scholars who had studied negotiations did understand what was happening in specific situations. They had mastered the details of bargaining rounds in major industries, and their approach had the flavor of telling "war stories." But they were not able to conceptualize or formulate principles. Herbert Northrup, one of the best-known and highly experienced union-management researchers of that era, probably spoke for many of his colleagues in his review of our book: "A new language justifies itself when it leads to new insights previously unknown, or even if an esthetic improvement results. Careful reading of this book—and it takes just that for understanding—fails to produce such new insights. Esthetics are a matter of taste."[21]

The back-and-forth process, necessary for two colleagues to move a project forward, was facilitated by the fact that Purdue and the University of Chicago are only about a hundred miles apart. We would often work at one or another's office, but we also found a convenient midpoint where our two families would gather regularly for a picnic while Dick and I huddled with the latest draft.

The project was not without its moments of tension. I spent enough time working on the book that it led to a point in my relationship with George Shultz that I look back on now and wonder about. As director of the Armour Automation Fund, George recruited individuals who could guide demonstration projects in cities where Armour plants were being closed. Arnie Weber played this role for a plant in Minnesota; Jim Stern from the University of Wisconsin played a similar role at another site; and George asked me to tackle a plant in downstate Illinois. I told him I could not take on the assignment given my work on the negotiation book with Walton, especially because Dick felt I was not doing enough on my side of the partnership.

In any case, the result was a comprehensive study of the negotiation process. It took five years, but in 1965 our book *A Behavioral Theory of Labor Negotiations* was published as part of McGraw-Hill's Economic Handbook series.

Productivity Bargaining

I took a sabbatical during the 1965–66 academic year, electing to spend it at the London School of Economics (LSE). My host was Benjamin Roberts, a renowned scholar and editor of *The British Journal of Industrial Relations*. Henry Phelps Brown, a retired labor economist, appeared from time to time, and it was a treat to get to know him.

My yearlong stint at the LSE was memorable for several reasons. First, George Shultz had proposed a creative solution for how I could be there for the entire academic year at full pay. My application to the Ford Foundation for a fellowship was not accepted, so George suggested I teach in the summers both before and after the 1965–66 academic year.

My arrival was fortuitous in that Allan Flanders had just published a comprehensive study of the use of what came to be called productivity bargaining at the Fawley Refinery of Esso. Productivity bargaining generally involves negotiating changes in work rules that inhibit productivity in the face of changing technologies, in return for some quid pro quo to the unionized workers who might be negatively affected by the changes. In the United States, perhaps the best-documented example was the West Coast Mechanization and Modernization Agreement negotiated in the 1960s between the International Longshore and Warehouse Union and the employer association that ran the docks.[22]

Given the visibility of productivity bargaining on both sides of the pond, I jumped at the opportunity to explore how it was being carried out across Britain. I spent a wonderful year visiting companies in a variety of industries that were implementing productivity agreements. As someone from the United States, I was a nonthreatening visitor, and I received full cooperation, much more so than would have been the case had I tried to conduct a similar study back home.

In many cases these agreements brought real changes that enabled workers to enjoy larger wage increases than would have been allowed under the guidelines then in place. The most successful agreements involved fundamental organizational change, not simply specifying certain work rules that had to be changed. British government officials who had to approve the agreements expected Imperial Chemical Industries, a large chemical company, and Shell Oil Company to produce evidence that they were engaged in such fundamental organizational change. In other instances, however, the agreements were only pieces of paper, and little real change took place. Owing to some of these "pseudoagreements," the concept of productivity bargaining eventually fell out of favor, with commentators viewing the agreements as merely a cosmetic way to raise wages above the norms of the United Kingdom's income policy.

Productivity bargaining could generate positive results, but it was not an approach to be used often, because it had the potential to create anticipation by unions and their members of a payoff even before they agreed to implement changes that would increase the efficiency of operations. Rather than the quid pro quo method for increasing productivity, a better approach emphasized organizational change and a continuous improvement in how work was done. Years after my time at LSE, I had a chance to revisit these lessons when working with unions and public officials in Nassau County in New York to improve productivity in their public services (discussed in chapter 4).

The fact that a book eventually emerged from my experiences was due in large part to my recruiting Laurence Hunter as coauthor. Hunter was a scholar on the faculty of the University of Glasgow and understood all the nuances of industrial relations in Britain. In addition, as is always the case, it was helpful to have a PhD student available to dig into the various aspects of the subject. For this project it was Werner Sengenberger, who was interested in the subject and willing to spend time in England as part of his studies at the University of Chicago. Ultimately, after several follow-on trips and additional work by Sengenberger, we published *Pay, Productivity, and Collective Bargaining* in 1973.[23]

Productivity was also very much on the minds of *New York Times* management in the 1960s, who wanted something done about their labor costs—especially the high cost of overtime. Management wanted to understand better what was driving overtime, and the union was interested in understanding the problem of pay fluctuations. Sengenberger and I put our previous research to work by analyzing work schedules. The workforce supporting newspaper production, especially the mailing and delivery services, held substantial power owing to the need to get newspapers to customers on time—that is, while news was still news. We found that their workload varied widely depending on the season of the year, day of the week, and amount of print advertising in the paper. So we presented the data and left it to the parties to take the next step: better scheduling and a reduction in overtime.

One lesson I took away from the *New York Times* case helped illustrate a theoretical concept, integrative bargaining (which is detailed in chapter 5). The key point is that if labor and management work together to explore issues of deep concern to each other (in the *Times* case, it was reducing overtime costs for management and better scheduling for employees), integrative solutions can often be found that make both parties better off—or at least allow both parties to achieve something of value in exchange for allowing their counterpart to achieve a high-priority objective. The key is to design a process for putting one's key interests on the table and then exploring options for achieving them rather than simply exchanging demands, proposals, and counterproposals from positions of power.

My Involvement in the Civil Rights Movement

My work on the book with Dick Walton had taken considerable time and energy. So, too, did my involvement in the civil rights movement in Chicago during the 1960s, though in this case it was emotional energy.

The pull developed slowly. In the 1959 fall semester, I offered for the first time a course covering unions and collective bargaining. One of my students, Monte Brown, asked if he could write his term paper on a strike underway near our campus, to which I readily agreed. That led to an article in the *Quarterly Journal of Economics* that examined the campaign to organize nonprofessional minority workers at two Chicago health care institutions.[24]

The backstory is that the American Federation of State, County, and Municipal Employees (AFSCME) had called for strikes at the Home for the Incurables (an unbelievable name!), as well as at Mt. Sinai, a large teaching hospital on Chicago's West Side. The National Labor Relations Act did not at that time cover hospitals, so no procedures were in place to resolve the question of whether employees could be represented by a union. The two AFSCME leaders, Victor Gotbaum and Lillian Roberts, had signed up a majority of the employees, but management at both institutions refused to recognize the union. The only option left was to call a strike in the hope that the pressure of work stoppages would motivate management to recognize the union. This did not happen, and after several months (and with winter approaching) the union called off the organizing campaign.

This strike gave me a closer view of management's opposition to having a union on the premises. It would become a dominant theme later, at the MIT Sloan School, in my research for the *Transformation* book detailed in chapter 5.

The study of efforts by black workers to organize was done from the sidelines. Getting actively involved came as a result of inspired examples from two individuals, Alex Poinsett and Tim Black, who I got to know at the First Unitarian Church of Chicago. In a fundamental way, becoming active with the civil rights movement took me away from working with unions, because for the most part the two movements in Chicago were not involved with each other.

In Chicago there was even open hostility, especially between the craft unions and the civil rights movement. The craft unions traced their origins to the very earliest days of the union movement in the United States, and were organized based on a particular job or "craft" (as opposed to the industrial unions, which organized everyone in a given industry into the same union, regardless of job or skill). Historically they had been largely closed to black workers; in 1902, W. E. B. Du Bois, the great black historian, found in a study that forty-three craft unions had no black members and twenty-seven others barred black apprentices. The hostility in Chicago arose over the operation of the Washburne Trade and Continuance School, which offered courses that enabled students to gain entry into the craft occupations.[25] Minority students found it difficult to gain access to the school because their earlier education was typically deficient and, as a result, they tended not to score well on the entrance exams. The civil rights movement in the city mounted a campaign to increase minority enrollment in the school, whereas the craft unions insisted on maintaining "standards"—which was largely code for keeping out the black kids from the primarily white institution. When desegregation began in 1965 there were seventeen different unions in the school; by 1978 that number had dropped to eight.

Although my involvement in the civil rights movement created some tensions with colleagues, they did recognize that my interest in civil rights had opened doors in Washington, DC—the very chance to be involved with government and influence policy that any academic should shoot for. In early 1969, I accepted a presidential appointment to the Advisory Council for the newly formed Office of Minority Business Enterprise (OMBE). This certainly did not come about because of a vote for President Nixon; I had voted for Hubert Humphrey, his opponent.

I asked George Shultz, tapped by Nixon to be his secretary of labor, whether he had influenced my appointment. "Bob," he said, "you got here on your own." I attributed the appointment to my work with the Chicago Economic Development Corporation, an agency supported by the Small Business Administration (SBA). Both the SBA and OMBE were housed in the U.S. Department of Commerce. But it could also have been the wide dissemination of an article I wrote for the *Harvard Business Review* in which I advocated for black enterprises based on my work with Operation Breadbasket, as well as insights gained from my students, who provided technical assistance to struggling black businesses on Chicago's South Side.[26] I had also authored an article in the *California Journal of Industrial Relations* comparing the labor and civil rights movements.[27]

For me the civil rights movement dramatized the energy and impact of the labor movement of earlier decades. In both cases, injustices needed to be addressed. The labor sit-ins of the 1930s were now the civil rights marches and demonstrations of the 1960s. The status quo needed to be tackled with direct action, and mobilizing the aggrieved in large numbers was the only way to effect change.

Before accepting the appointment, I met with Jesse Jackson. He thought I should accept the assignment but also had some concerns, which I conveyed to then secretary of commerce Maurice Stans. I had advocated for black enterprises, but told Stans that black leaders such as Jackson were deeply suspicious of the ideas of "black capitalism" and "minority enterprise," fearing they would generate merely a token response given the larger problems facing the African American community: education, housing, community infrastructure, and so on. Leaders in that community felt the emphasis should instead be on economic development.

Members of the academic community, especially in the social sciences, like being called on to offer advice to public officials. It was heartening to be asked for ideas about how to improve minority enterprise and the employment position of blacks. At the same time, for me personally, it was a change of pace to be on the front lines of the civil rights movement. In fact, my involvement was considerably greater than what is conveyed here, and it was also deeply personal. It coincided with my desire to spend more time writing about the strategies and tactics of the movement as they unfolded, and conducting research on the employment of blacks in the Chicago labor market. Some years later I wrote *A Decisive Decade*, a book on the Chicago civil rights movement.[28]

Beyond that I also needed a research agenda that would help my case for tenure. An opportunity to obtain important data came in 1965 when I received a call from Phyllis Wallace, the assistant research director for the Equal Employment Opportunity Commission (EEOC) in Washington, who asked whether I would be interested in analyzing the first year of data being assembled as part of the requirements of the recently enacted Civil Rights Act. She brought together a cadre of scholars from around the country, including Orley Ashenfelter of Princeton University, Lester Thurow of MIT, and James Heckman of Columbia University, and we met several times in Washington to discuss our research findings. I assembled a team of research assistants, and we analyzed the data to identify patterns in the employment of minorities in the Chicago Standard Metropolitan Statistical Area. We found a big disparity for African Americans in the labor movement: 29 percent of all employers in Chicago counted no African Americans on the payroll; only 6 percent employed African Americans in both clerical and blue-collar occupations; and most African Americans were employed in low-level occupations. It is a disparity that still persists.

Once again a policy administrator had turned to the top labor economists of the day. Ashenfelter went on to lead the Industrial Relations Section at Princeton for many years and was one of the first scholars to transform labor economics from its institutional traditions to an emphasis on econometrics; later he would serve as president of the American Economics Association. Thurow would go on to a highly public career as the best communicator of economic issues to the public of his generation; he would later serve as dean of the MIT Sloan School of Management, where I was his associate dean. Heckman would one day win the Nobel Prize in Economics and become recognized as a leader in developing carefully designed experimental research and associated statistical tests to overcome biases in sample selection.

Following that, I embarked on a project for the Office of Federal Contract Compliance and Programs (OFCCP) in the U.S. Department of Labor. The OFCCP, created by executive order of President Lyndon Johnson in the early 1960s as the civil rights movement was gathering momentum, was charged with leveraging the purchasing power of the federal government to enhance the employment position of minorities throughout the economy. To fulfill this mission, each supplier or contractor to the federal government was required to develop a plan of action (eventually called affirmative action) that committed the firm to increase the number and occupational position of underrepresented minorities, then defined as African Americans, Asian Americans, Hispanics, and Native Americans. Rather than using a guideline that each business should "do its best," the OFCCP needed yardsticks that would help it evaluate and decide whether to approve a submitted plan. That is where I came into the picture.

Using EEOC data, and with the help of several research assistants, we constructed a target selection system that compared, for each establishment, the density (referred to as penetration) and occupational level for black employees in a firm against numbers for other firms in the same area. This system (which carried my name) identified companies that the OFCCP could then select as targets, directing them to submit revised affirmative action plans that we hoped would improve the employment position of blacks. The system was also used to justify budget requests and allocate resources for the affirmative action offices of various government agencies.

Eventually some government contractors complained that they were being targeted on the basis of "statistics" without any evidence of discrimination or deliberate exclusion of African Americans. The issue came to a head in a case that reached the U.S. Supreme Court, *Mississippi Power & Light Co. v. Mississippi*.[29] Mississippi Power & Light argued that as a government contractor it could not be targeted because its only involvement with the federal government was to supply power to federal agencies, a role about which it had no choice. The Supreme Court ruled against the company but told the lower court to review the company's charge that it had been arbitrarily selected for review by the OFCCP. In the lower court review, the OFCCP argued that the use of the McKersie selection system was proof that its actions were not arbitrary. The target selection system was substantially modified when George Travers, the OFCCP's director of research and a PhD graduate from the University of Chicago, moved to another civil service position in the federal government.

One other piece of the civil rights story merits mentioning: my public criticism of a large Chicago company closely attached to GSB. When the *Chicago Daily News* published my letter about Motorola trying to replace the chair of the Illinois Fair Employment Practices Commission after the commission found the company guilty of racial discrimination, Motorola threatened to withhold its support of GSB.

The Motorola saga offers another key insight into George Shultz's leadership. The GSB dean never said a word to me about the letter; instead, in a quiet and decisive way, he took the heat from this corporate sponsor. In effect, the buck stopped in his office, thereby protecting academic freedom without any fanfare. That same low-key style, backed by a highly analytical and principled mind, served our country well in many cabinet appointments in several Republican administrations, finally culminating in his service as secretary of state for President Ronald Reagan.

In a fundamental way, the Motorola case put academic freedom to the test and, thanks to GSB's leadership, this hallmark of university life remained unaffected; indeed, it was probably strengthened as a result of this episode. Shultz's example would later help me deal with a similar complaint from a powerful union constituent of the Cornell ILR School. George was a model without making a public point about his actions.

Helping the civil rights movement target employers and press for expanded job opportunities for blacks brought together my professional interests and personal commitments. One reason academics sometimes seek an active role in the domains they study is to test in practice the propositions they are developing in their emerging theories—even if doing so may involve risks. Indeed, my intense involvement in the Chicago civil rights movement coincided with my work on *A Behavioral Theory of Labor Negotiations* and afforded an opportunity to gather additional data on the negotiation process, sharpen my thinking, and test our framework (it even became an add-on piece to the study). The task of academic leaders (which George so ably demonstrated without fanfare) is to support and stand behind faculty who do take such risks.

Looking back more than a half century later, I am still not sure that I struck the right balance between my academic obligations and my desire to be involved in the movement. Being part of direct action is exhilarating and can easily lead to a full-time commitment. Others in the movement were "all in," so why shouldn't I have been totally immersed? As I will describe in chapter 4, several members of the Cornell faculty got so involved in the Human Affairs Program helping nascent community groups and union organizing committees that they did not publish and failed to get tenure.

Thanks to that involvement, though, I was able to use my vantage point to collect data that bolstered my résumé. But the word *use* can have another meaning: civil rights leaders may conclude that when an academic comes around it is precisely to "use" being up close to the movement solely for research purposes, in the way a reporter might get close to write a story. What are the trade-offs when an academic asks to attend strategy meetings and become part of the "team"? It can be a challenge. The implied quid pro quo in this relationship means the academic can no longer be the "outsider." I hope I found the right balance in being involved (as the insider) and at the same wearing my academic hat (as the outsider).

Getting involved in the civil rights movement presented another issue: it moved me away from my central interest in collective bargaining. Studying black employment kept me in the broad field of industrial relations, because understanding the functioning of the labor market has always been a central focus for our field. How did I justify my involvement with Operation Breadbasket and minority enterprise? Observing Jesse Jackson's campaign as it opened opportunities for black businesses by using consumer boycotts and negotiations with the large food chains gave me new insights into the various sources of power that he employed, and these were helpful in developing new ways of thinking about the important topic of negotiations.

It is almost trite to attribute a bright spot in one's career to being at the right place at the right time. But that saying has many layers of meaning. My dozen years at the University of Chicago also placed me in the right circumstances with the right examples that provided lessons never to be forgotten.

The right place, right time idea captures the hothouse atmosphere of a business school being transformed—bringing in George Shultz, building closer ties with a world-famous economics department, and so on. Among the many distinguished faculty, Shultz was the extraordinary leader who demonstrated the power of analysis, thus leading to important policy prescriptions. His strong connections, especially with corporations and policymakers, created research and consulting opportunities for all of us, his colleagues. He was like a meteor that had come to Chicago from outer space, lighting up the industrial relations field for a substantial period.

In the hands of a lesser man, policy advice might perhaps have remained ideas on paper, but with Shultz it led to hands-on involvement dealing with the big challenge of worker adjustment. The Armour Automation project delivered valuable services to workers who had been displaced by major changes unfolding in the meatpacking industry. As I write this, I have been wondering whether there are other examples of business school faculty and their disciples going beyond consulting advice and actually implementing the policies that they advocate. One example would surely be the students of John R. Commons, who founded the field in 1920 when he created the first academic industrial relations program at the University of Wisconsin and who helped craft and administer the New Deal labor policies. Another example might be the various academics who helped draft the state-level policies for public-sector bargaining that were being enacted in the 1960s and 1970s.

Like those scholars, Shultz and his team acted as if they were skilled physicians—except they were treating "patients" with problems caused by economic change. Their model was very much in mind when the Continuity of Employment Committee was created during the 1970s while I was at Cornell, and my service to that project was very much in the Shultz tradition (as will be discussed in chapter 4).

Above all, perhaps the defining feature of my Chicago experience was the recognition that theory in our field is best developed inductively—grounded in empirical data but then digested, discussed, and debated with colleagues to draw out theoretical insights from disciplines of economics and the behavioral sciences that scholars from those disciplines who do not engage the real world of practice often can't see or appreciate. This interplay of discipline-based theory and practical engagement in the phenomenon of interest continues to be absolutely key to much of the best work in our field.

Curiously, George Shultz—and essentially all other industrial relations researchers of that era—got it wrong in terms of assessing the future of unionization and collective bargaining in the public sector. At the time there was plenty to do in the private sector, and no one writing in the late 1950s or early 1960s could foresee the explosion of public-sector bargaining or anticipate the impact it would have on our field. The door to research on public-sector issues, as far as I was concerned, would open only after I arrived at Cornell University and was in a position to foster attention to the subject.

Being in the right place at the right time certainly explains my involvement in the civil rights movement in Chicago. Although much of what I did could be considered "extracurricular," getting into the trenches gave me data for my research and standing that led to work in Washington for both the Commerce and Labor Departments. By doing so, I met a Shultz requirement he had offered in the form of advice: "Anyone interested in the field of labor should spend some time in government."

Timing was also working for me when I took a sabbatical break and spent a year in England, just as productivity bargaining was sweeping industry. I was an outsider, welcomed by both sides as I went to the field to study that development.

Finally, there is the right time, right place coincidence that Dick Walton and I ended up in our first academic posts just a hundred miles apart, which enabled us to continue a project—trying to make sense of the process involved in labor negotiations—we had started together as doctoral students at Harvard Business School. We certainly did not weigh our options with that in mind. Call it luck, or something else, but in any event, the decade of the 1960s at the University of Chicago was the best of times for my family and me.

Professor Sumner H. Slichter, working in his office around 1944. A member of the Harvard Economics Department, he was a strong presence in our lives as students at Harvard Business School. He had helped draft the National Labor Relations Act of 1935. (HBS Archives Photograph Collection: Faculty and Staff, Baker Library, Harvard Business School.)

Walter Reuther (third from right), president of the United Auto Workers, and other union and management negotiators after securing a contract in 1950 with General Motors that introduced the first partially paid hospitalization and medical program in a union shop. (Walter P. Reuther Library, Archives of Labor and Union Affairs, Wayne State University.)

Ford Motor Company workers on strike in May 1950, part of the wave of strikes throughout the United States in the decade following the end of World War II. (Walter P. Reuther Library, Archives of Labor and Union Affairs, Wayne State University.)

E. Robert Livernash, professor at Harvard Business School, in 1956, who served as my dissertation advisor. He treated me as a partner from the beginning to the end of my work on the dissertation. (HBS Archives Photograph Collection: Faculty and Staff, Baker Library, Harvard Business School.)

Benjamin M. Selekman, professor of labor relations at Harvard Business School, around 1960. It was Selekman who guided me as a case writer before I entered the doctoral program and who challenged Richard Walton and me to study negotiations. (HBS Archives Photograph Collection: Faculty and Staff, Baker Library, Harvard Business School.)

Victor Gotbaum and Lillian Roberts at a press conference in Chicago in fall 1959, at the time of strikes in that city against Mt. Sinai Hospital and the Home for the Incurables. Gotbaum, head of the American Federation of State, County, and Municipal Employees for the city, invited Roberts, a nurse's aide at the University of Chicago, to join his staff. Later, when he became head of AFSCME's District Council 37 in New York City, Roberts joined him, eventually becoming associate director. (District Council 37 Photo Collection, Robert F. Wagner Labor Archives in the Tamiment Library, New York University.)

Teaching my Industrial Relations class as part of the "190" evening MBA program at the University of Chicago Graduate School of Business (GSB) in the early 1960s. The program got its name from its location at the former training center of International Harvester, 190 E. Delaware Place in downtown Chicago. (Photo courtesy of University of Chicago Booth School of Business.)

UAW leader Walter Reuther (second from left), his wife May, and Harry Van Arsdale (right), president of the New York City Central Labor Council, marching from Selma to Montgomery, Alabama, in 1965. Reuther addressed the crowd as marchers gathered. Coretta Scott King later said of Reuther that he "was to black people the most widely known and respected white labor leader in the nation" who "was there when the storm clouds were thick." In 1963, Reuther had arranged for $160,000 in bail money to get Dr. Martin Luther King Jr. and other protestors released from jail at the time of King's famous "Letter from Birmingham Jail." (Walter P. Reuther Library, Archives of Labor and Union Affairs, Wayne State University.)

George Shultz in the business and economics library at the University of Chicago during his deanship of the Graduate School of Business in the 1960s. He later went on to serve as U.S. secretary of labor and U.S. secretary of state.

My lifelong friend Seymour Kahan, in Palm Springs, California, in the 1960s. I first met him in the early 1960s when he was an international representative for the UAW Farm Equipment Department—having worked at International Harvester in Chicago, where I conducted research. Years later Kahan became a regular in my classes at the Sloan School of Management. Photo by Patsy Leibik.

Arnold Weber, an economist and part of the core industrial relations faculty at GSB. Weber attended the University of Illinois on a scholarship from his father's International Brotherhood of Electrical Workers Local 3, and later earned a PhD at the Massachusetts Institute of Technology in the Industrial Relations Section. He served as assistant secretary of labor in the Nixon administration and went on to become president of the University of Colorado and, later, Northwestern University. (Special Collections Research Center, University of Chicago Library.)

My longtime friend Paul Goodman in his office at the University of Chicago in the late 1960s. Later I brought him to Cornell University's ILR School as a visitor, and he recruited Tom Kochan and Lee Dyer to go down into a coal mine. The highlight of his career was developing Carnegie Mellon University's distinguished international program.

Jack Sheinkman, then president of the Amalgamated Clothing Workers of America in Chicago, testifying sometime in the 1960s. Later, after a merger of unions, he went on to become the national president of UNITE (the Union of Needletrades, Industrial, and Textile Employees). (Kheel Center for Labor-Management Documentation and Archives, Cornell University Library.)

Former Teamsters president Jimmy Hoffa in April 1975, three months before he disappeared. Hoffa was touring the United States speaking on prison reform (he had recently been released from jail) and visited the ILR School campus for a series of meetings and lectures. I sat next to him at a luncheon that day. (Kheel Center for Labor-Management Documentation and Archives, Cornell University Library.)

The boycott movement against textile giant J. P. Stevens taking to the streets of New York City in the late 1970s. Photo by Bettye Lane. (Schlesinger Library, Radcliffe Institute, Harvard University.)

Harold Newman, chairman of the New York State Public Employment Relations Board from 1977 to 1990. He was associated with the ILR School for thirty years, serving on its Advisory Council and as a visiting lecturer. (Kheel Center for Labor-Management Documentation and Archives, Cornell University Library.)

Ronald Ehrenberg at the ILR School in the 1970s. Today he is the Irving M. Ives Professor of Industrial and Labor Relations and Economics, a Stephen H. Weiss Presidential Fellow, and director of Cornell University's Higher Education Research Institute. (Kheel Center for Labor-Management Documentation and Archives, Cornell University Library.)

In 1974, when members of the Advisory Committee on Federal Pay presented their report to President Gerald R. Ford, I missed the White House memo about who would be wearing what suit. Also pictured are the other members of the committee—Frederick R. Livingstone (with briefcase) and Jerome M. Rosow, the chairman (second from left, partially obscured)— along with some unidentified administration staffers and other participants. (Kheel Center for Labor-Management Documentation and Archives, Cornell University Library.)

Left to right: David Lipsky, Lois Gray, and Jean McKelvey at the the ILR School in the 1970s. Lipsky is today the Anne Evans Estabrook Professor of Dispute Resolution at the ILR School, an adjunct professor of law, and a Stephen H. Weiss Presidential Fellow at Cornell University. Gray, who passed away in 2018, was the Jean McKelvey/Alice Grant Professor of Labor Management Relations. McKelvey, who passed away in 1998, was one of the ILR School's founding faculty in 1945. (Kheel Center for Labor-Management Documentation and Archives, Cornell University Library.)

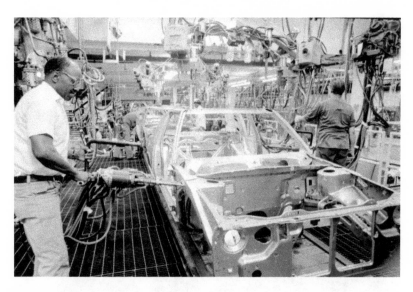

A typical scene in an auto plant in 1980: a worker on Chrysler's Jefferson Avenue Plant in Detroit helping build a Plymouth Reliant. (Walter P. Reuther Library, Archives of Labor and Union Affairs, Wayne State University.)

Phyllis Ann Wallace (right) at Mount Holyoke College in 1983, when she was awarded an honorary Doctor of Laws degree. She is pictured with Nancy Teeters (left) and Alice Rivlin, other honorary degree recipients that year. The first woman to receive a doctorate in economics from Yale University, she came to the MIT Sloan School in 1972 as a visiting professor while part of the senior staff at the Equal Employment Opportunity Commission. She was tenured as a full professor in 1974 and had a distinguished academic career that focused on racial and gender discrimination in the workplace—never giving up her activism. (MIT Museum.) *Source: Mount Holyoke Alumnae Quarterly*, Winter 1984, Archives and Special Collections, Mount Holyoke College

Professor Charles Myers teaching at MIT in the late 1970s or early 1980s. He held joint appointments in the Economics Department and the Sloan School and headed the Industrial Relations Section for many years. (MIT Sloan School of Management.)

Strikers from Detroit's Local 321 of the Professional Air Traffic Controllers Organization rally in August 1981, before President Ronald Reagan busted the union. Photo by Jim West/Alamy Stock Photo.

Don Ephlin, vice president of the UAW, in April 1982. He began his career working at the GM plant in Framingham, Massachusetts, headed the UAW's GM department, and was instrumental in bringing the Saturn plant to fruition in Tennessee. Later he lectured part-time in the Sloan School's executive program. (Walter P. Reuther Library, Archives of Labor and Union Affairs, Wayne State University.)

During the 1992–93 contract negotiations between HUCTW and Harvard University, rallies were held on a regular basis, centered on work and family issues. Here Kris Rondeau (right), the union president, poses with a union member at a "crazy hats day" rally. Rondeau is the president of the Labor and Employment Relations Association for 2018–2019. Photo by Ellen De Genova.

A "familiarization" tour of Inland Steel's East Chicago, Indiana, works that I took in 1993 after being nominated by the United Steelworkers of America to serve on Inland Steel's board of directors.

Abraham Siegel in 1999. After ten years as an economics instructor at the Sloan School, Siegel was named a full professor in 1964. He was dean of the Sloan School from 1981 to 1987 and later Howard W. Johnson Professor of Management Emeritus. (MIT Sloan School of Management.)

Richard Walton and I enjoying our time at a March 2015 symposium held at Harvard Law School to celebrate the fiftieth anniversary of the publication of our book *A Behavioral Theory of Labor Negotiations*. Photo by Susan Gershenfeld.

A rally by Harvard University dining hall workers and supporters during their three-week strike in the fall of 2016. It was the first strike at Harvard in thirty-three years, and it resulted in a five-year contract with a significant wage increase. (UNITE HERE Local 26.)

Joel Cutcher-Gershenfeld facilitating a multistakeholder dialogue involving a 2018 workshop on open data in the science publishing ecosystem. (Shelley Stall, American Geophysical Union.)

The cover of the January 2017 issue of *Hank*, the
magazine of the labor-management partnership at Kaiser
Permanente. (Kaiser Permanente Labor
Management Partnership.)

Tom Kochan (right) with David Rolf, founding president of Service Employees International
Union (SEIU) Local 775 in Seattle from 2003 to 2018. The local represents some forty-five
thousand health care workers. The two are pictured at the 2018 Sustainability Summit at MIT.
Rolf was a leading force in the successful fight to win a fifteen-dollar-per-hour minimum
wage in Seattle. Photo by Anna Demidova.

Chapter 4

Managing a Shop

New York State School of Industrial and Labor Relations, Cornell University, 1971–1979

My decision to leave the University of Chicago came about in steps. George Shultz and Arnold Weber left the Graduate School of Business (GSB) in January 1969 for appointments in the U.S. Department of Labor during the administration of President Richard M. Nixon, and I felt deserted. There were other faculty members—John Burton and Robert Flanagan—with interests in industrial relations, but I shifted my teaching away from industrial relations to business policy and small business administration. Was it because I had lost my cover of "respectability"? Shultz's presence in an environment with Milton Friedman and other economists who viewed unions as problems for the operation of the free market was a continuous validation of the importance of industrial unions. Or perhaps it was that I wanted to teach GSB's "high-status" courses. The business policy course even featured a business game—an advanced teaching method for that time—that relied on an IBM mainframe computer with data inputs on punch cards.

Most likely, however, what pushed me was my own need for a big change. I wanted to work on some different things, like teaching strategy. I convinced myself that I was uncomfortable with the direction GSB was going under the leadership of its new dean, Sidney Davidson, an accountant who stressed the corporate functions of finance and accounting. I was ready for a new challenge, and I began to explore the possibility of moving to Stanford University. I knew several faculty members in other subject areas who had moved from the University of Chicago to Stanford. The business school there lacked a senior faculty member interested in collective bargaining, and the weather there and California in general intrigued me. So I sent feelers to the faculty I knew and was invited to visit the campus. When I told Davidson I was exploring a move to Stanford, he was adamant that he was not going to let a faculty member move to a competing business school.

Then I was contacted about the deanship of the New York State School of Industrial and Labor Relations at Cornell University (the ILR School). It was not, and never has been, a business school. Established by the state legislature in 1945, the ILR School was the first college-level school of its kind in the world, and to this day is regarded as one of the leading institutions for the field of industrial relations. The school has an undergraduate curriculum, offers professional and doctoral degrees, and promotes executive and union education programs throughout New York State.

I told the provost I was very interested. I had no administrative experience in the academic world, and for the most part I was not well informed about the institution. But leading a school with a broad mandate for teaching and research in industrial and employment relations was very attractive. I knew a few of the faculty from meetings of the Industrial Relations Research Association, and certainly admired the school's journal, the *Industrial and Labor Relations Review*; it was the best in the field—even if the editors had rejected my first article.

It soon became clear in my discussions that the university's central administration wanted to hire an outsider who could help rejuvenate the ILR School at a time when the founding faculty members were approaching retirement and overall research output was not deemed satisfactory. Those discussions led to my first leadership position in academia.

Rejuvenation and Research

When I took over as dean in 1971, a number of key faculty who were considered charter members of the ILR School were already in their early sixties. They had been at the school since its establishment, and were cherished by alumni as mentors and revered as sources of wisdom. During my initial interview for the deanship with Cornell provost Robert Plane, however, he emphasized the need to bring "new blood" to the faculty.

With that mandate, I began to develop a plan for some faculty to retire, draw their state pensions, and at the same time be rehired on "college" funds at half-time salary.[1] This plan would not reduce their income; in fact, with a state pension, plus half-time salary, some would see their take-home pay rise. I thought it was a brilliant concept, and expected the targeted faculty to step forward enthusiastically.

I approached one individual who had not published for decades, urging him to retire at age sixty. He did—but he never spoke to me again. Then I moved on to three individuals who represented the "heart" of the school: Milton Konvitz, Jean McKelvey, and Morris Neufeld, all then in their early sixties. I pitched them my pension/half-time salary idea in terms of renewing the school's faculty, but they saw it as diminishing their status; they got the impression I viewed them as "tired" faculty who needed to be "put out to pasture." Nevertheless, the plan was put into effect.

Freeing up those senior faculty salaries from the state budget gave me the opportunity to hire additional junior faculty—in fact, more than just one-for-one replacements. In 1972–73, I brought on seven new faculty members: Samuel Bacharach, Clete Daniel, Thomas DeCottis, Lee Dyer, Tove Hammer, Roger Keeran, and Thomas Kochan. They all brought new energy to the school.

From the vantage point now of having myself been eased into retirement, I realize that I viewed my plan as a business transaction and failed to consider the emotional needs and interests of these senior faculty. I was not very popular with many of them. Later, Jean McKelvey said I should have explained my plan in terms of budget pressures, which she said would have made the quasi–retirement program more acceptable to her and her colleagues.

Hiring a cluster of junior faculty was only the first phase of rejuvenation. The second phase involved changing the direction of one department, Labor

Economics, which had become focused on the institutions of the labor market and was not in tune with the latest empirical research. One Labor Economics faculty member, Walter Galenson, believed strongly that the department needed to turn a corner. I decided to hold an off-campus meeting, with Galenson playing a key role, and invited Orley Ashenfelter, a scholar I knew from my days in Washington, DC, working for the Equal Employment Opportunity Commission (EEOC). More than anyone else, he was doing cutting-edge work and leading the field of labor economics back into the mainstream of economic theory and analysis, with a strong emphasis on modern econometric methods. Orley recommended that we hire Ronald Ehrenberg, then at the University of Massachusetts–Amherst and in a good position to move.

I visited Amherst and met with Ron at his home; he was impressed that the dean would travel all the way from Ithaca, New York, to talk to him. (I did not reveal that my in-laws lived a few miles away, and we saw them regularly.) We talked, and after some hesitation he agreed to join our faculty, first as a visitor and eventually as a full professor. Over the years Ron recruited other faculty, and presently the Labor Economics Department at the ILR School is one of the best in the country.

Later, after Ron had been at Cornell for many years, he received an offer to join the Department of Economics at Duke University, where H. Gregg Lewis—who had joined the Duke faculty after retiring from the University of Chicago—was based. I had many discussions with Ron as he deliberated; finally, he came into my office and told me he had decided on Duke. He had already told Tom Kochan, who said, "Good, you've finally made up your mind." But I told Ron he would regret his decision and he should stay at Cornell—which he ended up doing, going on to do pathbreaking research on the economics of higher education and, for a time, serving as Cornell's assistant provost responsible for research at the university.

I also set out to revitalize the school's Human Resources Department. Lee Dyer was hired in 1972, and in the late 1970s we recruited George Milkovich, a distinguished scholar from the University of Minnesota. He first visited for a term and then, and after a number of discussions, agreed to join the faculty. Like the Labor Economics Department, the ILR School's Human Resources Department has since attracted a number of other outstanding scholars and maintains the Center for Advanced Human Resource Studies, a highly respected and productive research center with links to leading human resources professionals.

Still, the widely held perception of the ILR School faculty at the time was that although it had an excellent classroom record, it was not keeping up with the field in terms of new research. Coming from earlier stints at Harvard University and the University of Chicago, where research was the name of the game, I looked for opportunities to foster a stronger research orientation at Cornell by encouraging projects that addressed cutting-edge issues. It turned out to be harder to move faculty in new directions than I had anticipated, but in the end the efforts paid off.

Productivity was a big theme in the 1970s; it became a rallying cry in business circles. As a measure of how well any economy is doing, productivity is key; after all, if our resources do not produce a steadily increasing number of products and services, then incomes stagnate and the expectation of an increasing standard of living for everyone cannot be realized.

In the 1970s Japan and several other industrialized countries were posting annual productivity increase numbers that far surpassed the performance of the U.S. economy. As a result, various public and private initiatives came forward. Jack Grayson, a classmate of mine in the doctoral program at Harvard Business School, established the American Productivity & Quality Center in Houston, Texas (where George Chandler, whom I introduced in chapter 2, had become executive director after leaving industry), after completing his stint as dean of the business school at Tulane University. At the federal level, the Nixon administration launched its Productivity Commission, which aimed, through various conferences and publications, to raise awareness of the importance of productivity for the health of the economy.

Getting unions to recognize the need for changes in the workplace that would improve productivity was not easy. Early in the 1970s, while working with Laurence Hunter on the book *Pay, Productivity, and Collective Bargaining*, I conducted a class for stewards from the large Bethlehem steelworks at Lackawanna, New York, focusing on my ideas for productivity improvement. I encountered substantial resistance. At that point in the history of the steel industry, competition from mini-mills and low-cost Japanese steel imports was on the horizon, but not apparent to this group of stewards.[2] They wanted to hold steady to their style of arm's-length collective bargaining rather than engage with management in efforts to boost productivity. The timing simply was not right.

In the years to follow, the climate changed considerably. The United Steelworkers produced a film titled *What Happened to Joe?* that chronicled the loss of jobs to imports. And in 1993, the union launched a comprehensive program entitled New Directions (described further in chapter 5) that envisioned union-management relationships with widespread and deep union involvement in productivity improvement efforts, as well as involvement in management decision making.

The question could be asked whether the Steelworkers (as well as other unions, especially in manufacturing) were playing catch-up. My answer has to be yes. The disconnect between management's orientation and that of labor is almost genetic. Management is always scanning the horizon for new methods, whereas the outlook of the workers and their leaders is to preserve what they view as hard-won gains in work practices and job protections. There is also the difference between the data about new technology available to management versus the union, especially at the local level. The Steelworkers at the national level—the union staff in the Pittsburgh headquarters—were well aware of the competitive challenge coming from new processes being adopted by steel companies in Japan and Korea, such as continuous casting. But the workers and their union representatives at the local level—in this case, at Bethlehem Steel's Lackawanna works, outside Buffalo, New York—were convinced that the methods being employed to make steel there would continue at the world-class level.

There were several other hot research topics in the 1970s, including worker alienation and quality of work life. I took the lead in making a proposal to the Ford Foundation for a fairly sizable grant, and though that specific grant did not come through, the efforts involved in applying for it generated sufficient interest to help keep the momentum going.

Worker alienation was an especially big topic. It was often said at the time that workers weren't dumb, they were just asked to work on dumb, repetitive jobs. The General Motors assembly plant in Lordstown, Ohio, became a national symbol for the discontent of many blue-collar workers. There a worker could make very good money in comparison to other jobs in the area, but it was a compulsory fifty-hour week, ten hours a day—at a high human cost. The assembly line moved at a relentless, unvarying rate, and the monotony of performing the same operation over and over gain forced members of the United Auto Workers there to a breaking point. In 1972 they struck for twenty-two days, during which one of their many tactics was to deliberately introduce defects into the Chevrolet cars coming off the line. Alienated workers at Lordstown believed they could do a better job designing their work than the General Motors industrial engineers who had developed the plant processes.

Soon enough, the term Lordstown Syndrome entered the lexicon as a reference to workers who were treated like automatons, with little attention given to the quality of their work life, and who struck back by disrupting production lines.

The issue of alienation captured more government attention, and in 1975 the administration of President Gerald R. Ford established the National Center for Productivity and Quality of Working Life. The nonprofit Ford Foundation (not related to the president) committed substantial resources to demonstration projects. At the ILR School, we put a team together and pushed ahead with fieldwork in several industries.

I had hoped we would be successful in receiving our own grant from the Ford Foundation. Its president, Mitchell Swirdoff, saw the need for encouraging research on the quality of work life. His officer, Basil Whiting, had been involved in the Michigan Quality of Work Program and served as the point person for stimulating a series of projects around the country. Paul Goodman, who was visiting at the ILR School, took the lead, helping Rushton Coal Mines introduce some of the concepts that Eric Trist had studied in Great Britain, especially the longwall method of mining in which a long, vertical wall of coal is mined in a single slice (typically 1.5 to 2.5 miles long) rather than the much older horizontal room-and-pillar method.

Paul recruited Lee Dyer and Tom Kochan to go with him on a trip underground—a new and unforgettable experience for those researchers. When Lee and Tom reported on their experience, they said we should imagine being two miles beneath the surface, sitting in the dark with water dripping down, and asking miners how, on a five-point scale, they would rate their working conditions—and getting consistent answers of "good" or "very good"! That's not quite how the miners would have rated their surroundings in the abstract, but all things are relative—and relative to other mines that those miners had worked in, that one was safer and a better place to work.

Paul and I were friends, and our families vacationed together in Maine. He had joined the faculty at the University of Chicago a few years after my arrival there, and he and his family rented our home when we were in England for a year during the mid-1970s. Paul did not get tenure at Chicago; being at Cornell gave him a year to search for other employment. He landed a position at Carnegie Mellon University, where he went on to have a very distinguished career and helped build and lead a very strong micro-organizational behavior group. But he never forgot his roots in studying and appreciating workers. He was a pioneer in producing documentary films that illustrated how workers from all over the world and from many occupations found dignity and meaning in their work and provided service to their customers and communities.

Although the ILR School did not receive the Ford Foundation grant, the biggest impacts for research came from opportunities the school received to engage in action research. Typically, most field research in industrial relations documented developments that had already taken place. The new role that the word *action* captures meant that that the researcher was not just an observer and a recorder, but was a member of the team that was designing and implementing an agenda for change.

I was uneasy about getting involved directly in that type of project. In my view, such projects should be left to the faculty. My job would be to make the rain—the opportunities—happen. But given the limited amount of research on topics that were not particularly important taking place when I first arrived at the ILR School, and with my mandate to change that, I justified spending time on projects as part of how I would involve faculty and bring them into engagement with topics that mattered.

Two Public Service Projects

I helped orchestrate two public service projects that provided just the right kinds of opportunities. In the first, we were asked to advise labor and management about how to improve productivity in the public sector in three municipalities in Nassau County on Long Island, New York. Vincent Macri, who contacted me at the ILR School to ask whether we could help, headed the project.

Having worked on productivity bargaining in Britain and with a strong personal interest in the effort to establish productivity improvement teams, I was interested in getting the ILR School moving on this contemporary issue. I recruited a staff member from the school's New York City office, Carol Wittenberg, who devoted half her time over a one-year period to the project, serving as a facilitator and conducting educational programs for the teams. Macri, realizing the need for joint union-management support, brought on board the president of the local Civil Service Employees Association (CSEA), which represented workers in the county's major towns.

Macri was the epitome of a young, ambitious lawyer who wanted to develop a reputation that would enable him to run for public office. He served as a special assistant to the county executive, and saw an opportunity to make his mark by securing funds that would facilitate establishing productivity improvement teams. He quickly generated extensive publicity about the project, and over several years orchestrated many press releases and public appearances to tout the program's success.

Even now the big question addressed by the Nassau Country project remains central: how to foster change and continuous improvement in any organization, particularly in a public-sector setting. The premise of the project was that without a "carrot" or some type of financial return for demonstrated results, not much would take place. In this case, the question took center stage at a hearing held before the Nassau County Board of Supervisors, where Vince's proposal that extra money should be offered for improvement was challenged. He wanted financial rewards to be paid for superior results. Several supervisors opined instead that improvements in productivity should come about naturally—that public workers should always do things more effectively and efficiently and, moreover, that because their pay and benefits had increased recently there was no need for extra compensation. Vince lost the argument, and no gainsharing took place.

I see this now through the prism of the evolving social contract that public workers experienced after World War II. Employment in the public sector had grown steadily in the first decades following the war, and although pay was lower than in the private sector, benefits were better. And though satisfactory performance on the job was expected, the pace of the work did not match that of jobs in the private sector.

Then, in the 1960s and 1970s, the public sector saw a wave of union organizing. As unions won recognition and their bargaining rights, public-sector workers made significant gains, especially in wages. This drove the unstated thinking of government officials that because they had improved the economic position of public workers, it was time for a quid pro quo in terms of increases in productivity.

The Nassau Country project came into being as a result of that very interest on the part of the federal government in increasing productivity in the public sector. The Department of Labor was helping fund the project. Indeed, the 1970s witnessed a surge of interest and activity on the part of the federal government regarding productivity (as exemplified in the 1975 establishment of the National Center for Productivity and Quality of Working Life), increases in which were important to the growth of the economy. Statistics were showing a decline in annual productivity rates.[3]

I am sure that somewhere in the archives of the U.S. Department of Labor there are reports that would shed light on the how much progress was actually made. Were I to go back to Nassau County, I doubt I would find anyone who could remember this important effort from the mid-1970s. And since that time, the emphasis on productivity in the United States has waxed and waned.

The other public-service project came about as the result of the CSEA's 1976 negotiations, during which the union demanded that New York State prohibit all future layoffs from mental health facilities—as deinstitutionalization was taking place throughout the state. With new treatment therapies available, many patients housed in state institutions were being released to smaller, sometimes privately owned facilities. As a result, more than ten thousand workers had already been terminated or were scheduled to be laid off in several waves. The union was under considerable pressure to end the disruption and dislocation caused by these massive layoffs.

The chief negotiator for New York State, Donald Wollett, responded that it was not feasible for the state to "tie its hands" by guaranteeing there would be no layoffs. He did, however, advance a counterproposal: the concept of advance notice and establishment of the Continuity of Employment Committee (CEC), mandated to conduct research and create demonstration projects to help the state as it moved through deinstitutionalization and help individuals affected by the layoffs find new jobs. The CEC members were four regional directors from the union and four high-level management officials from the state. Wollett, after consulting with the president of the CSEA, asked me to chair the committee. From the ILR School I recruited PhD students Leonard Greenhalgh and Todd Jick and MBA student Charles DeAngelo to provide staff support.

Early on, the CEC agreed to several ground rules. First, all decisions would be made only after a full discussion and consensus was reached among all CEC members. CEC recommendations would be submitted to the state's director of employee relations and to the CSEA president. A key ground rule involved what CEC members called the black box—namely, the CEC would concern itself only with the impact of program changes on workers, not with the rationale or the appropriateness of the changes being implemented. Further, the CEC agreed it would utilize existing state agencies and work toward incorporating its concepts and programs into those agencies rather than establishing a new and separate office. The CEC imposed a ceiling on research and administrative expenses of 25 percent of the $1 million appropriated for its work, meaning that most of its funds would be spent on services to benefit those who had been displaced.

The CEC established a readjustment center where workers could get help with résumé writing and access to job search aids. It also developed training programs that sought additional funding from state and federal agencies. Further, it conducted an experiment with a facility that was closing near New York City in which workers were urged to accept other jobs from New York State with the promise of training and relocation assistance; workers who chose instead to seek employment in the private sector would receive only minimal help. We found that even though most workers wanted to continue their employment with the state, many were unwilling to relocate. The CEC also emphasized the importance of achieving workforce reduction through attrition, thereby avoiding layoffs—especially if the closing could be done in stages.

About 35 percent of at-risk employees experienced no layoff, as they were able to move to other jobs within the state. About 45 percent were eventually recalled to state employment after a short layoff period, although about 10 percent needed to move to accept recall to state employment. The remaining workers were unemployed for periods that sometimes approached a half year. Most saw their savings decline. The financial impact of the layoffs mirrored other studies: on average, most workers experienced at least a 20 percent reduction in their long-term income. Many experienced stress and other emotional problems, and about 20 percent of the sample recorded heavy use of alcohol. There were several suicides.

The CEC operated for five years during the 1970s, and I count my involvement as its chair to be one of the most interesting and significant assignments I have been associated with in my career. While we did not conduct any systematic evaluation of the project, workers did receive advance notice about layoffs; many entered training programs, and still others received substantial counseling in their search for new jobs. The project's work was deemed successful. The initial allocation of $1 million was not fully spent, and some funds were returned to the state. A successor committee was formed with a focus on productivity and quality of work life.

The success of the CEC prompts a question: Why did this effort work while other initiatives involving labor-management cooperation did not produce comparable results? To address this question, some background is needed. Don Wollett saw the CEC as a successor to the Armour Automation Fund Committee that had been pioneered by Clark Kerr, Ralph Helstein, and George Shultz. As was noted in chapter 3, that committee dealt with the problem of workers displaced from large urban meatpacking plants that were shut down during the 1960s. The connection is not accidental. Early in his career, Don worked at the same law firm as Fred Livingston, who served as adviser to the Armour Automation Fund Committee. Both the CEC and the committee produced successful labor-management cooperation and robust outcomes.

It is interesting to compare these two examples with the work of the National Center for Productivity and Quality of Working Life, established in 1975 by the National Productivity and Quality of Working Life Act. One purpose, as stated in the legislation, was to "encourage joint labor, industry, and Government efforts to improve national productivity." In 1978 the U.S. Government Accounting Office reported that the center was "unsuccessful in accomplishing some major functions," giving as one reason the limited resources allocated by the administration of President Jimmy Carter and by the U.S. Congress.[4]

I would add that the National Center was "top-down" in contrast to the CEC and Armour projects, both of which were built from the ground up. Stakeholders defined what they thought was the problem—namely, the need to improve productivity and quality of work—and then the solution: labor-management cooperation. When parties at the operating level recognize on their own that they have a significant and immediate problem that can be worked on jointly, good results are more likely. Establishing a forum at the national level is good for bringing the parties together, but it generally does not extend beyond holding meetings, writing reports, and urging labor and management to work together.

While working on productivity bargaining in Britain, I learned that getting labor and management involved in designing and executing joint efforts has to be "copper-bottomed," which is a phrase the British use to mean "thoroughly reliable." In other words, if the effort is designed at the top and not related to problems experienced at the local level—that is, it does not involve the commitment of local actors—it will not stand the test of time.

Several lessons about what it takes to be a successful dean of a school stand out from these experiences in expanding research and public service. One lesson is that a dean must have a vision for where an institution needs to go, at least in broad outlines, or that dean will be nothing more than a simple caretaker of the status quo. The vision needs to be open and flexible to the circumstances and opportunities for innovation and the necessary development that gets clarified through faculty discussion and external engagement.

Another lesson is that making significant change requires bringing in new faculty with state-of-the-art training and fresh interests. Support and advice from more experienced and accomplished scholars from outside the school can help bolster the case for change so a dean isn't viewed as acting alone.

Finally, and perhaps most important, a dean has to have thick skin and determination to deal with the inevitable resistance that will come from those who may view *any* change as "not what we do here."

All of these lessons would apply to any dean, anywhere, but there is something unique about the ILR School that most deans never have to deal with: a highly complicated relationship with the labor movement.

A Complicated Relationship with the Labor Movement

The ILR School and the labor movement, especially those parts of it centered in New York State, have had a complicated relationship. The school has always been closely connected to the labor movement, and the state's labor movement has seen Cornell University—often referred to as "the people's university"—as a special province for advancing the interests of its members. This goes back to its founding in 1945, specifically to provide a "common training program" for labor and management that could help stabilize what were often contentious negotiations.[5] At that time, the Cornell University Board of Trustees was even expanded specifically to include two seats for trade union leaders.

Over the years, ILR School leaders were given many opportunities to champion the school to prospective students from union families. For example, each spring I attended the Scholarship Breakfast organized by Local 3 of the International Brotherhood of Electrical Workers (IBEW), where I met with parents and students who might someday apply for admission to the school. On other occasions, I spoke to the state convention of the AFL-CIO, which certainly helped promote the large number of programs in cities throughout New York State sponsored by the Extension Division of the ILR School that served the needs of the labor movement.

Despite these strong connections with the labor movement, the ILR School has always prized its independence and its ability to teach and conduct research without interference from *any* outside interests. By and large, the faculty wanted to remain neutral and not be seen as pro- union. At the same time, however, the school needed support from the labor movement— especially when help was needed to fight proposed budget cuts.

This issue of a school (by charter) being mandated to serve the labor movement but at the same time wanting to present a posture of neutrality naturally creates tensions. At the ILR School, these tensions came into focus in a variety of ways. At one faculty meeting, for example, a professor observed that some students who were enrolled in a field studies course were helping organize a union in a nearby plant; he objected to giving the students credit for this activity. The school's Human Affairs Program had placed the students in the field; William Whyte, who was committed to fieldwork, had been influential in getting the program started on a university-wide scale.

The impetus for the initiative grew out of complaints that surfaced during the late 1960s that much of the coursework being offered on college campuses was irrelevant and there should be a refocusing of the curriculum on the urgent problems of poverty and discrimination. So a number of ILR students enrolled in a course that took them to Cortland, New York, about twenty-five miles from Ithaca, to study working conditions in several plants. By chance, a union organizing effort was underway at one plant and, being partial to unions, the students—who were receiving credit for their fieldwork—helped with the distribution of materials to workers. This caught the attention of the faculty member who, though not anti-union, was certainly not pro-union.

Being open about whether one was pro- or anti-union was deemed "political," and given the academic mandate to be objective, faculty members did not express themselves publicly on the subject. Still, most ILR faculty were supportive of unions, although there were several members of the Labor Economics Department who—like economists at the University of Chicago profiled in chapter 3—saw unions as "restraints of trade."

The ILR faculty may have been more sensitive with regard to maintaining objectivity than industrial relations faculty at other institutions. I am quite sure that Jack Barbash of the University of Wisconsin, Philip Taft of Brown University, and George Taylor of the University of Pennsylvania—to mention several of the "big names" prominent in our field in the immediate postwar period—championed the role of unions and were very "partisan" in endorsing the view that unionism should be encouraged. The ILR School had been thrust on Cornell, and the faculty strived for acceptability from members of an institution located in a rural area.

Despite this institutional neutrality, there was the occasion when Walton Burdick, vice president of human resources at IBM, declined to join the ILR School Advisory Council. He did not explain his decision except to say, "You know, Bob, we do not have any unions at IBM." He did, by the way, support the school's Human Resources Department and helped establish the Center for Advanced Human Resource Studies.

Another example concerned the ILR School's prestigious journal, *The Industrial and Labor Relations Review*. The journal's policy required that it be printed by a union shop. An association representing nonunion printing companies complained, claiming the requirement violated the law. The associate dean at the time suggested we hire an ineffective lawyer to represent us in countering the complaint: it would appear we were fighting for the principle of a union shop, thus keeping our union friends happy, but the lawyer's incompetence would mean we'd lose the case. That would make the associate dean happy because he believed, in fact, that the requirement *was* inappropriate. In 2017, former dean Harry Katz confirmed to me that the school no longer requires the *ILR Review* to be printed by a union shop.[6]

The fact that public money was involved made this a complicated issue for me. I am uneasy in a situation where an organization uses public funds to require that a supplier be a union shop. As a consumer, though, I personally want to buy union-made products whenever possible, and I have always insisted that my calling cards be printed with the union "bug." At the beginning of the twenty-first century, however, it has become difficult to find a union printer.

A number of stories illustrate how this relationship between the ILR School and the labor movement played out during my time in Ithaca. As the school's dean, and also as someone who likes to solve problems, I thought at one point that it would be good to develop some guiding principles that could help resolve issues as they arose between the school and the labor movement. I came to realize that an overarching set of guidelines was probably not feasible and that each episode needed to be dealt with on a case-by-case basis.

Three events in particular, all of which unfolded or at least began before I had served a single semester as dean, are particularly telling. The first involved challenges in a project that would expand the ILR School's footprint.

The Labor College and Harry Van Arsdale

Soon after I arrived at the ILR School in the summer of 1971, Keith Kennedy, Cornell's assistant provost, called to say the two of us should drive that week to Albany, the state capitol, to meet with Chancellor Ernest Boyer of the State University of New York (SUNY) system. On the way, Keith told me that the labor movement in New York State, spearheaded by Harry Van Arsdale, had been pressing for the state government to create a labor college in New York City.

Harry was the president of the New York City Central Labor Council, and had been instrumental in getting the first labor contracts for teachers and taxi drivers. He also pushed to bring minorities into leadership positions in the labor movement. While he did not play a significant role in bringing about greater equality and recognition for women, he did appoint one woman to the staff of IBEW Local 3, his home union, at a time when there were no women on the staff of any building trades union. In Harry's view, management had business schools, and thus the labor movement should have its own school. Given that New York City had one of the highest unionization rates in the nation, one could understand his thinking.

The labor movement had for some time been on a campaign to persuade the ILR School to establish a degree-granting program specifically for union members. The school had offered a labor liberal arts program for many years, viewing it as general continuing education, first on a credit basis and then moving to offer a certificate. One source of the demand for a labor college was students from unions who had completed that labor liberal arts program.

Keith explained that Ernie Boyer was under pressure to get the labor college launched. The new Empire State College in the SUNY system, which emphasized education for working adults, could provide the ideal auspices. Keith agreed with Ernie that the ILR School, with its charter to provide labor education, needed to be centrally involved. "We need to protect our franchise," Keith explained.

It took many meetings, especially with ILR faculty, but Harry's dream became a reality in September 1971 with the creation of a partnership between the ILR School at Cornell and Empire State College that would grant a bachelor's degree. As part of establishing the Labor College, which would be housed in a building supplied by IBEW Local 3 at the southern end of Manhattan, the faculty agreed to give credit for the work done at the ILR School—but only after Empire State College stepped in to offer the degree. Originally, Ernie wanted the ILR School to take full responsibility for all aspects of the Labor College, including granting a bachelor's degree and later a graduate degree. But this was not to be, given the feeling of the faculty that a Cornell degree should not be given for work done outside of Ithaca.

I enthusiastically supported the Labor College, and even agreed to teach there. That meant commuting to New York City every week during the spring of 1972.

The Labor College stands as an impressive achievement by Harry Van Arsdale, labor leader turned education booster. Without his leadership, it would never have been launched. Harry's huge stature and influence were evident in June 1979 at an early graduation ceremony that took place in New York City. The program listed more than a hundred individuals who would receive either certificates, associate's, or bachelor's degrees related to industrial and labor relations. Toward the end of the program, Harry came to the podium and expressed his thanks to the public officials who were present. He was the only individual on stage not wearing a cap or gown. His direct manner marked him as a person accustomed to getting results. He addressed some of his remarks directly to Stanley Fink, the speaker of the New York State Assembly, who was present: "We know that the speaker will support the next step of building a full program—a master's degree."

Toward the end of the program, Jim Hall, the president of Empire State College, spoke about how important Harry was in supporting labor education. After Hall finished his speech and sat down, Harry turned to him and asked, "Is that all you're going to say?"

Following the ceremonies, we were invited to a reception at which Harry took the microphone and urged those assembled to recruit new students for the Labor College. I remember his emphasis: "I will ask the business manager to keep a list for each business agent of individuals who have been recruited and referred to the Labor College." To make sure there would be no mistake about his meaning, he asked several business agents from Local 3 to talk about the importance of education.[7]

Harry never missed a Labor College graduation, and demonstrated his commitment to education in other ways as well. College graduates from IBEW Local 3, organized in a group called the Futurians, were regularly invited to attend lectures and special programs. Additionally, the union owned and operated a residential center on Long Island named Bayberry. Over the years, approximately fifteen thousand members of the rank and file took up residence there for a one-week course in critical thinking.

At one Labor College graduation ceremony, Harry mentioned that he was going to spend the next few days at Bayberry, and asked if I would like to join him. I had planned to fly back to Ithaca late that night, so I hesitated, but quickly realized that I needed to say yes to this key person in the labor movement who was also a member of the ILR School's Advisory Council.

In retrospect, I use the term *win-win* to describe the outcome in establishing the Labor College, despite some faculty feeling that the school had been pressured into doing something it had some doubts about—namely, offering credited instruction in New York City.

As I think back to the creation of the Labor College, I realize the uniqueness of that development, which brought about an alignment of motivated students who had experienced college-level coursework (and wanted more), the strength of the labor movement in New York State (and its support of Governor Nelson Rockefeller), and the passion for education by a strong leader, Harry Van Arsdale. Labor education takes place in many places in this country, but the creation of an institution such as the Labor College has not been duplicated.

But what of the other two events and their outcomes? They were not win-win by any measure.

The Labor Day Fiasco

Another example of the tensions between traditional academia and the ILR School's unique mandate regarding the labor movement is illustrated by something that happened very soon after classes began in the 1971–72 academic year, my first as dean. I asked someone in the university's central administration about options regarding Labor Day. After all, it was a national holiday that most people had off from work. Cornell University didn't have classes on other national holidays of the same import.

"Cornell University will be in session," I was told, "and as part of Cornell, the ILR School must conform. Remember, students from other parts of the campus take courses in the school." In response, and being new, I did nothing more than make a feeble attempt to celebrate the day by announcing there would be a picnic on the ILR School quadrangle. To do nothing to draw attention to the national holiday, I thought, would be disrespectful. Soon thereafter, the Cornell Organization for Labor Activities (COLA), a student group, protested having to attend classes on Labor Day. They wanted to do what George Meany, then the president of the AFL-CIO, said all workers should be engaged in on the holiday: loafing. I wondered whether the *A* in COLA's name actually stood for "Agitation."

As the start of the next academic year (1972–73) approached, I thought we should develop a plan to treat Labor Day in a different way. We discussed several ideas at a meeting of the ILR School Administrative Council, including canceling classes. That was rejected on the grounds that there was already enough concern and even hostility around campus about the school—waggishly referred to as the Little Red School House. The most appealing idea was a convocation at which a distinguished speaker would help us reflect on the true meaning of Labor Day, which had been established in the 1890s but had grown to be a long "unofficial end of summer" weekend of activities largely unrelated to honoring the contributions of the American labor movement and workers generally.

So a joint faculty-student committee was appointed—when in doubt, organize a committee—chaired by Lawrence Williams. The committee went to work and, after a few turndowns, secured Howard Samuels as the featured speaker. His willingness to undertake the assignment was helped by the fact that Jack Sheinkman leaned on him; Howard was Jack's vice president in the Amalgamated Clothing and Textile Workers Union (ACTWU). Samuels gave what I thought was a fine speech, although toward the end he launched into some critical remarks about President Nixon, who was running for re-election. The convocation ended and classes resumed. At the end of the day, the school sponsored another picnic.

When I returned to my office, I found a note from the program committee apologizing to the students and faculty for Samuels's "inappropriate remarks" made earlier in the day. Now I was on the spot. This letter read as if it had been issued by a "truth squad": as soon as the speaker left town, the vigilantes fired off a note to the community. Should I let the letter stay in Ithaca? Or should I let Howard Samuels know what had transpired after he left campus?

I sent a copy to Howard. I didn't want him to learn about the letter secondhand.

It did not take long for Jack Sheinkman to call, asking for an explanation. "Howard feels he has been stabbed in the back," Jack told me. I agreed to send a copy of Howard's talk to Jack so he could form his own opinion. Subsequently, Jack called to say that some of Howard's comments about President Nixon were very partisan and that perhaps he did take advantage of the occasion to deliver a political speech.

On balance, I felt the action of the program committee went too far in the other direction and bordered on censorship—not the right message for an academic institution to convey. Howard went on to head the AFL-CIO's Industrial Union Department. Whenever our paths crossed, he was distinctly cool; clearly he felt he had been badly treated.

The Labor Day saga was pure lose-lose. No doubt I could have handled the aftermath of that convocation better, and to this day I wrestle with which of two alternative courses of action would have been correct: not sharing with Howard the program committee memo that criticized his speech, or talking to him face-to-face. Either option might have eased the tension. Both sides felt their values had been violated: the faculty was upset that an observance had been turned into a partisan event, and the union leader felt his freedom of speech had been violated.

A very different experience—involving an important strike—also speaks to the complicated relationship between the ILR School and the labor movement.

J. P. Stevens

In the fall of 1971 a major event took me to New York City—the first annual alumni award ceremony. To emphasize the ILR School's balanced approach to labor and management, we honored two individuals: Eric Jensen, a vice president of ACF Industries, and Jack Sheinkman, president of the ACTWU and a member of Cornell's Board of Trustees, occupying one of the two seats reserved for representatives of the labor movement.[8]

During the 1970s the ACTWU undertook a tough campaign to organize J. P. Stevens, one of the largest textile companies in the United States that was heavily involved in the production of broadcloth, which in turn was fabricated into many other products. Bruce Raynor, an ILR School alumnus who later succeeded Jack as union president, led the campaign and thought Cornell should follow the lead of Temple University and prohibit the use on campus of any J. P. Stevens products. The Cornell administration refused.

The legal contest between the ACTWU and J. P. Stevens came to a head in 1978 when the union decided the only way it could make headway in its efforts to organize the workers was to initiate a nationwide boycott. The union had plenty of grist for its campaign: the company had been found guilty of many unfair labor practices, and those complaints were slowly winding their way through the courts. In at least one instance where the union had gained representation rights, negotiations for a first agreement were proceeding very slowly.

ILR students quickly joined the campaign. They pressured Cornell's central administration to side with the union, but that didn't happen; the university made clear that a boycott was not going to take place. Then the ILR faculty was asked to endorse the boycott at its April 1978 meeting. After considerable discussion, the faculty took no action.

The students were not to be deterred. In the spirit of preparing to be mediators and arbitrators, and wanting to hear both sides of the issue, they put on their academic hats and invited Marshall Palmer, J. P. Stevens's director of administration, to come to campus. I suspect they could also have thought that Palmer might be persuaded to modify his position, or perhaps that he would say something that would give them more ammunition.

Sheinkman diplomatically asked about the school sponsoring the session at which Palmer spoke. In his letter, Jack attached a news story about Temple

University's decision to cease purchasing Stevens products; clearly this was the action Jack hoped Cornell would take. An exchange of letters followed. William Herbster, Cornell's senior vice president for administration, reaffirmed the university's neutral stand. Jack responded that the university should not remain neutral on such an important matter.

After the session, I wrote a letter to Palmer, thanking him for coming and complimenting him for exercising restraint in a situation fraught with considerable tension.

That fall, representatives of the ACTWU and J. P. Stevens met, and Jack outlined a framework for moving forward. It was clear both sides needed some kind of face-saver: the company needed assurances that free and open elections would take place, and that the union would not be recognized without an affirmative vote by the workers; the union needed to be able to say it had organized some plants and been able to negotiate initial contracts. Nothing came of the meeting.

Jack thought a third party could help, especially given that James Finley, the J. P. Stevens president, had been attacked personally by the union during its campaign. I decided I would approach Marshall Palmer about whether I might play a constructive role as facilitator or mediator. We met at the company's headquarters in New York City.

Marshall first took me to see the office of Robert Stevens, who I believe was then the board chairman and who had served in the administration of President Dwight D. Eisenhower as secretary of the U.S. Army. The entire boycott issue was somewhat of an embarrassment to the company, which resented being singled out by the union when textile manufacturing was largely unorganized throughout the South. Indeed, Jack and the union thought they could use the adverse publicity to bring J. P. Stevens into some type of settlement.

I told Marshall I had no idea whether the union was interested in further discussions (which wasn't true), but I wanted to offer my assistance nevertheless. I conveyed that I thought what was occurring was destructive, was hurting Stevens's image, and that the union might be compelled to go all out just to bolster its own image. Marshall said only that if they did get into discussions with the union, J. P. Stevens would probably want to limit the agenda to procedures for holding representation elections and nothing more.

Our meeting was brief. On the way out, Marshall introduced me to the company's general counsel and made the point that he had graduated from

Yale University. I knew Palmer to have gone to Princeton University. I got the not-so-subtle message: "You are representing a similar school, so don't rock the Ivy League boat."

Some weeks later, on November 20, Marshall phoned to thank me for coming and to tell me they didn't need my services "now." He asked me to keep in touch, and said they would get back to me "if and when." "I am in touch with Amalgamated," he told me, "and I know quite a bit about how to have discussions about discussions."

The ACTWU did win representation rights at one of the big J. P. Stevens plants and successfully negotiated a contract. But the union never gained representation rights at many other plants. Now, decades later, most of the plants no longer exist.

In the ACTWU effort to have Cornell boycott J. P. Stevens products, the university won, maintaining neutrality and not taking sides in a labor dispute. The company won by not agreeing to card check and by maintaining neutrality with respect to the union's organizing efforts. The union lost—in part due to the university maintaining that neutrality. The lesson to take away is that sometimes, when the labor movement reaches out to its friends for support in an important campaign, it will win some adherents and lose some. There is no guarantee of a positive outcome.

Had there been a more convincing case about the "bad behavior" of J. P. Stevens, would the university have been obliged to halt purchases from the company? The company had been found guilty of violating the National Labor Relations Act, but the cases were under appeal. Temple University had taken action, so Sheinkman argued Cornell should do likewise.

Sheinkman found himself in an embarrassing position, being a trustee and having earned two degrees from Cornell. Being unable to persuade his alma mater to change course was a big disappointment.

The J. P. Stevens affair raises big questions about the dilemma facing faculty in industrial relations: Should we speak out and weigh in on one side of an issue or crisis? Or should we not get involved, and instead follow along from the vantage point of an objective observer? As I noted in chapter 3, I did not hesitate to criticize Motorola for its actions with respect to the hiring of a qualified black worker. And, as I will discuss in chapter 5, I joined my colleagues in taking issue with President Ronald Reagan's firing of all air traffic controllers. There certainly are risks in taking a stand, especially when matters become polarized—which is not an uncommon situation when so much is at stake. But that is what makes the study and teaching of industrial relations so exciting.

Despite not taking sides in the J. P. Stevens matter, generally good relationships persisted between the ILR School and the labor movement. The school also began to build stronger *direct* ties with the labor movement and employers in the public sector.

Cooperation with the Practitioner Community

Collective bargaining in the public sector was relatively new while I was dean of the ILR School in the 1970s, and extending our involvement with the public sector had a major influence on the school's activities. We gave collective bargaining in the sector considerable attention and helped develop procedures and institutional relations in an orderly manner, which in turn helped establish it more firmly among public employees.

In a 1963 speech to the National Academy of Arbitrators, then secretary of labor W. Willard Wirtz had warned that "a statutory requirement that labor disputes be submitted to arbitration has a narcotic effect on private bargainers. . . . They will turn to it as an easy and habit-forming release from the . . . obligation of hard, responsible bargaining."[9]

There was concern that this "narcotic effect" would rear its head in the public sector, too, once collective bargaining became more commonplace— despite Wirtz's warning. Still, the public sector in New York provided a rich opportunity for collecting case studies and analyzing data. Tom Kochan, David Lipsky, and other ILR faculty members authored important studies that deepened the understanding of the process involved in reaching agreement in public-sector negotiations.

More than forty years after the 1967 enactment of New York State's Public Employees Fair Employment Act (also known as the Taylor Law), which legalized public-sector bargaining for local and state employees, Tom and David, along with Alan Benson and Mary Newhart, published a study that examined the long-run experience of interest arbitration for police and firefighters.[10] They noted positive results as well as issues that required attention, and showed that repeated dependence on the use of the procedure had not yet come to pass.[11]

The ILR School developed a close working relationship with the Public Employment Relations Board (PERB) in Albany. No discussion of public-sector labor relations in New York under the 1967 Taylor Law would be complete without a profile of Robert Helsby, PERB's first chairman. Helsby was a PhD graduate of the ILR School who received the prestigious Judge William B. Groat Alumni Award and served on the school's Advisory Council. He worked with Martin P. Catherwood, then the commissioner of the New York State Department of Labor; Catherwood later became the ILR School's second dean. Jerome Lefkowitz, who chaired PERB many years later, described Bob Helsby as a "man of rectitude" and a "superb administrator."[12]

Helsby reached out to professionals across the country engaged in dispute resolution in the public sector, and he helped create the Society of Professionals in Dispute Resolution, serving as its first president in 1972.

PERB staff and ILR School faculty forged a strong connection. PERB needed mediators, and fact finders, and many ILR faculty members welcomed the opportunity to be of service while earning additional income. (If I recall correctly, mediators and fact finders were paid the great sum of $150 per day.) While the joke goes that Ithaca is the most isolated part of central New York State, it is also nearly equidistant to each of New York's most important cities—Albany, Buffalo, and New York City. It's also not far from Horseheads, Lackawanna, and Oneonta (hardly bustling metropolises); faculty could move around the state readily to handle cases and conduct research.

One of Helsby's key decisions resulted in the creation of five statewide units of the CSEA. This caused considerable concern within the highest reaches of state government. The state, like most employers, preferred that the definition of the bargaining units be tied to specific locations rather than large and regional in makeup. Years later, Governor Rockefeller called Helsby to say that although he had been upset at the time, "he had come to realize that the success of the Taylor Law depended upon PERB's reputation as an agency independent from the governor, and that this decision had demonstrated that independence."[13]

Helsby was also responsible for a key hiring: Harold Newman as PERB's director of operations. Newman's association with the ILR School had many strands: he was a regular visiting lecturer, spent 1975 at the school on a year's sabbatical leave from PERB, and had worked in the labor movement for the American Federation of State, County, and Municipal Employees before joining PERB. The students loved his wit and benefited from his acumen about labor relations. He took over as PERB chair in 1977.

Harold drew heavily on ILR School faculty and even students as neutrals who could work on the many cases that needed mediation and arbitration, and many faculty members and even some students owe the start of their careers as neutrals to Harold. Marty Sheinman, a twenty-two-year-old graduate student, took on a case of school cafeteria workers who went on strike. "Fortunately for me," he said, "and I guess for Harold . . . I helped the parties reach agreement. My career as a neutral was born, thanks in large measure to Harold Newman." Richard Curreri, a later PERB chair, captured Newman's personality: "He was the elder statesman, even when he was not elderly. He commanded respect, but at the same time had an unexpected wit."[14]

The Extension Division of the ILR School played an important role in training and consulting with PERB officials and staff as well as conducting educational sessions for practitioners relating to the law and procedures. For several years, the Extension Division employed two full-time staff members for this work, supplemented by participation of resident faculty.

All of this points to a key aspect of how the ILR School functioned during my deanship. The role Harold Newman played illustrates well the close connection between practitioners and the faculty. When the state had a need for help, we responded; it was the best way to approach education and research. The school has always taken the word *State* in its official name—the New York State School of Industrial and Labor Relations—very seriously. During the 1970s almost three quarters of the budget came from state funds. And even a half century later, though state support has shrunk to around 10 percent, the ILR School is committed to working closely with state agencies.

One example was a fortuitous 1974 amendment to the Taylor Law providing for a three-year "experiment" that added interest arbitration as the final and binding step in the dispute resolution process. The idea was that at the end of the experiment the new provisions would either expire or be made permanent, depending on how they worked out in practice.

Tom Kochan, who at the time was one of our new junior faculty members, saw this as a researcher's gift—a natural experiment of sorts and an opportunity to extend his public-sector research interests to a challenging and controversial topic. Some of his senior colleagues discouraged him from taking it on, fearing it would become a political football that would cause researchers more headaches than it was worth. But Bob Helsby and Harold Newman offered Tom both PERB's full cooperation and their own personal support in opening doors to the key practitioners. Don Wollett, the governor's top employee relations official, also supported the ILR School doing a study when I discussed the idea with him.

I encouraged Tom go forward, suggesting that he ask Bob, Don, and Harold to help set up an informal advisory committee of key stakeholders to assist with the study. Tom undertook the work, but with real misgivings about needing an advisory committee. He got a National Science Foundation grant to support his research, and for three years engaged an army of graduate students to collect the data needed to track experience and evaluate the results of the experiment.

Three years later, in the midst of the New York City financial crisis, we were pleased to report out the results of this study at a major gathering of union, management, local and state government officials, and a number of leading academic experts from other states. My role was to introduce Tom, who would then present the results and recommendations. I used the occasion to say some nice words about him and his work, and then I turned to Tom and said, "Well, since we are under a statewide pay freeze because of the New York City situation, consider my nice words as your increase for this year!"

The important point of this story about that particular research project is that one could not have imagined then the coming together of a better mix of talent and professionalism needed to make such research possible. Neither Bob Helsby nor Harold Newman knew much about Tom at the start. They did not understand all the research design and methodological and statistical issues with which he had to grapple to do a thorough evaluation. And given the early stage of his career, Tom had only a vague sense of the political battles he would find himself thrust into when the experimental period ended. Don Wollett had no idea what the study might produce and had misgivings about the use of arbitration. Tom had to make sure the study would produce research of sufficient academic interest to justify the involvement of our PhD students while also advancing his own record of work on his way to tenure.

In the end, Tom acknowledged the wisdom of having the advisory committee. His report and recommendations served as the basis for discussion and debate as the state legislature took up the question of whether to scrap or continue the arbitration process. The report recommended continuation, but with several modifications based on an extensive array of quantitative and qualitative data. As a result of this joint effort, the arbitration process *was* made a permanent part of the statute; two PhD dissertations, a book, and numerous academic papers were published; and Tom Kochan got tenure a year later.

Helsby, Newman, and Wollett were not the only major figures in public-sector bargaining in New York with close connections to the ILR School. Arvid Anderson, a veteran mediator who cut his teeth at the Wisconsin Employment Relations Commission, was recruited to head up what was referred to as a mini-PERB for New York City: the Office of Collective Bargaining, which provided mediation, fact-finding, and, when necessary, arbitration services to bargaining units in the city. He made many trips to Ithaca to lecture in collective bargaining courses and played an informal mentoring role for many faculty as they began to deal with public-sector assignments not nearly as complicated as those he grappled with in New York City.

Anderson even cotaught a dispute resolution class with Tom Kochan. The semester coincided with Tom's drafting of his report on the police and firefighter study mentioned earlier. As Tom recalled, "Each week, I would give Arvid a draft chapter to read, and the next week he would come back with the draft in hand, marked up in red pencil with suggestions for revisions, all of which I gladly and gratefully accepted. He always described his comments with the wise words of an experienced and knowledgeable mediator: 'These little changes in wording won't change your conclusions or recommendations, but wording them this way will make them more acceptable to the parties.' Spoken as the modest, thoughtful, and world-class professional that everyone recognized Arvid to be."[15]

These contributions to public-sector research, teaching, and policy were possible because all the stakeholders considered the ILR School to be a trusted neutral resource. In turn, ILR faculty and students saw public-sector bargaining as a high-profile "laboratory" for teaching, learning, and interaction with the parties.

The Impact of Worker Dislocation

Although I saw my role as fostering research done by others—for example, pulling faculty together around productivity and quality of work life and encouraging evaluative studies of public-sector collective bargaining—I did undertake some research myself. Robert Aronson and I undertook a study of three plant shutdowns in communities near Ithaca and prepared a report for the New York State Department of Labor.[16]

In the 1970s Ithaca and nearby communities, including Binghamton, Cortland, and Elmira, were home to a lot of important manufacturing. Aronson and I learned about a series of factory closings in these communities through newspaper accounts and student term papers submitted for courses we were teaching. We became aware that the GAF Corporation in Binghamton and Westinghouse in Elmira were in the process of closing plants, affecting the lives of many workers and their families. These closings were a harbinger of things to come in the U.S. manufacturing sector: foreign competition and the pull to relocate to lower-wage areas of the United States, particularly the South, were driving the strategic decisions of management to shift production.

Those forces, though, could not explain the shutdown of Brockway Motor Company in Cortland. A division of Mack Trucks, Brockway manufactured custom-made, heavy-duty trucks of the highest quality. The plant had been in Cortland for many years, tracing its origins to Brockway Carriage Works established in 1875 by William Brockway. His son George converted the company into a truck manufacturer in 1909, which Mack Trucks purchased in 1956. Over time it became a high-cost operation, which led top management at the Mack Truck headquarters (then in Allentown, Pennsylvania) to conclude that major changes needed to be made in the plant's cost structure. So management proposed substantial changes in the contract.

The union dug in, unwilling to accept the changes. This was all long before the concept of concession bargaining had gained currency. Management decided to institute the changes when the contract expired, and the union went on strike.

I spoke with Arthur Shy, the international representative from the UAW, whom I knew through my work with International Harvester. Arthur had recommended that the union members go back to work because he knew the company was going to play hardball. But the local union leadership opted to continue the strike. That provoked the company to announce, several weeks later, that it would shut the plant permanently and shift production to another plant in Hagerstown, Maryland. The union leadership, the rank and file, and indeed the entire town of Cortland reacted in disbelief.

The Brockway story is a classic disconnect that can occur in collective bargaining: the union and its members want to protect their hard-won benefits and good wages, whereas the company—facing what it sees as an increasingly competitive market—feels compelled to force changes. Living and working in a small community in the middle of upstate New York with no other industrial activity nearby, the union workers were largely unaware of the changes taking place across manufacturing more widely: an emphasis by employers on lowering costs and increasing productivity in an effort to be more competitive.

Many of the findings in our report describe a reality still faced by many workers: they are displaced from their jobs, spend a lengthy period unemployed, and then find new work at a permanent reduction in income. When we conducted the study back in the 1970s, the reduction we found was 20 to 30 percent. In the early twenty-first century the loss in income is considerably higher, and the impact on local economies is also severe.

I was also involved with a project for Browne and Williamson, the big tobacco company, which had decided to close its home plant in Louisville, Kentucky. Management reached out for guidance on the plan it would put in place. I asked Felician Foltman of the ILR School's human resources faculty whether he would be interested in helping the company think through issues of advance notice, helping transfer rights to other plants in the company, and assisting in other aspects of a comprehensive readjustment plan. He agreed to take on the assignment.

Between Harvard, Chicago, and later MIT, most of my academic career has been spent at business schools where consulting work for companies takes place regularly. Faculty affiliated with labor centers, though, are rarely called upon to give policy advice in the area of labor-management relations. We do play a role in helping settle disputes, but the parties generally prefer to keep "outsiders" away from issues of structure and process—which leads us to focus our research elsewhere.

While we were engaged in research on job loss at the local level, the Nixon and Carter administrations were also embracing the subject as a top priority. William Batt headed an office within the U.S. Department of Labor that focused attention on the importance of advance notice and other measures that would help displaced workers adjust to job loss. He and Secretary of Labor Ray Marshall took a keen interest in exploring possibilities for legislation that would require advanced notification about plant shutdowns, and they both undertook an internal study of the issue and encouraged case studies of best company and union practices for dealing with such situations.

My son Bill, then a student at Tufts University, wrote several case studies representing best practices, and together we authored a report that was published by the Department of Labor.[17] But it would take another decade before passage of the Worker Adjustment and Retraining Notification Act of 1988, which required advance notice. Some of the provisions built on the best practices we had identified, such as requiring sixty days' advance notice, notification and engagement of union representatives of affected employees, and notification of local and state government officials.

In our work on job losses in New York State in the 1970s, as well as reviewing studies of job loss in general, we noted the many examples and graphic accounts of divorce, suicide, and other social consequences stemming from the trauma of involuntary displacement. The social, personal, and health consequences that we observed have since been widely documented in studies that depict the shorter life spans, family stresses and divorces, suicides, and other health problems of individuals who experience layoffs. Communities suffer, too. And if there was ever any doubt that there are political impacts from significant losses in manufacturing-sector jobs that largely built the middle class, the 2016 U.S. presidential election sealed the case.

It is clear that there remains a lot more work for those of us in industrial relations to do to help workers and communities adjust to economic changes that produce significant job losses. Many workers seem to take it as a given that their employment with any specific employer will only be for the short term, and when they are ultimately terminated they join the ranks of the displaced.

Returning to my time in Ithaca, though, there are two additional stories to tell. While they are about very different things, they reveal the scope of what a dean confronts in the course of leadership, and just how important it is to take the right stand.

The Ehrenberg Saga

The first of these two final stories—the multiyear saga and turmoil of Ronald Ehrenberg's research on wage levels for telephone workers—illustrates again the complex relationship between the ILR School and the labor movement and how it played out during my time at Cornell. It reminded me of how I had benefited from George Shultz's protection as a faculty member at the University of Chicago when I went after Motorola.

As a state institution, the ILR School responded affirmatively to requests from other state agencies—especially requests to do research. Ehrenberg, who was one of our highly respected labor economists, received a request from the state Public Service Commission (PSC) to study whether the wages of telephone workers were inflated. He first contacted me to make sure that such a study would not create difficulties for the ILR School. He knew that the staff of the PSC was convinced that the union had been able to increase wages significantly above the market and that having a faculty member from the school identified with such a finding would create political problems in terms of union support for our state budget. I told him not to worry and to move forward with the research because it was an interesting policy question that could provide useful guidance to the PSC.

Ehrenberg's study found that (controlling for education, experience, and skill levels) telephone workers were paid from 12 to 27 percent more than their counterparts in other industries. Ron suggested in his 1976 report that although the telephone company was free to pay those higher wages, the additional costs involved should not be passed on to consumers but instead should be charged against profits. Newspapers soon began to run stories along the lines of "Ma Bell" overpaying its workers.

The Communications Workers of America (CWA), which represented the telephone workers, was incensed that a faculty member had tackled such a sensitive subject. The ILR School came under intense criticism, and I was asked to disavow the research report—which I chose not to do.

CWA leader Morton Bahr was also a member of the ILR School's Advisory Council. He sent a strong letter condemning Ehrenberg's report and then issued a press release leveling several charges against Ron and the PSC. In the press release, Bahr claimed he had talked with Ron and was told the PSC had hired him to undertake a study that would "show" telephone workers were being paid more than workers with similar skills in other industries—the implication being that the results were cooked from the beginning. When I spoke with Morty Bahr, he began by saying, "I'm for academic freedom, but this is going too far. The school, which is supported by state funds, should have used more discretion."

Morty's strong negative response surprised me. I thought to myself that the study could have just as easily been interpreted as showing the union was doing a good job, which could help it in its organizing campaigns with unorganized workers. I responded that I supported Ron in his effort to shed light on the pay for telephone workers in New York State. I felt he had gone about the research in a very careful and professional manner.

Shortly thereafter we learned that Ray Corbett, the president of the state AFL-CIO, had shifted a meeting of the Committee on Political Education to a location in Albany; it had been scheduled to take place at the ILR School. Changing the meeting site made it difficult for Cornell students to participate. The CWA also canceled two summer education programs scheduled to take place at Cornell. A long period of strained relations followed.

One reason Morty was so incensed was that he thought the Ehrenberg study would give management a weapon to use against the union. In May–June 1976 he led the New York State members of the CWA in negotiations with AT&T—and, in fact, AT&T did bring up the study a number of times as it tried to hold the line on wage increases. In each instance, the company identified it as the "Cornell study" that "proved" telephone workers in New York state were paid a higher wage than their counterparts in other industries.

Whether the study had any real impact on the outcome of the negotiations is questionable. A new contract was reached without a strike, and it was hailed as one of the best the CWA had ever achieved. But given Morty's aspirations to become president of the national CWA (a goal he would achieve in 1985, serving for twenty years), he had seen it as a problem for the study to be on the record.

Ron Ehrenberg's report ricocheted around for some time, and the saga was not over. His study and a subsequent telephone rate case hearing were important learning experiences that launched him on a major study of regulatory agencies and collective bargaining that later resulted in a book.[18] Still, to some in the labor movement, he wore a sort of "black mark" for having released the report before the CWA negotiations with AT&T.

When Ron came up for promotion (the list of those being considered for full professor always goes before Cornell's Board of Trustees in a very pro forma way), Howard Molisani, first vice president of the International Ladies' Garment Workers Union, who also served on the board, raised a question about Ehrenberg's qualifications. I was in my office that Saturday morning when the provost, David Knapp, called to ask me what that was all about.

Ron's promotion did go through, despite the stir within the board. No other faulty member on the promotion list had ever received even the slightest scrutiny from a trustee.

For me the episode illustrated the almost lockstep approach the labor movement often takes once word is out that an institution is on the "wrong" side or that a faculty member is "doing damage" to the unions. I will never know whether Molisani was just going through the motions or felt strongly about the issue. Still, I considered him a friend, and he helped the ILR School a number of times in Albany.

As the 1977–78 academic year began, we had a general strategy to restore harmony with the labor movement. Associate Dean Lois Gray knew Morty Bahr personally, and she had a lengthy discussion with him about the issues involved in the Ehrenberg report.

I also called on Morty. He told me he no longer had a problem with the school because the negotiations were over and the CWA had won an excellent contract. He instructed his education officer to reschedule conferences at the ILR School. Still, even after being told everything was back to normal, a CWA local in Syracuse and another in Niagara Falls refused to cooperate with a new labor studies program. It turned out that the fallout from the CWA attack on the ILR School took longer to subside, even after Morty had issued a bill of "clean conduct."

Even with relations between the school and the CWA restored, however, there were no signs of a rapprochement with the state AFL-CIO. Indeed, we learned that one of the key unions in the federation, the Transport Workers Union, had canceled its Michael Quill Scholarship with the ILR School. It took at least another year before relations between the school and all corners of the labor movement in New York State returned to normal. As with any boycott, changing a particular mind-set and returning behavior to the status quo does not always take place swiftly.

Looking back, a good deal of the Ehrenberg story was also lose-lose. The union felt that its bargaining position with AT&T had been weakened by his report, and the school had to cancel many extension programs as a result of the boycott. As with the J. P. Stevens story, there was probably no chance for a better outcome. Too much was at stake: telephone workers were committed to protecting the wage levels they had negotiated over many years. From my perspective, it was extremely important to protect the right of a faculty member to conduct research and describe the results—even if those results created difficulties for labor.

Were there any instances where labor won and the university lost? No, but labor might have enjoyed a short-term victory, and the university would have lost had other trustees joined the labor trustee, Howard Molisani, when he challenged Ehrenberg's promotion. Holding that up would have been a big loss for the academic side of the relationship. Over the long term it would have been bad for a union to have squelched research.

A dean and other university leaders need to know when to take a principled stand against interference with the work and careers of faculty members, and I was pleased we did so in the Ehrenberg case. Thanks again are due to the model of academic leadership I learned firsthand from George Shultz in Chicago.

It is important to note that there were many examples of positive relationships between the ILR School and the labor movement. Having the support of the labor movement, especially during budget deliberations in Albany, was crucial during my deanship. Yes, there were moments when each side felt the relationship had deteriorated, but keeping in touch and being honest about interests helped the parties move on to areas of mutual benefit.

By the way, Jack Sheinkman and Morty Bahr became my lifelong friends.

Dealing with the Issue of Race

The second of these two final stories concerns the issue of race, which was a very hot topic on the Cornell campus and at many other universities, as well as in workplaces across the country. In 1969 a group of black students had occupied the Student Union, demanding that an African American studies program be established along with a black residential unit. Across the country, African American students were making similar demands, but what distinguished Cornell was what happened when the occupiers agreed to leave the student union: they emerged with guns and rounds of ammunition strung over their shoulders. These images were published nationwide and created an incredible public relations problem for Cornell.

At a faculty meeting soon thereafter, President James A. Perkins announced disciplinary action against those who had occupied the Student Union. Quickly, though, there was a groundswell on campus for amnesty, and Perkins was pressured to convene another faculty meeting—at which the penalties were reversed. One of the effects of this was that among the ILR faculty, where there were strong voices both for punishment and amnesty, some individuals ended up never again speaking to one another.

As a result of my involvement during the 1960s with the EEOC and the Office of Federal Contract Compliance, and having spent a few years deeply involved in the civil rights movement in Chicago before coming to Cornell, I was ready to do what I could to advance the position of minorities in our country and especially at the university. Some of that determination may have stemmed from a desire to create for myself, in a small way, what I had left behind in Chicago, the site of so many important initiatives and direct action, and moving to a very different environment in upstate New York.

Whatever the reason, it didn't take long for race to come up after my arrival.

ILR professor Leopold Gruenfeld and his family had escaped the Holocaust, leaving Germany just in time and moving first to Shanghai, China, and then coming to the United States. At one of my first faculty meetings, Gruenfeld put forth a resolution directing the school (and, indirectly, Cornell University) not to comply with a federal requirement to record race and gender numbers in reports to the EEOC. Actually refusing to comply would have been illegal had it been implemented, so the resolution was offered as a symbolic statement of opposition.

There were no African Americans on the ILR School faculty or staff when I arrived, and one of my first efforts to address this disparity was to recruit Donald Chatman, a member of the first class of the University of Chicago's African American MBA program. The ILR School needed a development officer, and Don came with enthusiasm, bringing new ideas and launching the Founders Fund to honor retiring faculty. Unfortunately, during one of the severe budget cuts that required layoffs, I had to shift the development function to the Alumni Affairs Department and let Chatman go.

I did not fully appreciate how sensitive the subject of race was at Cornell until I gave a speech on affirmative action in November 1971 to alumni in

Washington, DC. The following March, Cornell's administration, anxious to move forward with affirmative action and thinking my speech might help educate the community, published the full text of my talk in the *Cornell Chronicle*, the university's official weekly newspaper. All hell broke loose.

Several faculty focused on a brief section of my talk in which I criticized faculty members for raising questions about the academic standards for minority students enrolled in a summer preparatory program. "Recently, the leaders of a special program for black students," I had said, "have created a handbook in which they asked black students to really do a good job and maintain high academic standards. The faculty objected to this as the setting of academic policy."[19] I went on to comment that the concerned faculty members were scrutinizing the program far too much, and doing so precisely because it was for black students. Several faculty members said I was accusing them of being racist.

Throughout the controversy I discussed my views on affirmative action one-on-one with a number of faculty members. One thing led to another, and soon the Faculty Council of Representatives cited me for a "breach of decorum," setting in motion considerable discussion in both the student and official university newspapers about academic freedom and standards for civil discourse. I met with the faculty and acknowledged that several individuals had been improperly associated with my "negative" remarks. Initially, I was open-minded about whether to say something approaching an apology, but several key faculty advised me to keep quiet.

In private conversations with faculty I noted that a group of trade union students in one of the ILR School's courses in New York City had been told not to miss classes, stating that missing two would result in flunking the course. This also set academic policy, but no one raised an objection.

I soldiered on, attempting to put the entire episode behind me. Over the next couple of years, however, the issues of affirmative action and keeping records that listed personnel by race remained a sore point with many of the school's faculty members on both sides of the issues.

Looking back, it is clear that the subject of race was much more controversial and sensitive than I had anticipated when I accepted the Cornell appointment. Had I to do it over, I do not think I would have changed the content of the speech I gave in Washington, but in retrospect, the advice from faculty members who said I should not apologize ("Bob, this whole thing will blow over very quickly") was wrong. I should have apologized.

These early episodes also awakened me to the scrutiny Cornell faculty members—and perhaps faculty at most universities with strong faculty control norms—give to public statements of their deans. I learned I was under a microscope and that people would view anything I wrote or said as speaking not just for myself as a professional in our field but also "for the school." Leading a faculty comprised of individuals with very different interests and worldviews requires lots of dialogue and thick enough skin to live with the reality that not all will agree with everything one says or does. To worry too much about such things will paralyze a dean and ultimately lead to overemphasis on the status quo at the expense of adapting to changes in the environment.

A dean who gets too far out ahead of the faculty risks becoming a commander without a following!

As I reflect on my stint as dean of the ILR School, I want to take stock of how successful the faculty and I were in responding to the mandates I received as I came on board. The first mandate came from Cornell's provost, who wanted us to begin recruiting the people who would become the ILR School's second generation of scholars. By encouraging retirements, we were able to hire eight new junior and young tenured faculty members who have since led their disciplines into the future—especially in labor economics, human resources, and collective bargaining—with important work on the gender wage gap, executive compensation standards, and conflict management systems (to mention a few topics).

One of the decisions of which I am proud is the appointment of Lois Gray (since deceased) to be associate dean of the Extension Division. The statute that created the ILR School emphasized the dissemination of information, or "extension," as the third leg of the tripod, alongside instruction and research. It was a new activity for me, and one I strongly embraced.

When John Drotning resigned as the Extension Division's associate dean, I consulted with the Extension Committee and advanced the idea of promoting Lois, who had been heading the Extension Division's office in New York City. Extension faculty members had several qualms. One was whether it was fair to ask a woman to undertake the considerable travel around the state required by the position (keep in mind that this was 1976; few would dare raise such an issue now). Another concerned Lois's close relationship with Harry Van Arsdale and the labor movement, as her husband was a regional director for the UAW. Would she support extension programs that served management? But neither the Extension Committee nor I were persuaded that those concerns were valid. Lois has served the school with distinction for many years and, after stepping down as associate dean, continued to work full time as a professor and researcher. Now in her nineties and an emeritus professor, she is at the office every day and remains very active pursuing scholarly interests, especially studying the role of industrial relations in the arts.

It is important to note the resiliency of the ILR School and its ability to adapt—slowly, to be sure—to the declining labor movement by diversifying and strengthening other parts of the school less tied to the study of union-management relations. At America's business schools, most labor groups have declined substantially (a point to which I will return in chapter 6); at Harvard Business School and the University of Chicago's GSB they disappeared entirely after the luminaries retired. Meanwhile, at the ILR School, the academic Human Resources Department is the best in the country and the Department of Labor Economics has become a significant player in that field.

The second mandate came from Chancellor Ernest Boyer of the SUNY system, who wanted the ILR School to open a labor college in New York City. That urging created some difficulties between competing interests of the labor movement and the school's faculty. On the one hand, I inherited a faculty that treasured the tradition of faculty control and academic freedom; on the other hand, there was a very powerful set of external constituents, particularly labor leaders, anxious to have the school support its agenda and the labor movement more broadly. I had to live in two worlds, straddling both without getting totally captured by either. By offering professional courses for credit and at the same time cooperating with Empire State College to provide the degrees, we were able to implement a creative solution.

That same tension existed in what came to be called the Ehrenberg Affair. By supporting Ron Ehrenberg's right to conduct research that the labor movement felt weakened its bargaining power, we affirmed an important principle of academic freedom. At the same time, though, the school suffered the consequences of disaffected unions canceling programs. The trade-offs were clearly not as good as in the Labor College story.

On a personal level, my time at the ILR School supported my interests as a faculty member with a deep desire to understand collective bargaining as it was playing out in the 1970s. Faculty experts for specific industries, such as Don Cullen for construction and Pete Jensen for the maritime and long-shore industries, guaranteed that the school and I kept up to date on important developments. Many other activities and features of the ILR School helped feed my appetite for keeping informed: interacting with the labor trustees on the Cornell University Board of Trustees; invitations to speak to state AFL-CIO meetings; our Extension Division's education programs for union members, especially stewards; establishing the Labor College in New York City; appearing at the Scholarship Breakfast organized by Harry Van Arsdale for sons and daughters of IBEW Local 3; my stints in Washington with panels on pay; chairing the Continuity of Employment Committee; and many faculty performing mediation and conciliation work for labor and management, especially in the public sector.

I realize in retrospect that these activities lulled me into thinking that unions were here to stay. New York State had the highest density of union members in the United States during my time in Ithaca, and the state's labor movement continued to have a lot of clout in Albany, the state capitol. I did not see the writing on the wall in the form of national data at the same time that showed a steady decline in union density in the country as a whole.

While the overall role of labor continued to decline in that decade, the public sector was "hot" and my stint with the CEC kept me busy. I continued to teach courses in negotiation and collective bargaining, but I was not focused on the bigger picture.

The most rewarding aspects of my role came from association with members of the Advisory Council. Many, such as Jack Sheinkman and Harold Newman, became friends, and to this day I keep in touch with their widows.

Of course, I interacted frequently with Tom Kochan, Dave Lipsky, and other members of what we used to call the collective bargaining department (our shorthand for the Department of Labor Relations, Law, and History), and Tom later became my colleague at the MIT Sloan School of Management.

Chapter 5

RETURNING TO THE BENCH

Sloan School of Management, Massachusetts Institute of Technology, 1980–2018

My time at the Sloan School of Management at the Massachusetts Institute of Technology, now approaching four decades, far exceeds the combined number of years I was at Harvard Business School, the University of Chicago's Graduate School of Business, and the ILR School at Cornell University. Making the decision to leave Cornell and join the Sloan faculty in 1980 was not easy. One "pull" was my favorable experience at business schools, first as a graduate student at HBS and then the twelve years I spent at GSB. Compared with a specialized institution such as the ILR School, a business school provides a wider range of perspectives on the economy and society.

Just as important was the strength of industrial relations talent and the impressive history of the group at MIT Sloan. In the late 1930s, with help from the Rockefeller family, MIT established the Industrial Relations Section, initially housed in the Department of Economics. The group boasts an illustrious history, with individuals such as Douglas MacGregor heading it up, and PhD graduates of the stature of George Shultz and Arnold Weber— the former my mentor and the latter an important colleague at the University of Chicago.[1] Other prominent alumni from the section include Les Aspin, a former member of the U.S House of Representatives and secretary of defense in the Clinton administration; David Lipsky, who became dean at the ILR School some years after I left; Daniel Mitchell, who directed the Institute of Labor Relations at the University of California–Los Angeles; and George Strauss, who went on to become director of the Institute of Industrial Relations at the University of California–Berkeley.[2]

When the Sloan School was established in 1952, having worked its way up from 1914's "engineering administration" curriculum in the Department of Economics and Statistics to a master's degree program in 1925 to an actual school, the Industrial Relations Section shifted its base from the Department of Economics to the new school. Charles Myers headed the section, and at the time I was considering shifting my appointment to Sloan, he was very much in charge.[3] Other luminaries, such as Doug Brown, had officially retired but were still on the scene.

By 1980 most business schools had shifted their attention away from industrial relations in favor of human resource management. Faculty members such as Michael Piore were continuing the tradition of pioneering work in labor economics.[4] The successor to the Industrial Relations Section at Sloan—currently known as the Institute for Work and Employment Research (IWER)—has, however, remained focused on labor-management relations and labor market studies.

A dozen companies contributed funds annually for the support of research by faculty and PhD students in the section. For example, as I was being recruited to join the Sloan faculty, I was told to expect a visit each year from a Shawmut Bank executive who would present a check to support the section as a quid pro quo for MIT's banking business.

Several other aspects of the Sloan environment were particularly appealing. For instance, as part of the initial funding for establishing the Industrial Relations Section, the Rockefeller Foundation had provided seed money to support the Industrial Relations Collection in the Dewey Library. This collection quickly became recognized by scholars affiliated with universities throughout the Boston area as the place to find the best collection of materials related to industrial relations and the labor market.

As regards curriculum, industrial relations courses included labor law, collective bargaining, and labor economics. A seminar for PhD students and faculty—with regular attendance almost an obligation—takes place to this day, every Tuesday at 1:00 p.m.; it is a tradition that has been in place since the 1940s, before the Sloan School had even been established. The seminar continues to build rapport and provide valuable guidance to members of the community presenting research—especially work in progress.

Sloan faculty members maintained close ties to the Boston-area labor movement. Boston can speak with pride about the Archdiocese of Boston's Labor Guild, one of the remaining labor centers in the country, which traces its roots back to the Depression and was opened in 1938 by Jesuits as the region's first "Catholic labor school" to provide educational services to the labor movement. To this day, through its School of Labor Management Relations, the Guild offers courses for union leaders and rank-and-file members and has served as a meeting ground for the Boston labor movement.

Another draw was the presence of labor leaders nearby as students in the Harvard Trade Union Program, established in 1942. When I first came to Sloan, every January and February saw a cadre of leaders from all over the world take up residence in the program for seven weeks of instruction. It is still going strong today.

There was also a monthly dinner on campus that drew scholars and practitioners from around Boston. It was another thing that attracted me to the school (and I talk about it at length later in this chapter).

This lineup of resources was very attractive, so when I visited the Sloan School during the fall semester of 1979 I decided to accept an appointment that would begin a year later.

My Arrival at a Turning Point for Labor Relations

I first took up residence at Sloan during the fall 1979 semester to check out the school's courses for a potential fit, and spent the following spring on sabbatical in England. I then accepted a full-time faculty appointment to begin in the fall of 1980. Thomas Kochan, who had spent the 1979–80 academic year at the U.S. Department of Labor in Washington, DC, also joined Sloan's Industrial Relations Section at that time.

We arrived to witness what, in retrospect, became one of the major turning points in labor relations in the last half century. Our first inkling that times were changing was when we began to see firms we knew from previous research initiate much more aggressive behavior toward their unions than we had ever seen. No one had a good explanation of what was going on. Was it simply a response to the deep recession that was beginning to be felt as the Federal Reserve raised interest rates to record levels in an effort to break the inflationary pressures of the late 1970s? Was it the change in the political balance of power that ushered Ronald Reagan into the White House? Was it that top executives of unionized firms were not seeing their industrial relations directors taking strong enough actions to cope with the growth of international competition and domestic nonunion competition in their industries?

With respect to international competition, Toyota—which early in its penetration of the U.S. market had exported cars from its plants in Japan—had begun to build substantial manufacturing capacity in the United States. The integrated steel companies that had assured themselves that nonunion "mini-mills" like those of Nucor (in the early twenty-first century, the largest steel producer in the United States) would not be able to produce high-end steel for the auto and appliance industries were finding their assumptions terribly flawed. Whatever the cause, it seemed as if the labor relations system that had grown out of the New Deal and established industry and national patterns through collective bargaining was under severe pressures.

One event brought home the change in the environment for unions and collective bargaining more than any other, and it happened in dramatic fashion. Early in the morning of August 3, 1981, the twelve thousand members of the Professional Air Traffic Controllers Organization (PATCO) went on strike. A few hours later, President Reagan declared the strike illegal and ordered the air traffic controllers back to work, reading to reporters in the White House Rose Garden what he called a "solemn oath" and "sworn affidavit" each PATCO member had signed promising not to strike against the U.S. government. He gave them forty-eight hours to go back to work or lose their jobs.

On August 5, Reagan followed through and fired every one of the 11,345 strikers who had refused to return to work. Reagan's action set the tone for labor relations in the years and decades to follow, encouraging employers to adopt a hard line vis-à-vis unions.

As soon as the PATCO strike began, but before President Reagan took his action, I wrote a letter to the editor of the *Boston Globe* drawing attention to the stressful working conditions experienced by controllers; it was never published. Quality of work life was a major theme in the 1980s, and the long hours and demands for attentiveness associated with occupations such as air traffic controller in particular led to a widespread realization that changes were needed.

I also deplored strike action in this case and observed that mediation and appointing a commission to study the industry would be the preferred resolution to the problem. I thought about my years in Chicago, when academics were routinely called upon to help with major labor policy issues. I thought third-party help in this situation would be the best course of action—but it was not to be with President Reagan.

The firing of the air traffic controllers caught all of us in academia by surprise. Robert Poli, the PATCO president, was shocked. Why would President Reagan, who had once been a Democrat and also had been president of a strong union, the Screen Actors Guild, take such drastic action? No doubt, Reagan wanted to make a point and show his conservative supporters that he was on the side of employers.

In retrospect, the strike action taken by the union under Poli's leadership was indefensible. I have no doubt that Poli reviewed the history of other stoppages by controllers, saw that the government had taken no disciplinary action, and assumed the response would be the same this time around. Thus, because of a decision driven by poor assumptions, the union missed an opportunity to address the real concerns of the workers. As it turned out, thousands of new employees were hired, and it took until 1986 before any of the former air traffic controllers were allowed to reapply for their jobs and get rehired.[5]

At the time, I was reminded of a similar suicidal strike undertaken by the United Auto Workers at Brockway Motors in the 1970s (discussed in chapter 4). In both the PATCO and Brockway cases, the thinking of management had changed—but labor leaders assumed management was bluffing. Their view was governed by having taken strikes in the past and seeing management cave in. Albert Rees analyzed this tendency of union leaders and their members to look back at earlier negotiations while management looked ahead to new challenges.

The PATCO strike, with the other changes taking place in private-sector firms, prompted a return to the field to try to understand what was really going on, and why. It led to a major Sloan School project of the 1980s: a multiyear faculty and student collaborative effort focused on the transformations in industrial relations unfolding before our eyes.

One interesting question in retrospect is whether Tom and I would have "seen" these changes—the ones less obvious than the PATCO strike—had we not experienced a year away from our duties at the ILR School. Was it the fresh perspective of starting anew, at a new place, a school of management with new colleagues such as Harry Katz and Michael Piore who were also beginning to question whether the post–World War II model of labor relations and the even older mass production system had run their course? In that postwar model, it was largely unions that drove the changes that led to improvements in wages, benefit, and working conditions. Did being at Sloan, rather than a specialized school of industrial and labor relations, help us see how management now seemed to be taking the lead in driving change? Or was it simply the force of events that posed anomalies to our mental models and existing theories of labor relations that suggested the need to ask more fundamental questions and search for new understandings?

These questions illustrate how getting one step out of an academic routine and comfortable environment can provide fresh perspectives and opportunities to explore new questions with new colleagues and students.

The PATCO strike was perhaps the most significant single event related to our field, but happening outside academia, that took place upon Tom's and my arrival at Sloan. At the time, we did not appreciate the full impact of the president's action. Most of our discussion was about the poor strategy of the union in engaging in an illegal strike. Over the decade, it became clear that the strike—the most potent weapon in the union arsenal—could be blunted by management hiring *permanent* replacements and continuing operations—something that had never been done before in any major U.S. industry. In response, a lot of unions abandoned the time-honored tactic of striking at the point of production in favor of the "corporate campaign" strategy pushed by Ray Rogers.[6] It made the few militant strikes later on, such as those against Caterpillar, Hormel Foods, and A. E. Staley, all the more extraordinary.[7]

Inside the Sloan School itself, we also began a research project that had tremendous implications for our discipline of industrial relations.

The *Transformation* Project

Soon after Tom Kochan and I joined the Sloan faculty, Dean Abe Siegel asked the industrial relations faculty whether we would be interested in submitting a proposal to the Alfred P. Sloan Foundation to support a major research project. The connection between the Sloan School and the eponymous foundation had always been close, and periodically the foundation provided significant funds for research.

Thus unfolded a five-year study that examined the state of industrial relations throughout the economy, culminating in a major book I coauthored with Harry Katz and Tom Kochan, *The Transformation of American Industrial Relations.*[8] In pursuing this topic, we recruited a number of companies and unions as sponsors, held several conferences, and provided resources and research opportunities for graduate students.

Our book broke new ground by viewing the relationship between labor and management in terms of three tiers. The bottom tier, the work group, and the middle tier, contract negotiations, were well analyzed in the literature. Our contribution was to add a third, strategic tier and document that although some employers chose to work cooperatively with unions, many were choosing to avoid unionism vigorously. How to explain these different choices and the consequences for shaping the future of industrial relations became a central intellectual question in our research.

The *Transformation* project could not have broken new ground or generated as much new empirical evidence without the involvement of a large number of graduate students, faculty, and a postdoc. It is worth commenting on how such a team came together. I had learned at Cornell that leading a group of academics to work together on a research project is a bit like attempting to herd cats. In this case, the cats succeeded in coming together to create something that approached what Theodore Leavitt described as an academic "hot spot."[9]

The first requirement for a team project is that there must be some big, shared problem around which researchers can rally. At MIT, there is a lot of lore about how faculty rallied together during World War II, building things such as the "rad lab," which focused on developing sophisticated radar systems. In our case, we rallied around an intellectual puzzle and our deep concern about what was happening in labor-management relations that seemed to be turning many accepted principles of collective bargaining on end. What was going on, and how could we understand the fundamental changes taking place?

Leavitt also suggested that it would help to have a debate with others to fuel the research. In our case, the debate was whether what was happening in labor-management relations was simply a temporary adjustment to the deep recession playing out between 1981 and 1983 or a more fundamental set of forces that would change the nature of industrial relations for the long run.

Our leading sparring partner on the issue was John T. Dunlop. Early in the 1980s, he railed against the notion that fundamental changes were occurring, insisting that "nothing new under the sun" was going on. The wage concessions, flurry of workplace experimentation with worker participation, and shifts in power within management structures we were observing were just temporary, Dunlop insisted, and things would revert back to past forms as the economy pulled out of the recession. But early on in the project, we began to see evidence that the changes underway were not likely to be reversed—and we started saying so in our various writings, conference presentations, and discussions with the media.

Having John Dunlop as your leading critic: what more could one ask for as a motivating force?

The creative power of a team project is unleashed not by trying to direct research from the top but rather by developing opportunities for students and faculty colleagues to pursue questions of interest to them and then using their work as pieces that fit together in solving a bigger puzzle. We were fortunate to have many contributors to this process. Peter Cappelli joined our group early on, as he prepared to defend his doctoral dissertation at Oxford University,[10] and helped get us started on a range of projects, particularly in the airline industry. Later he joined us in writing an article that introduced what eventually became known as our strategic choice framework. Harry Katz took the lead in working with two master's degree students doing research at General Motors who uncovered data from company files on grievances, work rules, productivity, and quality. Anil Verma wrote his PhD dissertation using rich data he and Tom collected on the different practices, wages, and performance outcomes in union and nonunion plants of a large conglomerate.[11]

Jan Klein worked closely with me to examine how supervisors and middle managers were responding to employee participation initiatives. I recall how she produced what we often still refer to as the 70-50-30 rule: when she asked supervisors whether quality of working life experiments were good for employees, for their firms, and for themselves, 70 percent said they were good for employees, 50 percent said they were good for their firms, and only 30 percent agreed they were good for themselves as supervisors!

Casey Ichniowski broke new ground in his dissertation,[12] working with Boise Cascade, a paper company where I had some contacts, to obtain data on grievances and plant performance. This was one of the first studies to demonstrate that industrial relations outcomes had significant effects on firm performance, and it opened our eyes to the importance of looking at the industrial relations effects on performance in other industries. A bit later, Joel Cutcher-Gershenfeld found similar results in his research at Xerox. In that study, he introduced the idea of combining different workplace practices into a "transformation index" that prompted others to "bundle" practices rather than treating each as a separate variable.

John Chalykoff worked with data from the Conference Board that helped us understand how powerful management ideologies and workplace practices were in avoiding unions in new facilities. Nancy Mower did much of the fieldwork in a study Harry and Tom directed, exploring how unions were responding to different worker participation programs.

I could go on to mention others who contributed in some way to the *Transformation* project, but the main point is that all of these young researchers used the project to advance their own research agendas while making significant contributions to the larger study. They identified specific questions of interest that could be pursued with rigorous research methods and that supported high-quality theses and peer-reviewed journal articles.

Harry, Tom, and I shared the task of helping orchestrate these efforts. We opened doors to companies and unions, served as advisors on PhD committees, and sometimes joined with students in writing papers. But our primary role in the project was as system integrators, looking at two key questions: What did all this evidence add up to? How do we make sense of it in light of the big puzzle and debate? Those were the questions we tried to address in the *Transformation* book, which would not have been possible without the work of the team members and without the many hours of discussion and debate in seminars, hallways, and small groups we had among ourselves, with colleagues at other universities, and with management, labor, and government officials eager to hear and debate what we were finding. Such is what makes for at least a miniature version of an academic "hot spot."

In our conclusion to the *Transformation* study, we focused on possible scenarios regarding the future of collective bargaining—hedging our bets, as the 1980s was a period of considerable change and uncertainty. One scenario, and the one that has dominated, envisioned a steady decline in union membership stemming from actions taken by employers (getting tough with unions, modeled on Reagan's firing of the air traffic controllers, and the introduction of human resource polices and practices designed to serve as "substitute unionism") and a loss of jobs due to domestic and foreign competition.

The *Transformation* study has received considerable attention from our colleagues, an award from the Academy of Management, and a thirtieth-anniversary symposium in the *Industrial and Labor Relations Review*. It also helped jump-start a new area of inquiry that came to be known as research on high-performance work systems. The basic idea, incubated in the work by Joel Cutcher-Gershenfeld at Xerox and Casey Ichniowski at Boise Cascade, is that employment practices are tied together in a system that affects organizational performance. Our students went on to document how these high-performance work systems led to high levels of productivity and product or service quality in industries as diverse as automobile manufacturing, airlines, telecommunications, and health care. Academics at other universities soon joined in, doing similar research in a variety of manufacturing and service settings.[13] At the time it was revolutionary to treat as bundles of complementary practices what had previously been viewed as separate human resource practices: job design, compensation, employee participation, and the like. It has since become a widely accepted idea—yet another major contribution of the *Transformation* project.

The industrial relations field has benefited periodically from a comprehensive look at the state of collective bargaining. Sumner Slichter took just such a look with his pioneering 1941 study *Union Policies and Industrial Management*.[14] Then, almost two decades later, Slichter and two colleagues, James Healy and E. Robert Livernash, published *The Impact of Collective Bargaining*.[15] Our own contribution to this continuum, the *Transformation* study, was issued in 1986 and helped frame the discussion of how industrial relations were changing and would continue to change in the years ahead.

As I write this history, the time that has passed since we published *Transformation* suggests the clear need for another update in the field of industrial relations scholarship. We are fortunate that Barbara Dyer has joined us at the Sloan School to help orchestrate a large new project focused on how good companies can create and sustain good jobs. She and the team she is building are determined to understand and promote the diffusion of "high-road" management systems that can address the biggest economic and social problem currently: income inequality and the effects of long-term stagnation of wages.

Thus, in the near future we might just benefit from another update.

Why the Focus on Industries?

There is a long and deep tradition in the field of industrial relations to use specific industries as units of analysis. John R. Commons at the University of Wisconsin began the tradition with his classic study of the evolution of shoemaking and the labor guilds and unions that rose and fell in that industry from the late 1600s to the end of the nineteenth century.[16] John T. Dunlop used industries as his unit of analysis in his 1958 classic *Industrial Relations Systems*, stressing the importance of understanding differences in market structures, technologies, the history of management, and labor organizations in specific settings to explain differences in the rules governing employment relationships across industries such as construction, manufacturing, mining, trucking, and others.[17]

As was noted in chapter 3, meatpacking provided a window into how work and automation were changing in that industrial sector in the 1960s; as was noted in chapter 4, the rise of collective bargaining in the public sector provided an excellent learning laboratory for many scholars, particularly for new participants in our field in the 1970s.

Much of our work on the *Transformation* project followed in this tradition. Harry Katz, for example, became the leading expert on the auto industry and in 1985 published the appropriately titled *Shifting Gears*, which tracked changes occurring in that industry.[18] As I noted in chapter 1, I have a long-standing fascination with various modes of transportation, and much of my work has focused on that sector.

Airlines

The airline industry has always captivated me. Because of the craft nature of the work and the special procedures of the Railway Labor Act (also governing labor relations in the airline industry), which made it easier for unions to organize, the industry holds considerable interest for those of us in academia.

Owing to our frequent trips, we have been able to function as participant-observers of the airline industry. Those who have traveled on flights with me over the years will attest to the fact that I like to use my time in the air talking with flight attendants about their work and, if the opportunity ever avails itself, with pilots. There is no better way to learn about the state of airline labor relations than from those living it firsthand, and no better opportunity than to take advantage of a captive crew—even when they would rather be resting during a long flight!

The 1980s witnessed turmoil in the airline industry stemming from deregulation and competitive pressure from new entrants. As a result, Eastern Air Lines, Pan Am, and TWA all filed for bankruptcy in the early 1990s. Airlines that emerged during the early days of deregulation, such as People Express, fell by the wayside. Eventually, JetBlue and other new entrants found a niche in the industry and succeeded—while at the same time remaining largely nonunion until early 2018, when JetBlue's flight attendants voted to be unionized (after many earlier failed attempts). The Air Line Pilots Association had won representation rights at JetBlue in 2014, as expected; even Delta Airlines, with its strong nonunion culture across the company, bargained with its pilots.

Research opportunities in the airline industry have been many for those of us at the Sloan School. For her doctoral dissertation, Kirsten Wever studied the emergence of Western Airlines from bankruptcy and its eventual merger with Delta.[19] Peter Cappelli wrote an influential analysis of how airline industry unions would not make concessions unless faced with the threat of bankruptcy.[20] A bit later, Jody Hoffer-Gittel began a career studying relational coordination, initially at Southwest Airlines and then in health care and other sectors. Eventually her work blossomed into the Relational Coordination Research Collaborative at the Heller School for Social Policy and Management at Brandeis University. In 2009, Peter Belobaba, Amedeo Odoni, and Cynthia Barnhart published a study of the airline industry based in MIT's Department of Aeronautics and Astronautics and financed by the Sloan Foundation.[21]

The Eastern Air Lines story merits a deeper review of the history of the imbroglio to gain a better understanding of how union-management relations became so dysfunctional and personal. It was a contest of wills between CEO Frank Borman and Charles Bryant, president of the Machinists Union. From 1983 to 1985, the parties engaged in a much-heralded "partnership" that placed union representatives on Eastern's board of directors, gave employees a substantial share of stock in exchange for major financial concessions, created a system of joint committees to improve productivity (with the inducement that workers could earn back their wage cuts), and fostered unprecedented information sharing between labor and management.

The labor-management cooperation was genuine. During the early 1980s, I visited Eastern's offices at Logan Airport in Boston and talked with both management and union officials. Delegation of responsibility to the working level had occurred to such an extent that, for many operations, no supervisors were assigned. Workers formed task forces, one of which recommended a plan for using idle planes during the night to handle major shipments of U.S. mail in and out of Boston. Establishing a new hub in Kansas City was another example of the cooperative spirit. To undertake that project, labor and management signed a pioneering agreement that reduced the number of job classifications, created teams, and established a high-commitment work system that had been pioneered in a number of manufacturing industries.

Borman and Bryant traveled together to airports to talk with Eastern employees about the new era that had arrived, and the company appeared to be thriving—that is, until another round of fare cuts across all the domestic airlines in late 1985 sent Eastern's profits into a quick and disastrous nosedive. The cooperative spirit unraveled further when management approached the unions and asked for additional reductions in compensation to the tune of approximately 20 percent of salaries. Although Eastern's other unions grudgingly agreed, the Machinists firmly said no. Negotiations that began at that impasse eventually reached the make-or-break point, with management maintaining it needed a minimum package of 15 percent concessions from the Machinists or Eastern would either have to file bankruptcy or seek a buyer.

The union's response was that it would go along with concessions only if the board removed Borman, whom the union considered responsible for the company's economic woes by virtue of several poor strategic decisions. First, he had bought a fleet of fuel-efficient planes that added approximately $2 billion in debt to the company's balance sheet. The decision, made at a time when fuel prices were high and were thought to be going even higher, proved unwise. When fuel prices dropped, Eastern was left with a large amount of debt at high interest rates. Second, Borman expanded routes to the West Coast and offered low fares, an unprofitable move that actually cost the airline tens of millions of dollars.

Eastern's board of directors called the union's hand, voting to keep Borman and, at the same time, approve the sale of the company to Frank Lorenzo of Texas Air. The Machinists struck, and Lorenzo declared bankruptcy. Eventually, in 1991, Eastern Air Lines was liquidated.

How could a relationship that appeared to be so constructive sour so quickly to the point that the union demanded the departure of the CEO as its price for concessions? A number of factors provide some explanation. The workers, particularly the Machinists, developed expectations that labor-management cooperation would solve all the company's economic problems. They were not ready for further losses and the necessity of additional financial sacrifices. At the same time, management lost much of its enthusiasm for labor-management cooperation. At one point, an Eastern vice president said to me, "With this employee ownership arrangement, every day is a stockholders' meeting."

From management's point of view, the downside of employee involvement was that all decisions needed union approval, and the ensuing organizational gridlock slowed things down considerably. Some in management also believed that many of the productivity savings that justified restoration of concessions (for example, changing a supplier to reduce costs) were not joint accomplishments but reflected management initiatives.

Borman is said to have acknowledged later that the company probably paid too high a price with the partnership.

How big a risk was Charles Bryant running in insisting that the union was only willing to accept changes if the board was willing to make changes in management? Given that the skills of airline mechanics are not industry specific, Bryant may have been thinking that in the event of a shutdown his members could find employment elsewhere.

What are the major themes and lessons? Once matters become personalized, positions harden, new areas of dispute can develop, and the parties lose respect for one another. At Eastern Air Lines, the lack of trust—indeed, the lack of any communication—became so severe that whatever common ground that may have once existed disappeared. The battle became not about reaching agreement within an established framework but about changing the players and the basic relationship itself.

Unions are very adept at distributive bargaining when the pie is growing larger, but they have great difficulty managing the internal dynamics when the pie is shrinking and a type of reverse bargaining is required.

On the management side, it is difficult to strike the right balance between joint consultation and taking the initiative within a framework of labor-management cooperation. Management tends to commit two errors. First, it overlooks the potential of employee involvement for enhancing commitment and organizational performance. Eastern Airlines missed this opportunity for most of its history. The second error occurs when management assumes that labor-management cooperation will bring about substantial benefits and a new "team spirit" will eliminate all conflicts in the relationship. Such a perspective overlooks both the need for managerial initiative and an effective structure for participation. To sustain cooperation requires that all stakeholders be aware of the dangers that lurk around the corner, and avenues must be found for the partnership to confront differences and bad news as well as celebrating jointly improved productivity.

Once matters became so embroiled, and personalities and pride assumed undue importance, it would have taken intervention by a trusted official to help the parties reach a solution that would have left all sides in a better position. But during the time frame of the Eastern story, market forces seem to have been the preferred mode for resolving important issues in product and labor markets.

The Automobile Industry

Just as engaging for research as the airline industry, the automobile industry has been for decades what I would call ground zero for those of us in industrial relations. During my days at Harvard, I spent many hours at Ford Motor Company plants studying the operations of measured day-work. The Brookings Institution study during my time at Harvard devoted considerable attention to the auto industry, too, with the index for the final study containing more than twenty references to GM and Ford and more than sixty references to the UAW.

Some may even say that because I am based at the Sloan School, it stands to reason I would be interested in the automobile industry. After all, the school is named for Alfred P. Sloan, longtime president, chairman, and CEO of General Motors. Point well taken.

GM President Charles E. Wilson is often quoted as having said, "What's good for General Motors is good for the country."[22] It was a controversial statement, but even though it is actually a misquote (and one that got him in some trouble), it does express that historically, the health of the U.S. economy has often been gauged by the performance of the so-called Big Three automobile companies. Chrysler experienced two bankruptcies: first, between 1978 and 1992, when Lee Iacocca was president, and again during the financial crisis of 2008. GM also filed for bankruptcy in 2008, and the ensuing "bailout" became front-page news. Ford surprised a lot of people by refusing the same bailout and finding its way through the crisis successfully.

During my time at the Sloan School, the auto industry has experienced considerable change, including the closure of the GM plant in Framingham, Massachusetts, which was built soon after the end of World War II, and for many decades UAW members assembled Buicks and related models there. But in the early 1980s competition from Japanese automobiles caused a drop in GM auto sales and created considerable excess capacity.

In Framingham those global shifts played out along with some local issues. The town's political leaders had opposed GM's expansion of its facilities to include a paint and plastics plant, and the town had refused to sell a piece of property to GM to facilitate that expansion. In response, Governor Michael Dukakis acquired the property by right of eminent domain and made it available to GM. That expansion gave hope that GM would remain in Framingham.

By October 1982, though, GM suspended operations in Framingham, hoping to wait it out until demand caught up with capacity. In March 1983, a single shift was called back to work, and in December a second shift was added. By the mid-1980s, however, the penetration of foreign automobile imports had deepened, and GM announced it would close the Framingham plant for good. That happened on August 1, 1989.

Global competition was clearly not the only reason. There were poor labor relations at the plant, which had experienced many labor grievances—more than for all the other GM plants combined. It also was one of GM's poorest-performing plants on the two critical metrics auto executives use to judge performance: productivity as measured in work hours required to produce a car, and quality as measured by defects per one hundred cars coming off the assembly line.

The GM workforce in Framingham was quite senior. During earlier shutdowns, workers had earned close to their regular wages thanks to special unemployment funds the UAW had negotiated with GM. When the permanent shutdown occurred, the workers with considerable years of service were able to retire on nearly full pensions. It was clear that although programs of employment security and financial cushions were desirable, such benefits also lessened the financial urgency that would have served as an incentive to change rules and customary practices.

Economists use the term *moral hazard* to describe behavior like that of the Framingham workers. It's a term most often associated with health insurance: policyholders, because they have coverage, have little incentive to guard against the risk of getting sick. In Framingham it meant workers had little incentive to make changes to protect their jobs, especially because their seniority ensured good pensions.

Certainly the community had a stake, but it had no way of influencing GM's decision. The fact that some elements of the community opposed an earlier expansion of the plant probably had some bearing on GM's thinking. Public officials such as Governor Dukakis clearly had an interest in saving the plant, and he took action. But in the final analysis, he had no influence on the productivity of the workforce.

For management, the value of having a major assembly plant in New England—the only one there—had been outweighed by other considerations, such as lengthy distances for parts to reach Massachusetts from the company's main base of operations in Michigan.

The Framingham story carries with it an interesting connection. Donald Ephlin, whom many of us at Sloan got to know and admire as an effective labor leader for the UAW, began his career at the Framingham plant. At the time of the plant closing in 1989, some observers commented that GM might have resisted closing Ephlin's home plant while he was heading the GM department of the UAW.

Closing the Framingham plant, however, did not become national news like GM's actions elsewhere in the country—thanks in large part to Michael Moore's 1989 documentary *Roger and Me*, which became a big hit. Moore focused on the economic changes that were devastating his hometown of

Flint, Michigan, also home of the first UAW local and site of the famous sit-down strike in 1937. At its peak, Flint was referred to as Buick City, with GM employing more than eighty thousand workers. By the late 1980s, however, downsizing had dropped that number to fifty thousand.

Moore viewed management as a class and not just as a function within the larger economic system. Some of the most devastating scenes in his film showed members of the GM management group at their country clubs enjoying parties in luxurious surroundings. Moore as narrator observed that at the same time the shutdowns and job losses in Flint were taking place, General Motors CEO Roger Smith received a $2 million bonus.

Currently there is renewed attention on economic dislocation; it was a major theme in the 2016 presidential election. Back in 1989, while serving as deputy dean to Lester Thurow and wanting to feed material to him—he regularly authored op-ed pieces—I prepared a report on *Roger and Me*, which I quote from here:

> No doubt the acclaim being accorded the film is due to the fact that many members of the younger generation have not been subjected to earlier rounds of economic change, what some economists have called the "creative destruction of capital." The loss of textiles in New England; the closing down of the steel mills in Youngstown, Ohio; the elimination of meat packing from most of the rail centers in the Midwest—in their time these changes created more havoc than what General Motors has done recently in Flint.
>
> It is also the case that General Motors, in cooperation with the UAW and community groups, has done a good deal to help with cushioning the impact of unemployment in places like Flint. This is an aspect of the larger picture that the director chooses to ignore and helps explain why General Motors and the UAW are so irritated with the movie.
>
> While on the point of the movie being biased and omitting important pieces of information in order to make the director's points, it should also be noted that General Motors replaced its old factories in Flint with Buick City, an impressive complex of new plants. This change was prompted by the need to improve the competitiveness of this important division of the company and thereby the jobs and economic wellbeing of Flint. So the film can properly be criticized for advocating a type of Luddite approach to economic change and overlooking some important social processes other than the act of closing down excess capacity and antiquated plants.

Many experiments are underway today in the automobile industry aimed at eliciting from the workforce flexibility, composite skills, and in general a high commitment that makes it possible to produce high-quality cars at competitive prices. All of these programs have, as a key tenet of the new culture, equality of perquisites and elimination of management as a class. Separate dining facilities, reserved parking spaces, and the use of ties to denote status are all eliminated.

These ideas are modeled after the culture in Japanese plants. The question is two-fold: Will these "bottom up" efforts change the overriding belief system of management in the automobile industry as depicted in this film? Or have the interests of class become so entrenched that when the tough decisions have to be made, production will be cut back (as is currently being done) in order to preserve quarterly earnings, and the interests of workers will be given second standing?

Measured against what we saw in *Roger and Me*, the behavior of Japanese managers in the face of economic adversity is dramatically different. Japanese managers usually take cuts in their own salaries long before taking any other action to reduce costs. If an event that brings personal or economic tragedy to a family takes place, top executives visit the homes and apologize to the families. In this case, individuals who hold key positions in the enterprise are acting as representatives of the larger community of interests and not as members of a class.[23]

Around the time the GM Framingham plant was closing and *Roger and Me* was becoming a hit in movie theaters across the United States, Don Ephlin and other GM leaders were bringing a new assembly plant online in Spring Hill, Tennessee. Saturn Corporation made history, reflecting a commitment made to Ephlin by General Motors CEO Roger Smith to put aside traditional ideas about how to set up an automobile plant.

The two men charged a joint team of management and union leaders to design "the plant of the future." The team spent two years and designed an organization with innovative ideas: participation by union representatives at all levels of management, the use of joint labor-management teams throughout the plant, and a commitment to partnership. After it opened in 1990, I had a chance to observe the new Saturn plant in operation for several weeks.

Tom Kochan and Saul Rubinstein wrote a book that captured the promise of this experiment. What they couldn't foretell was its demise when the leaders of both GM and the UAW could not figure out how to nurture their child and ultimately ended up halting the experiment.[24]

In abandoning Saturn, were GM and the UAW as shortsighted as we academics might like to think? When I was in Spring Hill, I saw an amazing organization. I observed meetings of the strategic council that brought top management and union leaders together to discuss major issues affecting plant operations. I saw the teams in operation, with supervisors and union stewards jointly running the departments. All in all, it seemed like a remarkable innovation.

The Saturn line of automobiles created considerable excitement in the marketplace, but the cars did not sell as well as had been hoped. Some commentators blamed top management for delaying the decision to invest in new models in time to replace the initial vehicle offerings and, when they finally did, not reinvesting in more exciting models for this new brand. Part of the reason for the delayed decision was that the UAW president at the time, Stephen Yokich, was a union traditionalist who opposed the innovations at Saturn and argued with GM leaders to channel new product to other plants.

Saturn may represent one of the biggest strategic missed opportunities— or strategic opportunities not pursued—for both the American labor movement and GM. The answer may never be known as to whether this is an example of what might be called organ rejection—namely, GM and UAW leaders (especially in Detroit) not knowing how to sustain the experiment and diffuse it to other parts of the vast company. Ultimately, the Saturn experiment passed from the scene.

When Ephlin retired from the UAW in 1991, he accepted an invitation to join us on a part-time basis to do guest lectures in our executive programs at Sloan and advise and work with students in MIT's Leaders for Manufacturing Program. His quiet demeanor and deep understanding of what the U.S. auto industry needed to do to meet mounting competition from abroad and reform its outmoded labor relations practices enabled countless students to see his vision and appreciate the wisdom and value of labor-management partnerships. Perhaps the industry and the UAW could have avoided some of the trauma of shrinking market share, jobs, and eventual bankruptcies had they heeded Ephlin's advice.

To be sure, not all the attention we paid to the auto industry was focused on General Motors. Several colleagues and I studied the implementation of what Chrysler called the modern operating agreement. These were initiatives that embraced the best ideas among new concepts for work organization, including worker responsibility for quality, a culture of teamwork, and high commitment to excellence. My part of the study focused on the Chrysler electronics plant in Huntsville, Alabama, where I spent a number of days interviewing key leaders about the implementation of the modern operating agreement.[25]

Two main questions arise for me as I think about summarizing the lessons to be taken away from the automobile industry. First, did the auto companies, while trying to work cooperatively with the union, become distracted and not recognize the importance of competition and new manufacturing concepts coming from Japan, such as lean manufacturing? The same question could be asked about the UAW: Was the union leadership myopic? Numerous reports have been written about NUMMI (New United Motor Manufacturing), the assembly plant in California jointly operated by GM and Toyota, often citing GM's failure to understand and capture the essence of Toyota's high-productivity operation.[26]

Second, did we researchers pay insufficient attention to the opening of many new auto plants by foreign companies in the U.S. South? Our research for the *Transformation* book identified the strategy of companies phasing out old plants, opening new ones and keeping the latter unorganized. Our contacts at that time were with the Big Three in the industry; we were not in touch with BMW, Subaru, Toyota, Volkswagen, and others. When I began field research in the auto industry in the 1950s, the UAW represented almost every plant. As I write this in 2018, 40 percent of the workforce is in nonunion plants.

Like management in the auto industry, we old-timers in academia remained too focused on familiar territory and often failed to investigate new developments. Our students and younger colleagues did explore the new developments, however, building on the earlier study of the industry by Harry Katz and examining practices beyond the Big Three and in union and nonunion auto plants around the world.[27] For instance, as part of the MIT International Motor Vehicle Program, John Krafcik and John Paul MacDuffie did seminal research on the relationships between workplace practices linked to lean production and plant performance (using measures of productivity and quality described in the discussion of the Framingham GM plant).[28]

The point here is that it is important to encourage and support young researchers to follow their instincts and go where the action is. A lot of that action, we came to see, had to do with an expanding view of negotiation as a "discipline."

Labor Negotiation Theory Goes Generic

I'm sure that when Dick Walton and I published *A Behavioral Theory of Labor Negotiations* in 1965, while I was at GSB, we had no idea that the subject of negotiations would become so pervasive and that our ideas—which were developed in the context of collective bargaining—would have relevance in so many other arenas. Our work took a fascinating journey, as the topic of negotiation became a major one for research and education.

Many of the stops on that journey were in the Boston-Cambridge area. The first stop involved the shift in university courses from a focus on labor negotiations to teaching about negotiation more generically.

Max Bazerman and I launched the first "generic" negotiations course at the Sloan School with a seminar in 1984. At the time, the National Institute for Dispute Resolution and the Knight Foundation were promoting generic negotiation courses in law schools, but the same systematic attention to teaching negotiation had not yet surfaced in business schools.

For me the transition was easy because I had taught labor negotiations at both Chicago and Cornell using the *Behavioral Theory* book as the intellectual foundation. Drawing on it again, Max and I adapted the framework, centering on distributive and integrative bargaining and adding cases and simulations from a wide range of business and social settings.[29] Max, who is now a professor at HBS and has published many books on the topic, was a great partner who expanded the process we called attitudinal structuring to take into account biases and other psychological processes.[30]

Mary Rowe also used the framework of negotiation theory in designing her course "Negotiations and Conflict Management," bringing a very valuable perspective honed by her many years as MIT's ombudsperson. Rowe developed conceptual tools, including a systems approach to illustrate the workplace institutionalization of collaborative, mixed motive, and distributive methods of conflict management; the importance of dealing with very diverse populations; and a framework for understanding sources of power in ways that go beyond traditional positional, expertise, sanctions, and reward power to include factors such as the power that comes from use of force, information, expertise, elegant solutions, charisma and moral authority, relationships, and persistence. Mary also added to the traditional theoretical framework of avoidance, competition, compromise, accommodation, and collaboration an analysis of negotiations when the aim is to *harm* opponents.[31] She extended traditional teaching about coalitions from her many years of working with dozens of affinity groups, pointing out that coalitions can expand and contract, and become more or less powerful, as they confront different issues. This thinking is an extension of the original behavioral theory about negotiations *within* teams that Dick Walton and I developed to illuminate the existence of subgroups on a given team that do not necessarily agree with each other about successive issues—and that may occasionally even "cross over" to join opposing groups on some issues.

These courses became very popular, with almost 80 percent of Sloan students opting to take an elective in the subject. As a result, many of us shifted our own course offerings from a focus on labor to a focus on negotiations in an effort to follow the changing interests of our students. The proliferation of negotiation courses moved beyond business schools and law schools to other professional degree programs across the country. These courses continue to be very popular; students recognize the value of learning how to negotiate in a variety of settings regardless of their specific career interests.

Many of these courses draw on concepts developed in *A Behavioral Theory*, and many more use terminology developed by colleagues. Whether it is the contrast between integrative and distributive bargaining, creating and claiming, or other terms, students instinctively understand that certain issues and certain situations are more collaborative or more competitive. New learning happens when they come to see their own personal strengths and blind sides as well as the many complex ways these two aspects of negotiations interact with each other. Addressing attitudinal issues—the human biases and various forms of influence—is also mind stretching. Students know these issues to be important, but are not always clear about their options. It is heartening to see that these important parts of *A Behavioral Theory* are still at the core of negotiation courses, with applications that span labor, business, legal, policy, community, and many other negotiation settings.

The fourth part of *A Behavioral Theory*—the internal negotiations within each party—was the last part of the theory to be added to these generic elements. Parts of our field data just could not be explained without taking into account these internal dynamics. Most simulation exercises aren't set up to illustrate both negotiations *between* parties and negotiations *within* each party, yet these dynamics are often the most challenging in real-world settings.[32]

Scholars have since applied agency theory to what Dick and I termed internal negotiations, and I wrote a chapter on collective bargaining in a book examining the concept in a variety of settings.[33]

By the early 1990s strategic changes at both the adversarial and cooperative extremes were taking place that exceeded what was going on when Dick and I wrote *A Behavioral Theory*. In response, we teamed with Joel Cutcher-Gershenfeld and wrote *Strategic Negotiations*, which added further consideration of strategy and structure to a focus on process in our earlier book.[34] We were motivated to expand the theory through strategic developments along a spectrum that ranged from the collaborative transformation of labor-management relations to the complete destruction of the relationship. At the time we were observing what we called a strategy of escape—companies abandoning the entire relationship. In Poland we saw the same thing on the union side, with the trade union Solidarność (Solidarity) escaping the Communist regime. At the same time, some U.S. unions were entering far-ranging strategic partnerships with companies. There were structural developments as well: changes in pattern bargaining, multilateral bargaining, new levels of complexity spurred by the growth of multinational corporations, union mergers, and the increasing importance of teams and frontline relations. As in *A Behavioral Theory*, we focused on labor-management negotiations.

In our new work we drew a sharp distinction between forcing and fostering. The forcing strategy seeks to realize what is desirable; it places heavy emphasis on maintaining control and ensuring that the results of negotiations meet specific goals and timetables. In contrast, the fostering strategy emphasizes building better relationships and addresses the value-added dimensions of change; it pays more attention to feasibility by emphasizing attitudes and a readiness for change.

Both strategies have limitations in their extreme forms. Unrestrained forcing is problematic, but so, too, is superficial fostering. When applying the forcing strategy, management will often insist that the other party accept its agenda without understanding the shortcomings of advancing its position too aggressively. The approach can cause dynamic moves and countermoves; in a labor context, that often results in strikes, lockouts, and other escalating conflicts. The limitations of a fostering strategy are that the parties meet and emerge from the negotiation with "a good feeling," but then little or nothing else happens. The status quo persists, and the journey to change never really begins.

In *Strategic Negotiations* we highlighted how labor negotiations involve not only a substantive contract but also a social contract. In effect, the relationship is on the table at the same time as the traditional contractual issues. This led us to recommend a combination of more restrained forms of forcing and more robust forms of fostering in order to achieve substantive gains and maintain a constructive relationship.

In our study we each applied the framework to a different industry. Dick had been a director at Champion Paper, so he used that company to do a case study of the industry. Joel selected the auto parts industry, one he had studied closely while on the faculty at Michigan State University. My long-standing love affair with railroads led to that being my industry for study. I arranged to visit the headquarters of Union Pacific in Omaha, Nebraska, where a graduate of the Sloan Fellows Program was an executive. But a relatively new carrier garnered most of my attention, one that emerged over time from the bankruptcy of the Penn Central railroad.

When there was an opportunity to split off some of the Penn Central's smaller branches, several entrepreneurs—with money from the Mellon family fortune—put together a plan to buy the Maine Central Railroad, the Boston & Maine Railroad, and the Delaware & Hudson Railway and create a new company, Guilford Industries.

With its new name and headquarters in a new location—Springfield, Vermont—Guilford announced that it was a "new" company and therefore that all labor agreements with the predecessor carriers were void. In quick order, Guilford changed crew sizes, mileage limits, and other restrictions. When the unions went out on strike in response, charging management with taking a union-busting stance, Guilford continued to operate the lines using management personnel and replacement workers—a highly unusual tactic in the rail industry.

It was a clear case of unrestrained forcing. The management of Guilford Industries undertook a pseudo-reorganization and then did an end run around negotiating changes in work rules. When I went to visit what was supposed to be the new headquarters, I found nothing more than a switching facility overgrown with weeds.

The strike wreaked havoc for freight shippers and commuters in the northeastern United States and, for a time, threatened nationwide rail service.

It was only the intervention of federal courts in several states that prevented the latter: they blocked the Brotherhood of Maintenance of Way Employees from staging sympathy strikes at the Santa Fe Railway, Burlington Northern, and other major railroads. And even after ten weeks, when President Reagan issued an order creating an emergency panel to help end the strike, workers who tried to return to their jobs were turned away by the company—more proof that union busting was a big part of Guilford's initial motivation. Finally, after five months, Guilford offered union members 15 percent of company ownership, along with a wage increase, to settle. But the next year there was an even longer strike.[35]

Was it cynicism run wild? Was it a clever move to get around entrenched labor interests clinging to outmoded work rules? Could there have been a more rational transition from old to new railroading? The railroad industry had been on a change journey for some time, with a steady decline in crew size, elimination of brakemen, and efforts to get train crews to work longer shifts. So why did Guilford management not continue the journey by seeking a new round of concessions? The answer goes to an ideology present in many quarters that champions a crusade to break union power. I continue to believe that constructive engagement on both sides would have yielded better results for each.

Meanwhile, the expansion of negotiation as a discipline continued—specifically, into *interest-based bargaining*.

Interest-Based Bargaining

The Program on Negotiations (PON), established in 1983 at Harvard Law School, was in full swing by the 1990s, complete with a journal, regular seminars, a clearinghouse for cases, and simulations and activities that brought together faculty members from a range of colleges in the Boston area. I was part of the group that helped launch PON.

I brought labor negotiations into the mix, but it wasn't until a decade later that we offered a formal seminar on the topic. The motivation was, in part, a growing number of stories of parties that had attempted to set aside the adversarial approach to collective bargaining and turn negotiations into an entirely cooperative process. There were a few notable successes, but also a number of failures. Constituents were not always ready for their representatives to be cooperative. Both sides were unprepared for shifts that would dramatically shrink the available resources, such as happened during the recession of the early 1990s. Having just completed *Strategic Negotiations*, we knew success would require a mix of forcing and fostering, with attention to internal negotiations and attitudinal dynamics. It couldn't just be a shift to a pure "win-win" approach.

Joel Cutcher-Gershenfeld arranged to take a sabbatical in 1995 at PON. It was an opportunity for us to develop a two-day seminar focused on practitioners and the institutional complexities of labor-management relations. We had been hearing stories of employers and unions that were experimenting with the approach described in the book *Getting to Yes* (the authors were from the Harvard Negotiation Project) having difficulty taking into account issues such as the requirements of union constitutions, questions on how to handle the traditional role of a single spokesperson for each side, what to do when one side or the other needed to call for a caucus, complexities around the use of subcommittees, the challenges of union ratification meetings and management executive review, and planning for joint implementation of negotiated agreements.[36] We wanted to show that such a focus could deliver on the promise of mutual gains while also attending to the complex challenges of collective bargaining.

We recruited Tom Kochan, Nancy Peace, and Phyllis Segal to be part of the instructional team. The program acquainted participants with the tools and concepts of interest-based bargaining.

Over a ten-year period we offered approximately thirty of these seminars to more than four thousand individuals. In follow-up telephone surveys, we documented success stories in which interest-based bargaining moved the parties to arrangements that were mutually beneficial. In other cases, the process worked fine for some subjects, but when the economic agenda items came on the table, the process reverted to traditional bargaining, with back-and-forth exchanges of positions.

I wanted to understand how the process worked in actual practice, so I conducted a video interview with managers at a trucking firm that had sent a team to our seminar. Using the interest-based bargaining process, the parties had agreed on a new scheduling plan that enabled it to compete with nonunion carriers that had lower wages and fringe benefit costs. How representative was that experience?

Earlier research showed that in 2003, more than 65 percent of managers and 75 percent of union leaders were at least aware of the principles of interest-based bargaining—figures I suspect are largely still the same. Almost as many—60 percent of managers and nearly 75 percent of union leaders—reported having also utilized the approach, which was a substantial increase from surveys conducted in 1996 and 1999, when the numbers were approximately 35 and nearly 60 percent for managers in these two years, respectively, and approximately 45 and 55 percent for union leaders, respectively.[37] One limit on the use is that unions associate interest-based bargaining with efforts of management to roll back various fringe benefits and secure other concessions. Union members are often nervous about their negotiators engaging in interest-based bargaining for fear they will not represent the interests of rank-and-file workers with sufficient vigor. They often assume that winning a satisfactory contract requires distributive bargaining. They may not see interest-based bargaining—which is largely an elaboration of integrative bargaining—as doing the job when there are also distributive elements present. Leadership turnover, especially on the union side, has in some cases brought the process back to what a labor leader I got to know when I was on the board of directors of Inland Steel referred to as "professional adversarialism."

When parties have followed the interest-based bargaining process, it has led to mutual gains agreements that would not have likely been achieved otherwise. For example, here is Article 24, "Creating and Sustaining a Collaborative Culture," from the contract between the San Juan Unified School District in California and the San Juan Teachers Association:

> The District and Association agree to take responsibility and be held accountable for the improvement of the quality of teaching and learning which represents an expanded role in public education. It is in the best interest of the San Juan Schools that the District and the Association cooperatively engage in activities and communication which demonstrate mutual respect for all stakeholders and results in the improvement of student achievement through the development of common goals, a cooperative, trusting environment, and teamwork. It is the belief that actively and constructively involving all relevant stakeholders contributes significantly toward achieving these goals.
>
> Shared responsibility and accountability for results are at the core of a continuous improvement model. Joint responsibility for student success means

that educators share in celebrating what works and share in identifying together areas that are not working and are in need of improvement.[38]

This language is then supported by commitments to joint training, joint school leadership teams, guidance on collaborative decision making, and other provisions. Both labor and management are signaling to the broader community a joint commitment that goes well beyond the traditional focus of collective bargaining on wages, hours, and working conditions.

So interest-based bargaining continues to make a contribution, although it needs to be seen as having limitations. The most success seems to be with a hybrid model that is matched to the history of the relationship, the leaders at a given moment, and the challenges on the table. Interest-based bargaining can be seen as a second-generation building on the conceptualization of integrative bargaining as a key feature of constructive labor negotiations.

Can we take credit for the increased awareness, if not the use of interest-based bargaining by labor and management negotiators? To some extent, that is the case. The postseminar surveys we undertook with participants showed that they gained a thorough understanding of the new process—its potential as well as the challenges in coping with distributive issues and leadership turnover. But the surveys revealed something even more significant: that the most effective implementation of interest-based bargaining occurred when the two sides came to the seminar as a joint team. In fact, in one case, the parties used the evening between the two days to negotiate a new contract.[39]

From Negotiation to Collaboration

In the language of negotiations, the *integrative potential* of collective bargaining is something many industrial relations scholars have sought to analyze so that more of it can take place. The expansion of negotiation, and especially the rise of interest-based bargaining, gave me hope that something I have always been anxious to see—namely, for collective bargaining to embrace labor-management partnerships that would benefit all interests—would become more widespread.

Most of my 1990 address as president of the Labor and Employment Relations Association highlighted the potential for labor-management partnerships.

It was also my theme in talks I gave under the auspices of the Collective Bargaining Forum (CBF). At the Sloan School, I focused on two examples of what could be characterized as sustained labor-management cooperation. The first was the Scanlon Plan.

Although it has mostly passed from the scene, the Scanlon Plan was very much in place in the 1980s, my earliest years at Sloan. This innovation in labor-management relations was pioneered by Joseph Scanlon in the 1940s and 1950s after he retired from the United Steelworkers of America and joined the MIT faculty. Scanlon's core vision was of management and labor working together to improve productivity and share the economic rewards generated by achieving productivity objectives.

I first heard about the plan while a doctoral student at HBS in the late 1950s, when I attended one of the biennial Scanlon conferences. The gatherings brought labor leaders and managers to the MIT campus to share their experiences with representatives from other companies and unions interested in learning about the plan and possibly adopting it.

I never had an opportunity to meet Joe Scanlon, who died in 1956. But it was clear from accounts by George Shultz and Fred Lesieur, who succeeded Joe Scanlon in guiding the Scanlon Plan Association, that Scanlon impressed everyone with his knowledge of factory operations and his insights about how to motivate workers and improve productivity—the result of his background as a steelworker and union official.

During the Scanlon Plan's prime, the more than fifty companies and their unions that had implemented the plan provided important research opportunities for faculty and graduate students at MIT, as well as financial resources derived from the conferences.

As was mentioned in chapter 3, George Shultz at the University of Chicago took the template of the Scanlon Plan and adapted it to Esso refineries and their marketing departments; the proposal was never implemented, but he and I published two articles summarizing our work. After all, academics who "fail" at consulting assignments typically recover by writing about them.[40]

In the 1990s the Scanlon Plan principles caught the attention of Mitchell Rabkin, then the CEO of Beth Israel Hospital in Boston. He designed what came to be called PREPARE/21 as a way of motivating workers to improve the effectiveness of operations. I served on an advisory committee along with Warren Bennis, a distinguished scholar who had been on the MIT faculty and then took an appointment at the University of Southern California, where he authored best-selling works on leadership.[41] Workers at the hospital could earn a small bonus, and over the period of the plan rewards on the order of 5 percent were paid to employees. Beth Israel had no unions (and still does not), so this was not a Scanlon Plan in the strictest sense, but it was grounded in the plan's principles.

The secret to the success of the Scanlon Plan was the association of firms using the plan, regular visits from consultants to these companies, and biennial conferences that brought representatives together to share lessons about issues encountered in day-to-day operations. Studies have found a relationship between this form of gainsharing and improved performance.[42] Although there are still a number of consultants offering to help establish Scanlon Plans, and a number of organizations in manufacturing and service sectors utilizing these plans, the idea of gainsharing has mostly fallen out of favor with management.[43] Instead management has come to believe that a formal plan of gainsharing is not needed to elicit superior performance, so long as there is competent oversight of the workforce.

Still, I believe the Scanlon Plan is an idea that may yet come around again. It has a logic everyone can appreciate: people will work together better when they can clearly see their shared opportunity to benefit from the gains.

Would the appointment of someone like Scanlon, who was a senior lecturer at the Sloan School (initially in the Department of Economics), be appropriate in the early twenty-first century? Yes, if such an individual could be found. MIT prides itself on finding solutions to big problems. Scanlon formulated a plan to deal with the challenges of the workplace, designing a system that generated increased motivation and productivity from a workforce and thereby creating resources that could be shared as bonuses. He wasn't the only person to do so, but his plan captured the attention of many companies and unions, and for many decades served as a reminder that labor-management relations could contribute to the interests of all stakeholders involved in the economic enterprise. Joe Scanlon was way ahead of his time.

The second example is the labor-management partnership at Kaiser Permanente, the largest managed care organization in the United States. It is the largest and longest sustained example of such cooperation seen in decades in this country. It has certainly faced challenges, with leadership changes requiring the establishment of new social contracts, but it has also delivered improved pay and benefits for the eighty-six thousand employees whose unions are members of the coalition. Tom Kochan led a team that told the full story in our book *Healing Together.*[44]

The highlight of my involvement with Kaiser was observing a national negotiation. The parties created task forces that utilized interest-based bargaining, and our team was given full access to and cooperation with tracking these deliberations.[45]

As of this writing, the Kaiser Permanente partnership is approaching three decades of making a difference. It has remained robust for so long because of alignment at the strategic level between management and the leaders of the various unions. Also, size makes a difference: Kaiser's size helps facilitate the commitment of resources and the ability to share best practices across divisions to create a learning environment. This is vividly illustrated by the way the organization rolled out the concept and practice of unit-based teams that foster problem solving across the different specialties employed in Kaiser's clinics and hospitals.

Currently there are more than three thousand of these unit-based teams, each implementing improvements—large and small—on a regular basis. *Hank*, a newsletter named after Kaiser Permanente founder Henry "Hank" Kaiser and published several times a year, highlights examples and challenges in the partnership experience and, by sharing best practices, helps foster a learning environment. The most well-established teams (Kaiser Permanente refers to these as Level 4 or Level 5 teams on its five-point maturity scale) are associated with reduced medical errors, increased patient satisfaction, and other key outcomes.

Who knows whether this labor-management partnership will endure? Even robust partnerships are challenges to govern and sustain in a setting where the overall national (and perhaps industry) climate is hostile toward union participation in broad-based organizational affairs. But it has already defied the odds, lasting three decades. And even were the partnership to have ended by the time you read this, it will be recorded not only as the largest and longest-lasting such partnership but also the one that accomplished the most—in this case, for Kaiser Permanente as an organization, for the union members, and for the patients they serve together.

The example of Kaiser's labor-management partnership poses two big questions for our field of study that remain unanswered: What would it take to sustain a successful partnership like Kaiser's indefinitely? What would it take to see more like it adopted? Answering the latter was a major reason

Tom Kochan and I served as resources for the CBF, sponsored by the National Planning Association. It was part of an effort to foster collaboration at a national level.

Malcolm Lovell, a former U.S. undersecretary of labor and former director of labor relations at American Motors under George Romney, chaired the forum. Lovell brought together top labor and management leaders to discuss important issues and formulate policy proposals regarding the future of unions in American society. He believed that unions could help their employers achieve and sustain competitiveness and that, in turn, employers would endorse the premise that unions are good for the economy, and companies should not fight unionization.

Robert Crandall, CEO of American Airlines (AA), joined the CBF hoping for ideas to restructure the relationship between his carrier and its unions—in particular, some wisdom about improving the labor relations climate. He thought that the collaborative approach endorsed by union officials who were members of the CBF might rub off on the leaders of AA unions. But at one point, Crandall walked into the room as Jack Sheinkman, president of the Amalgamated Clothing and Textile Workers Union, was describing the positive role several companies had played in regional economic development programs by working with his union. Crandall listened for a bit and then leaned over to one of us and asked, "Who is that guy talking? We never hear things like that at the Business Roundtable!"

But none of what Crandall was hoping for happened. He had attended several meetings before and concluded that the CBF was fine for airing issues and talking about policy but did not provide leverage for what he wanted to accomplish.

The CBF did develop good personal relationships among some of the highest-ranking union leaders and CEOs in the United States, and it did foster dialogue that produced consensus statements on the core principles that should guide American labor-management relations. But what Bob Crandall saw was true: the CBF was not a vehicle for changing outlooks or resolving contentious issues between labor and management in specific relationships.

Still, for nearly two decades, the CBF persisted. Eventually, though, it closed in 2003 as interest in continuing dialogue between management and labor leaders dissipated.[46] Certainly the CBF effort did not set back industrial relations in any way, but did it do any good? The CBF gave labor leaders an opportunity to put their points of view in front of top management, advancing the premise that unions should be viewed as a positive force in the economy. Participant CEOs learned how unions felt, and some gained a new appreciation for the value of working together with their union counterparts. But these CEOs participated as individuals and did not engage in any type of bargaining. Position papers on a variety of subjects were prepared, one of which called for a new labor-management compact. But none influenced the course of national labor policy.[47]

The CBF can be thought of in the same vein as the Joint Labor-Management Conference that President Harry Truman convened shortly after the end of World War II. Truman underscored his purpose in an address to its opening session: "I am convinced that if labor and management will approach each other, with the realization that they have a common goal, and with the determination to compose their differences in their own long-range interest, it will not be long before we have put industrial strife behind us."[48]

At present there is nothing that duplicates these earlier efforts to develop better understanding between business and labor. Perhaps, given the divisions laid bare by the 2016 election and the dysfunctional national politics that have followed, the time is again ripe for labor and management to come together and demonstrate that there can be civil discourse among leaders of divergent interests. They can serve as role models to demonstrate that, when necessary, participants can draw on some broader and deeper shared values to bridge their divides.

Pushing the Boundaries of Negotiation Theory Even Further

As much as I learned from everything that took place as negotiation became a "discipline" and its parameters expanded well beyond the labor-management domain with which I was most familiar, there was nothing that specifically prepared me for an opportunity that came to Dick Walton and me a little over a decade ago.

At some point in 2007, as the administration of President George W. Bush wound down, Mary Rowe and her husband Robert Fein asked Dick and me whether we would be interested in working on a project together. The project had been launched by the Intelligence Science Board to study what was known scientifically about interrogating people detained because they were believed to possess information critical to national security.[49] The group we soon joined included several individuals who had worked for the Federal Bureau of Investigation and the Naval Criminal Investigation Service, along with an air force reserve officer, a Harvard Law School professor, and several other researchers and practitioners. We met regularly in Cambridge, and once traveled to the National Defense Intelligence College just outside Washington, DC.

Dick and I had been asked to join because of our behavioral theory of negotiation. Of interest was whether negotiation, as we understood its theory and applications, could be a useful approach for understanding interrogation. After all, the reality is that every interrogation is fundamentally an interaction between parties with different interests, and that certainly meets the initial qualification to be a negotiation.

Like some labor negotiations, the relationship between the interrogator and the interrogatee—in interrogation lingo, these people are the *educer* and the *source*, respectively—is very likely adversarial. It may even be characterized by intense hostility from the potential source and a refusal to cooperate. Unlike in a labor negotiation, however, the protagonists commence the journey—if that word can be used to describe the process—with few, if any, common interests. Furthermore, the interaction itself may be very short, lasting only a few hours, or go on for months.

Thus, although the relationship between educer and source in an interrogation is most likely to fall on the negative side of any spectrum of possible relationships, the task in all negotiations still matters: to design a process that creates and makes salient interests that can be harmonized, even if only for a short period. That takes all the skills and wisdom of the educer, who must establish some degree of relationship by probing to understand the source's background details about family, hometown, work, and so on.

The challenge our study group faced was that there were very few, if any, detailed descriptions available of processes that government agencies involved in the so-called War on Terror had followed. We were briefed about the successful interrogation that Ali Soufan had conducted with terrorists suspected in the bombing of the USS *Cole* in the Middle East.[50] But for the most part, the kinds of case studies with rich detail that Dick Walton and I used for labor negotiations were not available to our committee.

We were also well aware of the controversy surrounding events in 2003 at Abu Ghraib prison in Iraq, where personnel of the U.S. Army and the Central Intelligence Agency had subjected prisoners to what Amnesty International characterized as human rights abuses. It became a national scandal a year later when photographs emerged.

No members of our group advocated abusive interrogation techniques. Vice President Dick Cheney and Secretary of Defense Donald Rumsfeld claimed that useful information had been obtained with what the Bush administration euphemistically called "enhanced interrogation techniques"— which we viewed as unacceptable. Although there may have been instances, here and there, in which useful information was obtained in that way, our view—consistent with how most military people regard what is usually characterized as *torture*—is that it doesn't work, that any "successes" were coincidental to the method used, and that the harm created by making a suspect even more of an enemy far outweighed such "successes." One well-documented shortcoming of enhanced interrogation techniques is that most suspects will say anything to get the process to stop. We felt that the chance of procuring useful information would be much higher by building relationships—an approach with no downsides.

Notwithstanding the absence of case studies, Dick Walton dove into the subject and developed a framework for thinking about the interrogation process. He built on the work we had done with Joel Cutcher-Gershenfeld while developing our *Strategic Negotiations* book. Dick fleshed out the strategic approaches of forcing and fostering as a way of thinking about the interview process and the techniques that might be used for building a relationship and eliciting actionable information.

When President Obama took office in 2009, he immediately banned the use of enhanced interrogation as CIA operatives had practiced it and directed that there be an interagency task force review of U.S. interrogation efforts. In August 2009 U.S. Attorney General Eric Holder announced the formation of the High-Value Detainee Interrogation Group (HIG), which was charged—among other responsibilities—with developing a research program on interrogation. In his comments, Holder mentioned the work of our group.

HIG has functioned since 2010, and U.S. policy has banned coercive interrogation. Now, as we fast-forward to the present, President Donald Trump has made statements endorsing the form of torture known as waterboarding. So the controversy persists.

I learned several things from the Intelligence Science Board experience. First, when it comes to the intersection of human values—in this case, treating suspects in a humane way versus the mission of gathering information and protecting the country—the trade-offs are very complicated. Second, it is challenging to do research when so much of the data that are needed to inform better practice are simply not made available to researchers. Third, the subject—with its heavy political overtones—remains very contentious and a topic of considerable debate.

Finally, Dick Walton's framing of the process illustrated once again that the basic concepts and processes of negotiation can be used in a wide variety of settings, most of which were never on our minds when we first proposed them in 1965.

Negotiation, Mediation, and Public-Sector Labor Relations

Another extension of my own knowledge and experience with collective bargaining and negotiation has been into the world of mediation, especially involving public-sector unions. Unions may have declined in the private sector, but anyone still interested in labor relations can point to the public sector, where there is still plenty of "action." Particularly in state and local government, unions have a significance presence. Even in Arlington, Massachusetts, the suburb of Boston where I live (with a population under fifty thousand), we've experienced the shock waves of contention that have hit the public sector across the country—and sometimes mediation, in this environment where strikes are often "illegal," is the only way to resolve differences.

Why has collective bargaining in the public sector become so contentious? Certainly one reason is the increasing costs local municipalities and state governments face to fund benefits for their workers. Further, teacher contracts in particular have come under scrutiny for the practice of providing annual step wage increases. These cost pressures are exacerbated by the realities of static or declining budgets as citizens exert pressure on their governments to curtail tax increases or even implement tax cuts.

Most municipalities use fact-finding and/or arbitration to settle contract negotiations with police and firefighters. Typically, third-party recommendations include cost-of-living adjustments, and in many cases these regular wage increases have moved the salaries of public-sector workers ahead of those in the private sector, where wages for most workers have been stagnant for nearly forty years.

Health care costs have been escalating for all employers, making them the top agenda item in most collective bargaining. Such negotiations have been very difficult in the public sector, especially for municipal workers. I have been involved in facilitating negotiations in Arlington, where the town manager approached the unions to gauge their willingness to switch from a Blue Cross/Blue Shield–type plan to the state health care plan for Massachusetts— at substantial savings to the town. As an inducement, the town manager offered to share half the savings with the unions. But union members feared any change would be disruptive, and especially that most of them would lose options such as their indemnity plans. So their leaders opposed the town's proposition, and negotiations ended in a stalemate.

Unions and their members tend to look back to hard-won gains in wages and benefits and want them protected. For its part, management looks ahead and focuses on budget uncertainties and the prospects of further cuts in state and federal funding.

Defined-benefit pension plans have also come under attack, and public-sector unions and their members resist changes in these benefits. As a mediator in Arlington, I frequently heard union members argue that most of them had accepted jobs in the public sector, even though the wages were not as high as in the private sector, because they knew the benefits would be better, making up for wage differences. Public-sector workers view themselves as career employees, and they count on scheduled pensions and health care programs that are affordable and flexible.

The Arlington town manager also proposed that the union forgo a scheduled wage increase—a tough sell, as is convincing a majority of union members to accept no wage increases in a new contract. It's difficult even when there is a potential for job losses and acceptance might mean fewer employees will be terminated. The latter is often management's main argument: "If we don't get these concessions, we'll have to lay off X number of workers." Given the principle of seniority in layoffs, the jobs of junior workers are most at risk with any projected (or threatened) reduction in the workforce. So a majority of the membership votes to oppose any revisions (and the majority rules for most votes taken in the union).

Given how pension benefits are calculated, public employees are, in the end, focused on their salaries—particularly the salary levels they will achieve by retirement. As one union member told the Arlington town manager, "I've just done the calculation, and what you're asking will cost me two thousand dollars per year in pension benefits."

I have sometimes wondered in retrospect whether I could have done things differently and had a more positive effect when I mediated negotiations in Arlington. Ultimately, Massachusetts passed a law that gave municipalities unilateral authority to shift employees to the state health care plan. The Arlington unions missed an opportunity to share in the savings because of the union leadership's inability to educate the membership about the new economic realities facing municipal government. Even when it became clear the legislature was going to take action, the union leaders remained committed to their position.

Should I have tried to convince the union members that it was in their best interests to accept the management proposal? They had heard the arguments directly from management about both the need for change and its inevitability. I suspect that adding my endorsement would not have made a difference, and instead I would have jeopardized my mediator role, in which remaining neutral on the issues is central.

Clearly these are not easy times to be a labor leader in the public sector. Most are aware of the financial stresses governments face but are also aware that politically they must oppose changes that many (perhaps even a majority) members find objectionable. Labor leaders do not want to run the risk of accepting changes in pension plans and health care plans, take their members into new and uncertain environments because of it, and end up being voted out of office. On top of all that, the Supreme Court in late June 2018 made things even more difficult.

In *Janus v. American Federation of State, County, and Municipal Employees, Council 31* the Supreme Court—as expected—eliminated mandatory dues collection (often referred to as the checkoff) for unionized public employees, creating considerable consternation among those of us who, like unions leaders, have accepted this decades-long arrangement as necessary and beneficial. Several states had already passed legislation eliminating the dues checkoff; in one case, Wisconsin, the reported result has been a dramatic drop in union membership and dues collections.

That is not to say that the checkoff mechanism (in which the employer deducts the dues and transmits the funds to the union) is ideal. Its automated nature can result in de-emphasizing the need for union leaders to be in close touch with their members. Instead of active servicing, they turn to other priorities such as lobbying. The court's decision does not say that union members are prevented from paying dues, but that they cannot be forced to pay dues. So, like cultural organizations that must make the case for financial support by offering attractive services, union leaders will have to respond appropriately to keep their organizations funded.

At the 2018 annual meeting of the national Labor and Industrial Relations Research Association, held less than two weeks before the court's decision, I was impressed by the attitude of several union leaders whose unions had already taken steps to deal with the anticipated negative consequences. Although they did not say that the restriction was something they would have endorsed, the long-term results may be positive.

One irony that comes to mind as I think about the impact of this decision is that unions, under the mandate of what is called duty of fair representation, are required to represent an employee in the bargaining unit who has a grievance. At first glance it seems unfair that a union is required to pursue a grievance—even all the way to arbitration—for an individual who may not be financially supporting that union. The question is whether this situation can be turned to an advantage, to a selling point: "We will handle your issue and pursue settlement, but we are expecting that you will pay dues on a regular basis." The alternative allowed under the *Janus* decision is for a union to say to a worker who is not a member of the union but is in the bargaining unit: "Okay, we will handle your grievance and take it all the way to arbitration, but you have to pay the costs that will be accrued." That number would run into the thousands of dollars.

As the saying goes, the jury is still out on the impact of the *Janus* decision on the health and well-being of unions as institutions; regardless, the need for mediation involving public-sector employees will continue. Through the many hours I have spent in such activities, I have come to see that the elements of mediation are actually quite simple. Often my role has been little more than to set the dates for meetings and make sure everything is in order so the parties can function effectively. Other times I have been engaged in "shuttle diplomacy" between the parties, holding potential concessions in "escrow" to see whether they can be made to work.

On occasion I have played much more of what Deborah Kolb describes as a directive or orchestrative role.[51] In the 2015 round of negotiations between Harvard University and the Harvard Union of Clerical and Technical Workers, at a point in the process when the parties were very far apart on compensation, Lawrence Katz and I asked the two chief negotiators whether they would be willing to consider our recommendations. They said yes, and we proceeded to outline an economic package for the parties to consider. It served as a basis for the eventual settlement they reached.

Fortunately, the issue of acceptability—the "coin of the realm" in arbitration that requires not only neutrality but also professional bearing and recognizable smarts about industrial relations—was never an issue in the Harvard or Arlington cases. But another time it certainly *was* a problem.

I have always been on the lookout for ways to get involved, and in 1987 I thought I had a brilliant idea for settling a strike by National Football League players. I hatched a mediation plan that involved creating a three-person fact-finding group—me included—that would interview both sides and make recommendations.

To ensure acceptability I recruited George Burman, a former PhD student of mine at the University of Chicago who had played offensive center for both the Los Angeles Rams and the Washington Redskins under the legendary coach George Allen. At the time, Burman was on the faculty of the Syracuse University School of Management, where he later became dean. For the employer side, I had in mind William Ford of the Ford Motor Company. While at MIT as a Sloan Fellow, he had taken my class in industrial relations—and he just happened to be one of the owners of the Detroit Lions football team.

I thought this "dream team" would be readily accepted, but when I called the representative for the owners—someone I knew casually who had graduated from the Cornell ILR School—they weren't interested. That was the end of that effort. It underscored the reality that most parties, even when engaged in difficult negotiations, want to keep control and avoid opening the process to outsiders.

Closer to home, Tom Kochan and I learned that managers want to keep would-be "helpers" at arm's length. During the early 1990s, when MIT broke ground for several new buildings, Tom and I received a call from Mark Erlich, business agent for Local 40 of the Carpenters union. He was anxious for MIT to enter into a project agreement with his union: in exchange for a commitment from the union of no work stoppages, the contractor could only employ union labor. I agreed to contact William Dickson, MIT's senior vice president, and urge a meeting with Erlich and consideration of such an agreement. In short order, Dickson fired back a tart note: "We will decide what to do—I don't tell you how to run the Sloan School."

Eventually Dickson and the union did enter into a project agreement, but the episode reaffirmed George Shultz's sage advice when I was at the University of Chicago: "Giving unsolicited advice to your employer is very risky."

Still, if serving as a mediator teaches anything, it is that there is tremendous value in being able to maintain a neutral posture and hence an open mind. For a professor of industrial relations, doing so can create new opportunities to serve outside the ivory tower. Several such opportunities have come my way in my years at the Sloan School. Two of them involved the same union.

Up Close to Two Strikes

When I first plunged into the subject of labor-management relations, trying to understand the causes and consequences of strikes became a major subject. Indeed, strike activity in the decade after World War II was extremely high. Early in my Sloan career the PATCO strike and the strike at Eastern Air Lines were both noteworthy events. Over the succeeding decades, however, strikes have become rare enough that their mere occurrence generates newspaper headlines. Part of this is due to the decline of unions, another part is that unions have become more skillful at bargaining for new contracts and thus the parties settle their differences without a strike.

The combination of my academic standing and my neutrality as a mediator brought me up close to two strikes, both of which involved the same union: UNITE HERE.[52] In 2004, a lengthy strike took place in the hotel-casino industry in Atlantic City, New Jersey. Management wanted a five-year contract to bring negotiations there in line with those in Las Vegas, and union leadership felt its Atlantic City members had become complacent and were not as energized in their support of the union as were their counterparts in Las Vegas.

It is hard to see how the strike could have been avoided. The union leadership wanted to mobilize the membership and used the pressure of a large negotiating committee—an intimidating sight and a way to limit the union's own flexibility to make concessions—to persuade management to continue the three-year contract duration. Picket lines and rallies were viewed as a way to build solidarity and a committed membership.

After a four-week strike and all the time and costs that accumulated in preparing and waging that strike, the union ended up accepting a five-year contract with safeguards in the contract's outer years that would guarantee adequate company contributions to union health and welfare funds.

Soon after the strike ended, the president of the union and the CEO of the Harrah's casino chain asked me to analyze the reasons for the strike and make recommendations to improve the negotiating process (absent of threats and strike action) in the next round of bargaining.

In 2016, I was a mediator in the strike by dining hall workers (also organized by UNITE HERE) against Harvard University. As a rule, most of them are laid off during the summer months when Harvard has no undergraduate students, and for years the issue of no summer pay had been looming. Management miscalculated the importance of that demand and thought that by introducing the same summer compensation plan that had been put in place at Columbia University an agreement could be reached. The union demanded a much better compensation package than the Columbia "pattern." Ultimately, after a three-week strike, the union won everything it had demanded.

These two strikes illustrate many of the points that have become accepted wisdom in the industrial relations field. I remember Bob Livernash at HBS saying that if management wants to win a strike it had better be willing to withstand a long one. That certainly describes the casino strike in Atlantic City: management endured a four-week strike, and every indication is that the hotels and casinos were prepared to hold out much longer. In the end, the union agreed to the employers' main demand and signed a five-year agreement.

At Harvard, the union won after three weeks. Could Harvard management have won had it been willing to hold out and take all the public relations "hits" of a well-endowed university denying what the union considered "adequate compensation" for its food service workers?

Strikes have both tangible and intangible outcomes. The short strike at Harvard not only won important economic gains for the workers but also produced greater involvement on the part of the union members. The longer strike in Atlantic City also achieved solidarity, but failed to deliver a contract any better than what the union would have gotten had it settled at the deadline. Perhaps the bottom line is that even putting aside various efforts by economists to model strike behavior using rational calculations of expectations and assumptions about having full information, strikes serve a variety of functions that can't be valued by such a seemingly straightforward calculus.

Strikes can also be a mechanism for releasing pressure. They may be a last-ditch effort to protest in support of a matter of principle. They can be about building solidarity; in some cases, though, they destroy solidarity. Above all, strikes reflect a core democratic principle in a society that values and protects freedom of association, expression, and action.

Another opportunity to employ my neutrality skills outside the ivory tower came my way in the form of a newly recognized challenge in workplaces.

Mediating Supervisory Behavior

Historically, unions have emphasized wages, hours, and working conditions, the latter embracing all aspects of health and safety for the workforce. These are challenging enough, but in 2003, I became involved efforts to deal with inappropriate behavior by supervisors; it was new territory. Now it seems that every day brings a new report of sexual harassment in every kind of workplace, broadly defined, and a militant movement against it has exploded virally, especially since October 2017 and the use of the #MeToo hashtag on social media. But in this case, the harassment was not exclusive to any gender relationship but was instead about old-fashioned, out-of-control supervisors bullying members of the workforce.

Bill Bowe, the manager of labor relations for Airborne Express, called me at the Sloan School to tell me that his company and the Teamsters were organizing a panel to study the problem of bullying. (I am not sure how he came to make the contact; my guess is that he had read the book I had coauthored with Tom Kochan and Harry Katz, *The Transformation of American Industrial Relations*.) At the time, Airborne was the third-largest private express delivery company in the United States. The topic of "unfair treatment" had surfaced during the last contract negotiations as the number one concern of union members. The rank and file was fed up.

I agreed to join a panel of three neutrals to investigate instances of bullying, track incidents, and design a training program aimed at addressing the problem. The assignment took me directly into the culture of how labor and management leaders in some industries get along.

I first met Bill over dinner at a Boston restaurant. George Cashman, who led the large Teamsters Local 25 in the city, was also at the table. Cashman was the point person for dealings between Airborne and the union, so it made sense that he would be there to discuss how to address the pervasive problem of bullying. What did not make sense were the multiple rounds of martinis and glasses of wine that appeared. I had been exposed to this culture before; it seemed to be the way the "big guys" in labor relations conducted their business, but I had never felt comfortable participating in such rituals.

Several subsequent meetings took place, including one at the Teamsters headquarters in Charlestown, a neighborhood of Boston. As we approached Sullivan Square in my car, one of the team members spotted a sign for Local 25 and said, "There's the building." It was, however, Local 25's Health and Welfare Center. Many unions have these centers; offering health services in such outpatient clinics is a very important way unions provide significant value for their members. We found the actual headquarters in a building right on the Sullivan Square traffic circle (what Bostonians call a rotary), a particularly large and somewhat treacherous one to drive into. The building sits in the shadow of a large building that houses state offices and several businesses but that for many decades was the production plant for Schrafft Chocolates. The company's name still looms from a neon sign atop one of the building's clock tower.

As we pulled into the Local 25 parking lot I expected to be greeted by an attendant; the last time I had been to a meeting there, I had been "checked out" before being allowed to park my car. On this occasion, however, there were plenty of empty spaces.

The outside of the building that houses Local 25's offices is unremarkable: a simple red brick, square structure. Inside, however, it became clear that the building was unlike any typical union headquarters. It had a decidedly "scrubbed" look; in fact, it gleamed. The colors used to decorate the head-quarters were not the customary drab, uninspiring beige or gray; instead, the walls glowed with yellow, and the rugs were a vibrant green.

I observed two young men with cleaning equipment, wiping and polish-ing, to ensure that the attractive, shipshape appearance was maintained.

We signed in at the reception desk on the second floor, were issued visitor passes, and were shown into the conference room.[53] Fred Shrank, one of our panel members who had worked in trucking for many years, had complained to me earlier about having the meeting at the union's headquarters. He had thought we'd be meeting at MIT, and when it was changed to Local 25 he was distressed. Our academic venue would be more "spiffy" than a union hall, he had said. Now Fred had second thoughts. Looking around, he quietly admitted, "This is quite an impres-sive facility."

Our panel held a working session to formalize our conclusions and rec-ommendations. At around 6:30 p.m. we went downstairs to meet with union stewards from three Airborne terminals in the Boston area. Two bodyguards kept a watchful eye at one side of the room. They took their orders from a man named Lou, the business agent, who also stood off to the side, observ-ing but not saying a word.

One of the most arresting accounts about the behavior of company su-pervisors came from a female Airborne driver the union had recruited to talk to us. She recounted a sexual harassment incident that was under inves-tigation by the company; it involved physical contact from a supervisor, and Airborne had forced her to take a medical leave for a month after reporting the incident. I think it was quite difficult for her to have been thrust into the limelight—not the glow, but the glare—to tell her story to three male strangers.

We listened to story after story about the behavior of different supervi-sors, and I began to wonder whether every supervisor was as bad as those who had been singled out as examples. So I asked whether there were any "straight shooters." Yes, the Teamsters members present reluctantly agreed, there were some.

At these sessions the negative reports always seemed to dominate. Of course, the role of a union representative dictates an emphasis on the trou-blesome aspects of employment.

Later, Thomas Germano, a panel member and research associate at the Cornell ILR School with extensive experience developing training programs, designed a two-day module that could be rolled out for supervisors across Airborne. A budget was developed, and several sessions were held at locations around the country. Supervisors were directed to attend.

We also recommended establishing a procedure whereby workers could file complaints about alleged worker harassment. It was separate from the grievance system and would not involve arbitration. Complaints would be forwarded to Airborne's main office in Seattle. Our committee would be the final step in the process. We monitored the program on a regular basis, and were mandated to hear a dispute if it was not successfully resolved at lower levels.

A surprise development occurred while this project was underway. In April 2003 George Cashman, the president of Local 25, pleaded guilty to theft and embezzlement from an employee benefit plan and was sentenced to three years in prison. I was reminded of my first assignment with Benjamin Selekman at HBS decades earlier: preparing a case on corruption in the Teamsters Union uncovered by the McClellan Committee.

Initially there was a flurry of activity with the antibullying program, even with DHL buying Airborne later in 2003. Workers with pent-up complaints about particular supervisors used the system to bring their issues into the open. Generally, management took the complaints seriously; supervisors were put on the spot and asked to apologize, and in some cases they lost their jobs. By the second and third years, the number of complaints had dropped dramatically. We concluded that by drawing attention to the problem in negotiations and setting up a program to address the subject, the work culture had improved. Eventually, though, when DHL terminated the domestic operations that had been the core of Airborne's business, the program to deal with bullying faded from the scene.

The Teamsters Union deserves credit for being sensitive to the driver complaints about the behavior of supervisors in what is a high-pressure industry. Decades earlier, no one would have given a second thought to challenging the hard-hitting behavior of the "bosses." Having the Teamsters in place and able to channel the drivers' concerns about the unacceptable behavior of supervisors produced a much more humane workplace.

Union-Nominated Directors

One test of your connection to the real world as a professor is whether you are asked to serve as a consultant or in some other capacity that creates a connection to the business scene while also enabling you to make an academic contribution. For those of us in the industrial relations field, being selected as an arbitrator or mediator is one such validation. Another measure is being asked to serve on a corporate board of directors. That opportunity came to me twice: in the 1980s, for a large trucking company, and then again in the 1990s for an integrated steel company. Together these two opportunities spanned thirteen years.

The academic literature says little about individuals who came to boards of directors because of union nominations, as was the case in my personal examples, and whether they made a difference—but it ought to. I hope that by telling my own history it will at least close that gap a little.

The two examples that follow are dramatically different. The trucking company was privately held, in financial trouble, and run by inexperienced managers. By contrast, the steel company was publicly held, in sound financial shape, and enjoyed high-caliber management. My connection to the two unions as a board member was also very different: the Teamsters allowed its nominated directors at the trucking company to operate quite autonomously, while the Steelworkers union was keenly aware of my role on the board, which it monitored closely.

My first such board experience was with PIE Nationwide, a large trucking company headquartered in Florida.[54] Norman Weintraub, research director for the Teamsters, phoned me in 1986 to ask whether I would like to be considered for membership on the company's board, and I immediately said yes. I welcomed the opportunity to observe top management.

It was the period not long after a concerted effort to deregulate the trucking industry had resulted in the Motor Carrier Act of 1980, which significantly increased competition and the number of trucking companies in operation. This legislation also resulted in a sharp decrease in the number of truckers who were unionized, which in turn drastically lowered overall pay for drivers throughout the country.

PIE was among the many trucking companies that found themselves in financial difficulty in the newly competitive environment. One of its first steps to remain solvent was a 1983 merger with Ryder Truck Lines to form Ryder/PIE Nationwide, which eventually became PIE Nationwide. Seeking to avoid bankruptcy, PIE's parent company at the time, IU International (a large holding company in the transportation industry), had reached an agreement with the Teamsters to reduce wages by 15 percent, with a commensurate number of shares of stock put into an employee stock ownership plan (ESOP) fund, and to create two additional seats on the company's board of directors to be filled by Teamsters nominees.

At the first board meeting I attended, and much to my surprise, a representative from IU International was there to announce that the company had been sold to a group of Chicago investors who had acquired PIE Nationwide—which had revenues of $500 to $600 million per year—for the small sum of $5 million. No established company had been willing to touch PIE and its large unfunded pension liabilities for fear that if PIE went into bankruptcy, the liability would pass to the parent company and create a large obligation against that new owner's assets.

The other union-nominated director was Robert Harris, an attorney who had served on the National Mediation Board in Washington. Bob and I became friends and often compared notes about the task ahead of us: trying to keep the company from being plundered by its new owners, who had financed their purchase with debt. They quickly paid off the $5 million loan by charging large management fees. When they attempted to declare a dividend, we succeeded in blocking their action because there was no justification; the company had been losing money.

Even though it had sold the company, IU International had a commitment to stand behind the ESOP program it had established in its agreement with the Teamsters. When IU International reneged, I contacted an attorney friend, who subsequently filed a suit against IU International in federal court. I initiated this action as a director despite the fact that I did not have "standing," so I needed to recruit as plaintiffs several lower-level managers and rank-and-file workers who had been laid off. I also checked in with my contacts at Teamsters headquarters and was told that though they wanted to be kept informed they would not join as plaintiffs. Eventually, though, the Teamsters did assign Cleveland-based attorney John Peca to the case, and he joined the final negotiations that led to a settlement with IU International.

The lawsuit was an adventure. Soon after we filed it, some Florida lawyers, hoping for a piece of the action, recruited several hundred laid-off workers

and initiated a lawsuit similar to ours. Fortunately, a wise judge joined the
suits, and Marshall Patner was named lead counsel. It took several years and
many back-and-forth proposals before a settlement was reached.

The two-year period of negotiations would, by itself, make a fascinating
case study. Consider the parties of interest: IU International, the first owners;
two sets of new owners; PIE management; PIE employees; the Teamsters
union; and outside directors—namely, Bob Harris and me. The lead person
on the other side was William Waltrip, an IU International vice president
who was connected to my own interests because he was a director of TIAA/
CREF, the large pension fund for academics. Speaking of overlapping interests, Waltrip and Peca, the Teamsters' lawyer, also had a working rapport
because the Teamsters represented employees at other divisions of IU International.

On occasion I felt I was in over my head, but I acted as if I knew what I
was doing and had done it before, and I held to the objective of finding a
settlement that would benefit those who had been hurt by IU International's failure to stand behind PIE. Several times we thought we were close to
an agreement. At one point, I thought we had a solution: force the owners to
sell to the management group and create a close identity of interests between management and the employees. Several members of the partnership
group agreed, but they were vetoed when they took it back to the larger
group.

Someone (I think from IU International) suggested we ask the Teamsters
to request a thug to scare a couple of the company's partners. We never moved
on that idea.

Even small victories had moments of high drama. One New Year's Eve,
I was on the telephone with Roger Pugh, IU International's counsel. He told
me he was late for a party, already dressed in his tuxedo, and asked if we
could agree quickly so he would not have to keep his wife waiting. We did
not agree, we missed the deadline, and negotiations continued for most of
the next year before reaching agreement. I do not know whether Roger made
amends to his wife.

I got to know Kinsey Reeves, who had been PIE's chief operating officer
prior to its sale by IU International and who eventually became its CEO.
When he took those reins, he was wise enough to ensure that his own pension was fully funded. After the demise of PIE, I brought Reeves to MIT
for a conference held by the Center for Transportation Studies, which focused

on major changes in the various U.S. transportation sectors. Later I visited Reeves at his home in Florida; he had happily retired with a pension that would have been beyond the wildest imagination of any PIE trucker.

The Teamsters left Bob Harris and me alone. Although we had a point of contact in the union—Norman Weintraub, to whom we reported periodically—the top leadership never asked us to take a position on any of the issues before the company. On one occasion, Harris and I attended a Teamsters collective bargaining conference as the union prepared for upcoming negotiations with the trucking industry. PIE was not a lead carrier like Yellow Freight System or Roadway Express, so we were not asked for any input regarding strategy.

In some respects, the PIE story could almost be written up as a comedy— were it not for the lost livelihoods of the workers. The CEO who preceded Reeves had a background as a retail merchant. The partners from Bay Tree, the group that first purchased PIE from IU International, argued among themselves, and we learned at a subsequent meeting that Bay Tree had been bought out by a new collection of individual investors who called themselves Maxitron. Eventually, Maxitron was restructured and ownership passed to Maxitron II. From what Harris and I could tell, no one in the ownership group had any experience in trucking whatsoever—which is surely why they wisely kept Kinsey Reeves in place.

After five years, I left the board when I learned that yet another group had purchased the company's assets. The Teamsters had dealt with these individuals in several situations, and Weintraub advised me that the new group had an unsavory reputation, so I resigned from the board. Bob Harris remained on the board, and he kept me apprised of the company's final stages as it spiraled into bankruptcy. Ultimately, that last set of owners went to prison for absconding with company funds.

Looking back on the experience, I would say that our biggest impact was the lawsuit, which achieved a $6 million settlement for PIE workers who had been laid off as a result of the financial difficulties and sale of the company by IU International.

My second stint as a union-nominated board member came in 1993. As a result of negotiations with the United Steelworkers of America, Inland Steel agreed to bring a union-nominated director on its board. Arnie Weber was already on the Inland board, and he went to work behind the scenes to get me appointed. I had met Lynn Williams, the Steelworkers president, but did not know him well, so he interviewed me to satisfy himself that I could represent the union's interests on the board.

Compared to being on the PIE board, this experience felt like playing in the major leagues. The Inland Steel board counted among its members several impressive corporate CEOs, including James Henderson of Cummins Engine and Donald Perkins of Jewel Tea.

Soon enough, however, I ran against the grain when I asked for information about how the company was responding to an organizing campaign at one of its distribution facilities. Inland and the Steelworkers had entered into a partnership as part of what Williams called the New Directions Program, and I believed management had to observe a standard of fair play. Judd Gray, Inland's human resources director, was not happy when I asked to see letters and the campaign literature the company was using to keep that particular facility union free.

My stand probably won me some credibility with the union. And the example illustrates the potential value of diversifying board memberships: it broadens the issues discussed beyond the standard financials, bringing human resource and labor issues of strategic importance into board-level deliberations. I can't help but wonder whether it would better serve all stakeholders of American corporations if such issues were part of every corporate board's agenda.

Soon thereafter, however, I lost my rapport with union leadership over an issue of confidentiality. The union expected I would share strategic information I learned as a board member, but I could not confirm for the union that Inland Steel was exploring the purchase of a large steel company in Venezuela after a tech wizard in the union, while searching the World Wide Web, happened to come across a story that identified Inland as a potential buyer.

Such an acquisition would have had a substantial impact on Inland operations: labor costs were much lower in Venezuela, and the target company manufactured product lines quite similar to Inland. Union leaders expressed considerable irritation and asked why I had not given them a heads up. They were not satisfied by my explanation that the bid to buy the plant was confidential.

The confidentiality issue with the union remained unresolved throughout my tenure on the board. Later, after arbitrator Jay Siegel interviewed Inland Steel CEO Robert Darnell about the role of a union-nominated director, he offered this recollection: "Darnell said he had a conversation with George Becker, president of the Steelworkers who succeeded Williams.

Darnell told Becker that the union should not expect McKersie to be telling them about every idea that is floated before the board, as many do not come to pass and it makes no sense to seek union input. Darnell concedes that there is a fine line here about deciding at what point in time a situation is sufficiently ripe for the union-nominated director to advise the union of the company's proposed plans."[55] I should note that I never saw the issue as one of too much information, as Darnell suggested, but rather about the question of what I *could* report without violating confidentiality.

I served on the board's compensation committee, where my impact was minimal. The compensation process was run by a consulting firm that presented data on comparable salaries for top executives, and there was little I could do to slow down what was becoming a rapid uptick in executive compensation that was widening the wage gap with workers. I also served on the audit committee, where I sought to have the audit process cover more than just financial matters—for example, I tried to get Inland to schedule health and safety audits as a way of being proactive before accidents occurred.

The company also created a *partnership committee*—the term Lynn Williams used to describe the relationship he hoped would characterize his New Directions Program for the steel industry. The partnership faced many challenges, especially when management instituted a program to reduce union clerical and technical jobs by four hundred. The union did not object to a voluntary severance initiative, but it resisted any attempt to keep those jobs vacant. The union argued that many workers were still on long-term layoff, and in the East Chicago, Indiana, community where the company's sole plant was located, there were many young people who would have been delighted to get a job in the steel industry.

The company's position was that if it could not capture attrition and the union insisted on maintaining current levels of employment, then all jobs would be in jeopardy because Inland Steel would not be able to remain competitive.

Here the union faced a dilemma: How far could it go in accepting attrition and shrinking the number of jobs? How aggressive could it be in cooperating with management, improving productivity, introducing teams, and helping the company deal with its competitive pressures? Even though volume might increase, employment would continue to decline as a result of productivity increases realized through attrition. The union could propose that overtime be reduced or perhaps the workweek shortened as a way of maintaining employment—assuming management would agree to these adjustments.

However, it was clear that rank-and-file union members did not want these changes leading to a reduction in their take-home pay. Rather, they supported layoffs, letting junior workers take the hit.

By far the biggest event during my tenure on the Inland Steel board came when the company received a tender offer from Mittal Steel, a large international firm. The proposed merger prompted me to raise my voice and say I thought it was a "rip-off" on the part of the investment bankers. Indeed, Goldman Sachs submitted an invoice for $20 million—a small percentage of the money involved in the merger, but the kind of fee companies pay precisely because it is only a relatively minuscule part of the overall transaction value. I contended that it would be more appropriate for Goldman Sachs to charge a fixed sum or an hourly rate for services rendered.

Here again is an example of how adding more diverse voices to corporate boards might just change an established practice that serves the interests of only a very limited group of financiers, perhaps at the expense of the direct company stakeholders.

I was under considerable pressure from other directors to support the takeover, and ended up being the only director to vote no. I felt Inland could do just as well financially by remaining independent and exploiting the potential of the union-management partnership. And I was sufficiently troubled by what followed that I came to write the following long entry in my diary:

> In teaching courses in negotiations, I have often said that the key to effectiveness is never to get caught in the intersection of incompatible expectations— what I refer to as the "squirming" condition of a negative range. That has just happened, as I have ended up alienating both the union and management in the relationship where I served for 4-1/2 years as a union-nominated director.
>
> The story: the CEO and board members of the company are irritated with me because they see me as operating outside established conventions for a member of a board of directors. At the same time, the union is mad at me (although they say not with me personally, but with the constraints on the role) for not sharing more information, especially regarding the Mittal takeover offer.
>
> I sense that the union has come to the end of the road with me. They never have initiated regular contacts that would have pulled me into their camp

much more closely. Certainly they want to respect my independence and give me the latitude to decide how and when I report back to them; however, they would undoubtedly respond that it is the responsibility of the director to report back to the union.

On the company side, the Inland CEO still communicates with me as he does with other directors, but the tone is cool, sometimes downright angry. During the last phone conversation, the CEO, without any prompting on my part, told me what was wrong with my argument as to why I could not vote for the Mittal proposal. In short, he characterized my stance as fake, saying I was manufacturing reasons as to why I could not go along with the proposal. There may be a small element of truth to the charge, but the real story is otherwise.

I appreciate why Lynn Williams experienced a down period when he was removed from the board of Wheeling Paint after trying behind the scenes to get a strike settled. In a highly adversarial relationship, information is power, and anyone who seeks to mediate may get burned and is seldom praised. All parties would like to get the information directly, and feel diminished by the need for an intermediary.

This reminds me of the finding reported by Joel [Cutcher-Gershenfeld], namely, that mediators are never given credit for their role. The same is true here: the messengers get killed—or at the least, ignored. If they succeed, no one remembers!

So where does this leave me? When the Mittal takeover occurs, I am sure I will not be around, since the company is angry with my decision, and the union does not want to continue the role—at least not to trade it off against other priorities.

Fortunately, I have my niche as an academic, and this experience has given me some insight into life at the top. I understand the corporate suite since I have spent a good part of my life attached to business schools, yet I do not agree with the sole preoccupation with profit and the materialism that is involved. On the other hand, I identify with the lofty goals of the union movement, but I am turned off by the attitudes of some leaders at the top of the movement. They have been less supportive, less friendly, and less understanding than my contacts in management.

Corporations have the checks-and-balances of competition, and they are "inhuman" when they focus exclusively on profits. Unions, with their philosophical commitment to the goals of social justice, at least at the national level, do not have the same checks-and-balances. So corporations often pursue inhuman goals humanely, and unions at times pursue human goals inhumanely.

I doubt whether the union, if asked for an evaluation, would say that my role produced much value for them. Arnie Weber—an expert in industrial relations and human resource management—was also on the board, and he had far more influence on corporate policy than I did. The idea/innovation of union-nominated directors never became widespread because unions want to deal directly with top management on strategic matters. On the corporate side, the culture that pressures all directors to align behind the CEO means that a union-nominated director is often the odd man out. Without question, however, I gained an immense understanding of top-management thinking that I was able to use in the classroom. The other benefit to me was getting to know Lynn Williams. I know of no other labor leader who has come close to his passionate, wise, and principled leadership.

During the same time period I was serving on the PIE Nationwide board, Tom Kochan served in a comparable role at Transcom Trucking Company, which had entered a recovery program. We thought it would be a good idea to pull together union-nominated directors from companies in the airline and trucking industries, and held two forums at MIT. These sessions provided a rich source of material for articles on the subject. Corporate governance was becoming a hot subject, and the opportunity to talk about the contributions union-nominated directors made gave us plenty of material.

Given this considerable attention to the trucking industry in the throes of bankruptcy, I should address whether recovery programs made any difference for PIE and Transcom. Certainly their eventual demise was postponed, and as a result good jobs remained much longer than if the companies had been allowed to liquidate when difficulties first appeared. Drivers for both companies were willing to take a 15 percent cut in pay and work more cooperatively with management on productivity improvements, hoping the companies would survive. Economies of scale favored larger carriers, though, and these two medium-size companies with limited service across the United States did not manage to stay alive. In both cases, the presence of union-nominated directors on the boards had the potential to stave off actions to sell the companies to organizations that would have paid major shareholders at the expense of immediate job losses. In the case of PIE, the union-nominated directors joined the board after PIE had already been sold by IU International to a group of investors with no experience in trucking.

These trucking stories also point out something else: the dysfunction of pension plans that are supposed to pay defined benefits.[56] Both PIE and Transcom were members of large, multiemployer pension plans. All member companies were required to make payments into the funds to meet the actuarial requirements of the defined benefits. Had PIE's pension plan been on a defined-contribution basis, PIE probably would not have been sold by IU International, and would thus not have been taken over by a group that knew nothing about the trucking industry.[57]

The lesson of my experience with PIE and Inland—and, I suspect, Tom Kochan's with Transcom—is that although having union-nominated directors may provide some assurance that worker and union concerns will be voiced when important corporate and strategic decisions are being considered, it's unclear whether such input actually changes decisions. Further, a union-nominated director must cope with union expectations (from both leaders and members) that things will change as a result of the arrangement. If members believe they have given up some perceived economic gain to put a union nominee on the board, support for the arrangement will probably be limited. It is not surprising, then, that this practice—which was in play during the 1980s—never really expanded, and it has for the most part since passed from the scene.

Several questions can be posed. First, why has the concept of union-nominated directors mostly vanished from the scene? My colleague William Pounds, a former dean of the Sloan School, would probably answer by saying that boards necessarily operate on a "one-party system." The unitary board is the order of the day, and having a voice representing the workers/union is an unwarranted diversion. Boards do in some cases strive for diversity in their membership, and in that sense the worker point of a view could be there without having the institution of the union formally present.

The second question is whether having someone on a board representing the interests of the workers actually makes any difference. In the case of Inland Steel, I made little difference. The events that unfolded would have happened with or without my presence—as would probably have been the case at most well-run companies with diverse boards of directors.

I did, though, make some difference in the case of PIE. Perhaps in situations of bankruptcy, when worker interests are more or even most explicitly on the line, having a union-nominated director is necessary and advisable.

Did I gain any new insights about negotiation dynamics while serving on these two boards? In the case of PIE, my approach to protecting worker interests employed a forcing strategy by instituting a lawsuit. There were many meetings with representatives of PIE and IU International. And using the risk that a trial would rule in favor of the workers as leverage, I dug in until IU International upped its offer to an acceptable number. Thus the lesson: Sometimes sitting tight and allowing the pressure of an impending event (such as having to make court appearance) to build is an effective approach to inducing the opponent to change position.

By contrast, my time on the Inland Steel board involved elements of problem solving (e.g., getting the company to initiate safety audits), but there were also many times when the interests I represented were not in line with those of the company. My interactions with other members of the board and with management could not be construed as negotiations. Raising questions and asking for information alerted management to union concerns, however, and though that source of power—which is available to any director—may not have always made me successful at changing policies and practices, it did put management on notice.

Getting "up close and personal" with business executives is one thing that is definitely a feature of serving on a corporate board. During my time at the Sloan School, that has also happened through interactions with students in the executive education programs—both degree-granting and otherwise—and in at least one case, the long-term participation of business leaders from the Boston area in an organized discussion that began long before my arrival.

The MIT Industrial Relations Group

No one knows the exact date the MIT Industrial Relations (IR) Group was established; it was not documented. But its story is worth telling because it reflects in its origins and eventual decline much of what I have discussed in this book. Its history parallels a sixty-year period of great change in industrial relations.

It began right after the end of World War II. Two distinguished academics who had both served on various government boards during the war—John Dunlop of Harvard and Charles Myers of MIT—convened a group that met monthly at MIT in an informal setting over dinner. Robert Fuchs, regional director of the National Labor Relations Board (NLRB), was instrumental in providing a focus for the group. Early members came from a widely diverse group of unionized companies in the greater Boston area: Wyman-Gordon, a metalworks company; Hood, the area's major dairy; insurance company John Hancock; Raytheon, a manufacturer and defense contractor; chemical company W. R. Grace; the local telephone company, then part of the Bell System; and Stop & Shop, the supermarket giant.

The MIT IR Group was convening monthly from October through May at the time I joined the Sloan School faculty in 1980. The meetings provided a forum for discussing current events and issues arising in industrial relations activity across the country. It was a very informal, off-the-record environment of sharing professional interests and concerns—even ones beyond the strict confines of industrial relations. For instance, at one meeting, I found it very helpful to explore some of the issues I was facing while chairing the MIT search committee charged with finding a new vice president for human resources.

It is notable that even though much of the discussion focused on labor-management relations, no union leaders were part of the group. Had the group met at Harvard, Dunlop—who was very close to unions and served on many union internal dispute panels—would probably not have been able to convene an all-management group and maintain those relationships. Charles Myers, based at the Sloan School, was in a better position to provide sponsorship. We did, however, invite local union leaders to join our discussions from time to time, but they came as guests and were not considered members of the group.

I remember the representative from the telephone company showing up periodically with copies of recently negotiated labor agreements. With Fuchs in attendance, discussions often touched on legal questions before the NLRB. Dunlop would tell us about the latest developments at the national level, which he knew very well from his many contacts. Indeed, he had served as secretary of labor in President Gerald R. Ford's administration.

Over time, others were invited to join the group. Notably, we never included any managers from the public sector, where unionization was taking hold and many new issues worthy of discussion were being raised. Perhaps Myers, coming from a business school, did not feel comfortable reaching out to that domain.

As human resource management developed and became a respected function within business, the MIT group changed its name to MIT HR/IR (for Human Resources/Industrial Relations) and recruited executives from banks, insurance companies, health care, and hotels, and also expanded the number of academics, adding representatives from Bentley College, Boston College, Boston University, Harvard University, and Northeastern University.

When Charlie Myers moved to Florida, I assumed responsibility for the group. David Fine from Stop & Shop, and later Bill Vaughn, a Sloan PhD who also worked in labor relations at Stop & Shop, served as secretaries for most of the 1980s and 1990s.

By the mid-1990s it was becoming clear that the HR/IR Group was losing its value and standing. We made various efforts to sustain interest, including "field trips" for the group. I remember a valuable visit to the John Hancock headquarters, where we were briefed on the company's in-house day-care program. On other occasions we visited Beth Israel Hospital and became acquainted with its PREPARE/21 employee involvement program. We also welcomed new guests to meetings. James Jandl, who also served as the group's secretary, invited an executive he knew from the Association of San Francisco Hotels to present what was happening with an innovative joint labor-management program in that city. Students in Sloan executive programs who came from positions in industrial relations and human resources were invited to join the group as guests from time to time.

Over the years we tried a variety of meeting formats. We experimented with snacks and hors d'oeuvres from five to seven in the evening, in lieu of dinner, so group members could get home earlier. We met several times at Anthony's Pier 4, once among Boston's most famous restaurants (but now no longer in business).

In the early years of the new century, Jandl and Lewis Rambo drafted an attractive recruitment brochure to send to prospective new members, but not much came of that effort. By the middle of the decade, the meetings stopped. The group had clearly lost the energy that had once come from labor-management relations, but there were other factors that help explain its decline. Dunlop died in 2003, and then Fuchs in 2004, taking with them their magnetic pull. Meanwhile, Fred Foulkes at Boston University, who was a member of the group, brought together a similar group of human resources leaders at his school, where he had created the Human Resources Policy Institute in 1981 that attracted top executives, and over time its stature grew, eventually eclipsing the group at MIT.

All in all, the MIT group met for nearly sixty years. Those who participated attested to its value. Bill Vaughn said, "I first learned about this group as a PhD student at MIT from 1963 to 1968, majoring in labor economics. My principal advisor, Charlie Myers, often used anecdotes and stories learned from the group in his classes. Abe Siegel did as well. When I joined Stop & Shop in 1971, my boss David Fine (a member of the group) often referred to it."[58]

The group had a special meaning for me: it gave me a chance to engage John Dunlop in one-on-one conversation the many times I drove him to his home in Belmont after our meetings. He was a remarkable individual.

Reflecting on the makeup of this group and our wide-ranging discussions reminds me of just how much human resource management has changed. In a dinner group that included human resources professionals from both unionized and nonunion companies, as well as Bob Fuchs from the NLRB and, later, his successor Rosemary Pye, there was an openness to and recognition of the value unions and government policy played in balancing employment relations. These colleagues genuinely saw their role as one of finding and speaking up for that right balance in their organizations.

Contrast that with what we experience in the early twenty-first century in human resources circles. Many define their primary responsibility as something other than balancing the needs of workers and their employer; even fewer would seek out conversations with government regulators or union leaders. Instead, they focus on gaining or maintaining a "seat at the table" in strategic discussions with their CEOs or other senior executives.

Something valuable has been lost in that transition of roles and professional identity. It may not spring back unless and until workers, unions, and government policymakers regain some of the power they have lost.

The MIT IR Group was not the only way the Sloan School was already engaging business executives on campus when I arrived. There were executives who were on campus full-time.

Howard Johnson had left the University of Chicago for MIT Sloan, becoming director of the Sloan Fellowship Program in 1955. Early in my Sloan years, I taught a course in that program for senior executives that covered my favorite topics in industrial relations and human resource management.

I reached back to my own Chicago days to bring someone who became a regular guest in my classes: Seymour Kahan. A longtime UAW leader, Seymour's sessions were the best, despite the fact that the business leaders who were students were somewhat skeptical when they first met him.

Seymour would present the case for unions very professionally. Early in his career, he had led several wildcat strikes—a frequently used tactic in the late 1940s and 1950s at International Harvester—and was quite willing to engage in verbal warfare with management across the bargaining table. By the 1980s, though, when he appeared at MIT, dealings between International Harvester and the UAW had settled into an accommodative relationship, and Seymour's style—though still feisty—had softened into that of an articulate professional who could hold his own with any business type.

Soft-spoken but nevertheless intense, Seymour captured the attention of the executives. To be sure, he didn't persuade them to see unions as good for their workers, to get them to embrace their employees being organized and becoming union members, but I know they told themselves that if their companies ever did get unions, Seymour was a leader they could deal with.

Seymour had been in a bad automobile accident and suffered a serious back injury that required him to stand or lie down; sitting was extremely painful. As his health deteriorated, he could no longer show up in my class and had to connect by telephone and loudspeaker. But even physically absent, he held the attention of the class, and these sessions received high marks.

I end the saga of my time (so far) at the Sloan School with two vignettes about workers—unionized and not—at Cambridge's two most prestigious institutions. In both, I had experiences that reinforced much of what I had learned over a long career and that also taught me some new things about labor-management relationships.

The first involved Harvard University.

Harvard University's Relationship with a New Union

Earlier in this chapter, I described the successful outcomes that can occur when parties work together in partnership and utilize some of the latest ideas for effective negotiations, especially interest-based bargaining concepts and tools. When it comes to this kind of a relationship, Kris Rondeau was a visionary—and has remained one for thirty years. She is a unique union leader.

I first met Kris in the early 1980s when she called and asked whether she could come by my office to talk about a campaign underway to organize a union of clerical workers at Harvard Medical School (HMS). My guess is that she got my name from Tom Kochan, who had been following the initial organizing efforts. The hope of the organizers was to begin at HMS and then extend their efforts to encompass Harvard University's entire clerical and technical staff.

At our first meeting Kris explained that the organizers did not want to be affiliated with a national union. That meant finances were extremely tight, and they were relying mostly on contributions from like-minded support-ers. If they could stay the course, I said, an organizing effort run *by* employees *for* employees would present a powerful message. I offered to help. My wife and I even sent a check to the new Harvard Union of Clerical and Technical Workers (HUCTW; everyone calls it "huck-too").

Harvard University had long relied on a steady flow of employees willing to take jobs simply because of its reputation as the nation's most renowned institution of higher education, regardless of whether compensation was fair. The union organizers took this on directly in their campaign, declaring in literature and speeches, "We cannot eat prestige." They sold workers on the idea that the union would be a good outcome for them, and that they could be loyal both to Harvard and the union (and, by extension, to themselves). An early slogan was "It's not anti-Harvard to be pro-Union."

The battle HUCTW waged was truly epic, against tremendous odds. A full history of the fifteen years it took to prevail is impossible here. John Hoerr, in a 1993 magazine article that detailed much of that history, captured its essence, also very nicely profiling Kris Rondeau: "In 1988, against all odds and the great resources of the nation's wealthiest university, the union won a National Labor Relations Board (NLRB) election after two previous de-feats. In an earlier incarnation as labor law professor, Harvard's then presi-dent, Derek Bok, had championed the right of workers to have unions. But on his own campus, Bok continued a legal fight against HUCTW for months before the NLRB turned down his appeal. Bok then recognized HUCTW, ending a 15-year battle for the hearts of workers historically titled 'univer-sity servants' who really wanted to be loyal to both union and university— and subject to no master."[59]

Following their success at Harvard, Kris and her colleagues helped lead similar efforts at the University of Massachusetts Medical School and its affiliated hospital located in Worcester, Massachusetts. After substantial effort and time, they gained recognition and signed contracts for all the nonprofessional employees at both institutions. Then the organizing team set its sights on Tufts University in Medford.

I became aware of the Tufts effort when Kris phoned and asked me to contact Lawrence Bacow, the university's president, who had taken an open and very strong position against Tufts workers joining a union. Kris knew I had interacted with Bacow when he was MIT's chancellor, and I agreed to send him a letter.

If Tufts would not remain neutral, I told Larry Bacow, I urged him at least not to play "hardball" and not to emulate the negative behavior of most employers when confronted with a union organizing campaign. He responded by suggesting I speak with Patricia Campbell, his executive vice president for administration, which I did in a phone call. The conversation was cordial, and I tried to make the point that if Tufts was going to have a union, the university could do no better than one headed by Kris Rondeau. But it became clear that Tufts was going to go all out in its opposition. In the end, Tufts clerical workers were not organized, and they still remain without a union.

Nevertheless, Kris Rondeau and her colleagues taught me the power of organizing on a "retail basis"—building support for the union person by person. HUCTW organizers would visit their fellow employees' homes to persuade them that the benefits of joining a union and voting for certification far outweighed any reasons for remaining nonunion.

Kris has always taken the long view. She remarked to me several times that an effective organizing campaign takes years, not months. Her own experience at Harvard University certainly bore that out.

Later Kris asked me to help the parties at Harvard prepare to negotiate more collaboratively. I quickly agreed. Joel Cutcher-Gershenfeld, Nancy Peace, and I organized seminars and presentations by knowledgeable people from other labor-management relationships. In 2013, when the parties to the Harvard negotiations reached an impasse, Larry Katz, Arnold Zack, and I served as mediators.

For one round of the negotiations, in which we employed the principles of interest-based bargaining, we helped the parties establish subcommittees,

organized several plenary sessions, brought in talent from Kaiser Permanente to talk about its successful labor-management partnership, and assigned
academics as facilitators for each of the subcommittees. It was a huge investment in the process.

In subsequent Harvard negotiations, however, the process has become
much more traditional. Although the parties at Harvard still use the term
partnership to describe their relationship, over time the actual relationship
has "reverted to the mean."

There are a number of possible explanations. For one thing, it takes a lot
of hard work for any union-management relationship to continue to deliver
value for both parties. When the participants were meeting monthly in a
labor-management forum, Joel Cutcher-Gershenfeld put a lot of energy into
facilitating those meetings and focusing attention on constructive ideas that
could be implemented. (Larry Katz and I also would attend.) When Joel was
no longer involved, that energy was lost, and the parties' own energy toward
addressing problems on a day-to-day basis waned. The regular joint meetings came to a halt.

Kris told me of a pivotal event in the relationship's downward slide that
took place shortly after the economic downturn of 2008. Harvard saw its
endowment decline, and in response the university canceled all salary increases for nonunion employees. Then the university asked the union
whether it would defer the scheduled wage increases stipulated in its contract. There was considerable internal debate—Kris weighed in on the side
of agreeing to the deferral—but ultimately the union leadership decided
the scheduled increases should be paid. This decision created considerable
ire on the part of university administrators and nonunion employees, who
felt they were making sacrifices and that union members were not doing
their part.

Another reason for the arm's-length relationship is ongoing contention
over health care. In January 2013, Harvard implemented a change in health
care for nonunion employees, requiring (in most circumstances) an additional
five dollars on top of existing copays—which, given that most were set at ten
dollars, represented a 50 percent increase. The university opened negotiations
with the union to do the same, but it took three years to reach an agreement.
Five years later, many people at Harvard still feel the union dragged its feet
to save its members from paying. But from the union's point of view, the university was not responsive to union proposals to establish a new health care

premium tier and a safety net that would cushion the impact of cost shifting for its lower-salary members.

What should we take away from the almost thirty years of bargaining history between Harvard and this key union representing most of its nonteaching staff? The union has been very effective in expanding the agenda: it has vigorously represented the interests of its members, especially those in the lower-paid ranks, and has won some special benefits that really matter to Harvard workers, such as tuition reimbursement for continuing education. At the same time, the hope for a robust partnership along the lines of what has evolved at Kaiser Permanente has not materialized.

Harvard University likes to be known as the best in everything, but when it comes to the labor-management relationship it has settled for something that can best be characterized, in many respects, as traditional.

The second of my final vignettes concerns MIT itself.

MIT Stumbles

For many organizations, the recession that began in 2008 triggered dramatic moves, often prompting layoffs for a significant number of employees. In August 2009 Tom Kochan, in his capacity as chair of MIT faculty, asked Lotte Bailyn and me to conduct an investigation and write a report about staff layoffs then underway at MIT.

MIT had announced a three-year program that eventually involved several hundred reductions. The first wave, announced in the spring of 2009, involved approximately a hundred terminations—a number that ultimately nearly doubled.[60] In some cases, individuals took early retirement, but in many cases the layoffs put them back in the labor market.

One layoff became a cause célèbre at MIT. The employee had been at MIT for more than twenty years, and held a key administrative position that involved interacting with students and faculty on a regular basis. On the day she was told her employment was terminated, she was not allowed to return to her desk. Presumably, her manager feared an emotional reaction from her coworkers. Instead she was escorted out of the building and not allowed to return. Her belongings, she was told, would be sent to her. How could a major institution with such a fine Human Resources Department serving its employees treat a worker in such a cavalier manner?

From a negotiation point of view, termination can be seen as potentially provoking "endgame" behavior. Many managers assume a terminated employee will have the worst response—perhaps influencing other employees to protest the action, or even engaging in sabotage. Such behavior by a manager undermines any trust that may have existed before the termination.

Having managed budget cuts myself, I recognized it as a mandate that gives an organization the opportunity to terminate employees whose performance might be considered marginal—that is, not bad enough to be let go for performance reasons, but sufficiently marginal not to be kept for the long term given the particular circumstances. I wondered what might have been going on behind the scenes that would lead to a decision to terminate the twenty-year employee. Our investigation found evidence of friction between her and her supervisor and others in the department, so it was possible that the decision was based not on performance but on a desire to get rid of a "bothersome" worker.

Following her termination, there were several meetings of faculty and students to protest the approach being taken by the Institute. Some argued that the managers of MIT's endowment, who had been paid handsomely, should be the ones let go. Indeed, their stewardship of resources was below average for endowment returns across universities in 2008 and 2009, declining 20.7 percent in value in a year and ending a seven-year period of growth.[61]

As part of our assignment, Lotte and I interviewed many department heads and a number of terminated employees. We thought our best contributions would be to identify best practices as well as lessons from the instances in which terminations were not handled in a responsible and respectful manner. Given the decentralized nature of operations at MIT, we studied how the process was handled in various departments. To minimize layoffs, some departments reduced hours for existing employees; others urged workers to volunteer for furloughs. Thus, one lesson was that there were creative steps that could be taken to avoid terminations.

A big lesson learned from the budget crisis was that the initial plan to stage the layoffs over three years was not wise. The original thought behind that decision was that it would provide time for adjustments to take place and perhaps, as alternatives were found, even lower the number of layoffs required. Yet against this plausible premise was the reality that morale would suffer given the uncertainty that would be hanging over departments for an extended period. So, soon into the first year, a decision was made to consolidate

the projected second and third years of planned reductions so the terminations would happen as quickly as possible.[62]

Our report endorsed a theme heard in many of our interviews that "a
layoff is not something to be embarrassed about." A second point was a recom-
mendation regarding the situation with the twenty-year employee that had
generated so much attention: "The decision as to whether the person returns
to his or her office should be made by the employee."

Our report also summarized best practices that are essential elements of
any human resource portfolio regarding how to help employees who have
been terminated with the best pathway for pursuing their careers, if not
at MIT.

We presented our recommendations at a meeting of concerned faculty and
administrators along with another committee established jointly by the faculty chair and the chancellor to examine whether there should be additional
organizational changes outside of the layoff procedures to address issues that
the faculty had raised. Both reports were well received, and our recommendations were implemented to the satisfaction of both the faculty and the administrative officials.

Sometimes expertise in good employment practices and experience with
bad ones elsewhere can come in handy "at home." While at Cornell, I had
studied cases of worker displacement with many attendant problems and,
while chairing the Continuity of Employment Committee, drew on those
lessons in fashioning polices and practices to cushion the impact of job loss.
So at MIT, the same lesson surfaced: workers who are being terminated need
to be treated with respect and given resources for the future.

My nearly four decades' affiliation with the Sloan School—first in the Industrial Relations Section and then, when we adopted a new name in 1998,
as part of the Institute for Work and Employment Research—has been a
good one. It has been the longest stay of my four posts, and without a doubt
the most far reaching. That is certainly the case geographically speaking: my
research work has led to some very interesting trips to China, France, Israel,
Peru, Scandinavia, Singapore, and South Africa.

Would I have been happier had I returned to teaching strategy and small
business, as I did in my final years at the University of Chicago? It was clear
early in my time at Sloan that the labor movement was in decline, so why
did I hang on to a declining field? The answer lies in the interesting research

and numerous outside assignments described in this chapter. Faculty and student colleagues continue to keep me centered on the field, and I have always felt that I have been working on important issues.

Speaking of faculty, I want to recognize someone I first got to know while at the University of Chicago: Phyllis Wallace. Our association dates back to the mid-1960s when, in her role as assistant research director for the federal Equal Employment Opportunity Commission (EEOC), she asked me to analyze data on the Chicago labor market that was being released for the first time. As I mentioned in chapter 3, while working on that project I attended a number of conferences at the EEOC in Washington. It was at one of those sessions that I met Lester Thurow, who would later be my dean at the Sloan School.

My work with the EEOC expanded, and later I worked with the Office of Federal Contract Compliance. Both necessitated regular trips to Washington, and I kept in close touch with Phyllis. In 1971, when I assumed the deanship at the ILR School at Cornell, one of the first priorities that I discussed with the faculty was my desire to create an institute to study minority employment. Phyllis Wallace stood at the top of the list of candidates to head the institute, and she agreed to visit the campus.

Things did not work out as I hoped. After her visit, she called to say she had accepted an offer from MIT to be on the faculty of the Sloan School. When I arrived at Sloan as a visitor in the fall of 1979, Phyllis and I shared a laugh. "I couldn't persuade you to come to Cornell," I said to her, "so I had to come to MIT to have you be a colleague."

The list of potential candidates to head the institute at the ILR School back then is not the only one Phyllis headed. She is also on top when I am asked who has had a major impact with respect to the employment of minorities and women. While at the EEOC, she guided the research that led to a pathbreaking AT&T case in which the company agreed to pay millions in back wages and change its transfer, promotion, and recruitment policies. In Wallace's obituary in 1993, Thurow described the AT&T case as "one of the pioneering discrimination cases—opening up AT&T to women and minorities."[63]

While at Sloan, Phyllis tracked the careers of alumni, with special attention to women graduates. As of early 2018, thanks in part to her efforts, women made up 39 percent of the MIT student body, both undergraduate and graduate; it was only 16 percent around the time Phyllis joined the faculty. The increase in enrollment for persons of color has also been impressive: a mere 5 percent in 1977, it has now nearly tripled to 13 percent. The MIT administration frequently called on Phyllis for special studies and projects, and local corporations sought her counsel and her participation on their boards of directors.

Phyllis Wallace's sudden passing in 1993 hit all of us very hard. I am sure that if a center were established to study the labor market challenges faced by minorities and women, I would certainly hope that it would carry her name.

I would also like to recognize two other colleagues. Long before I arrived at MIT, I was aware of Mike Piore and his work. His book on internal labor markets, coauthored with Peter Doeringer, had made its mark, and we all knew that a graduate from the John T. Dunlop "shop" had to be very good.[64] Piore's ability to see past the noise of the present and spot uniformities and important subjects for the future is awe-inspiring. Our graduate students recognize his genius, and he has guided many of them during their studies at MIT. Mike participates actively in the weekly Tuesday seminars, and holds the record for the most seniority for this important event in the IWER community. His contributions are always mind stretching.

Mike was a member of the Reserve Officers' Training Corps (ROTC) faculty committee when I chaired it, and with his influence we made some headway in opening the ROTC program to all MIT students. In a frank discussion with the senior officers from the units, he helped them undo some of their misunderstandings about sexual orientation. This engagement took place at a time when individuals who were openly gay could not serve in the military; they were also barred from becoming ROTC cadets, taking advantage of the courses offered by ROTC (many with an emphasis on leadership), and receiving financial stipends. Mike helped shaped two initiatives that have continued into the twenty-first century and have even been expanded: leadership courses offered by ROTC would be open to all MIT students, and during the January intersession ROTC would offer a leadership seminar that would also be open to all students.

The second individual is Tom Kochan, whom I have known for half my lifetime and most of my academic career. He joined the faculty at Cornell's ILR School during my second year there as dean. It is easy to conclude that we have been "joined at the hip," but the actual relationship is one of leader

(Tom) and follower (me, tagging along.) Benefiting from Tom's wisdom and productivity has been a gift since the early 1970s.

In 2017 Tom authored a book with Lee Dyer detailing the challenges facing the United States, and especially the urgent need for a new social contract.[65] Teaching a course to several thousand participants via the World Wide Web has given Tom a deep understanding of the challenges facing our economy, as well as pathways forward for addressing these challenges.

We have hired an outstanding group of other faculty during my time at Sloan. We recruited Paul Osterman "back" from Boston University; with his PhD from the MIT Department of Urban Studies he quickly fit in and has gone on to author a range of very significant labor market studies.[66] Other recruits have since gone on to impressive careers at other institutions, including Katherine Abraham, professor of economics at the University of Maryland, who also directs the Maryland Center for Economics and Policy; Harry Katz, the Jack Sheinkman Professor of Collective Bargaining at the ILR School at Cornell; Lisa Lynch, provost and professor of social and economic policy at Brandeis University's Heller School for Social Policy and Management; James Rebitzer, who chairs the Markets, Public Policy and Law Department at Boston University's Questrom School of Business; and Ofer Sharone, who is a professor in the Department of Sociology at the University of Massachusetts–Amherst.[67]

The research undertaken by our PhD students reveals how, during each of my decades at Sloan, the agenda in our field has evolved. During the 1980s a majority of doctoral dissertations tackled some aspect of the changing nature of industrial relations: the role of employee participation; the effects of unions on firm performance; labor-management partnerships; the changing roles of supervisors and middle managers; and the growth of nonunion operations within unionized firms. During the 1990s studies of workplace innovations within specific industries dominated and led the way to the development of what became known as high-performance work systems; these industries included office equipment, automobile manufacturing, airlines, telecommunications, and health care. Since the beginning of the new century, students have selected a wide range of topics, often with an international focus, addressing issues related to economic development, the changing nature of work, careers, dispute resolution, the impact of technology, organizational change, work and family issues, and social movements.

So very many of these students stand out, and I could double the length of this book recounting my experiences with them; they have contributed so much to making my academic life so satisfying. Instead I will single out one graduate from the growing diaspora as representative of the many smart, stimulating, and enterprising people I have been fortunate to have as students.

Joel Cutcher-Gershenfeld is a great deal more than some "typical former student"; he has been my coauthor, colleague, and friend. Joel is a second-generation scholar in the field of industrial relations: his father, Walter Gershenfeld, taught labor relations at Temple University for many years, providing important leadership to the National Academy of Arbitrators (NAA), and his mother, Gladys Gershenfeld, enjoyed a career as an arbitrator and was NAA vice president. Not surprisingly, Joel was an undergraduate at the ILR School at Cornell, his mother's alma mater. He then worked for the Michigan Quality of Working Life Council—a labor-management nonprofit focused on employee involvement and labor-management cooperation—before coming to MIT to pursue a PhD. In January 2016 he joined the faculty at Brandeis University. Along the way he has dug deep into the industrial relations terrain at Ford Motor Company and Xerox and has led an interdisciplinary team studying stakeholder alignment in several industries. Joel's energy, initiative, and humanity are unmatched.

I am proud to be one of the many faculty who have helped bring to fruition about forty PhD dissertations in four decades, including Joel's, and to have helped train our many alumni who have gone on to fill key positions in industry and have held positions in government that help move the world forward. Of course, many have also continued in academia as professors, journal editors, deans, and provosts throughout the world; in fact, Sloan alumni have helped fill the faculty ranks in Australia, Canada, Italy, Mexico, Singapore, South Africa, South Korea, Spain, Switzerland, and the United Kingdom.

There is a thread that has run throughout this chapter: watching and helping the Sloan program, its faculty, and its PhD student body diversify and broaden to adapt to the changing nature of work, the changing workforce, and, as a result, a whole new teaching domain. The research of our students has evolved over these decades, reflecting the broadening of the field and aided by the arrival of new faculty members with different interests. IWER continues to thrive because it has adapted.

I could recite the accomplishments of many more of our students, graduates, and faculty, but in so many ways the sum is greater than the total of the parts because we have built and maintained a strong sense of community at MIT and with our alumni over all these years. Perhaps that is what emerges out of a group of highly committed and talented people who have tackled the big debates in our field and have taken the risks to lead the field in new directions. That's what has made MIT Sloan a great place to work.

Chapter 6

TAKING STOCK AND LOOKING AHEAD

Industrial relations has always been an applied field, one that makes its biggest contributions when there are big problems to be studied. These provide the energy to help identify and develop solutions.

There have been at least four periods during which this has happened. In the decades before the New Deal, John R. Commons and his students at the University of Wisconsin documented and helped invent state-level and private-sector innovations in collective bargaining and a variety of employment standards that came to be built into national policies. Later, in the decade after World War II, industrial relations scholars from universities all across the country were in the field documenting and helping shape collective bargaining practices. A comparable process took place in the 1960 and 1970s with the arrival of unions in the public sector. Industrial relations as a field of study made another significant contribution in the 1980s, when it became clear that management's embrace of the nonunion model had openly become the modus operandi.

Perhaps we are in another such invigorating and challenging period. The deep divisions in society made all too apparent in the 2016 U.S. presidential election and its aftermath, the recognition that the growth in inequality over the past thirty years is unacceptable and unsustainable, and increased concerns regarding the long-term consequences of union decline all suggest that the menu for employment relations research is once again filled with big problems.

I am not so audacious as to think that I know how to solve these big problems. But I do think that the lessons from the past sixty years of working personally and with others, and witnessing some of the masters of our field tackle big challenges, offers some insights into the questions that need to be posed to move industrial relations forward. Answering them is a task best left to the current and next generation of scholars, policymakers, and practitioners in our field.

Addressing Divisions

Our field of study arose out of the need to address the "labor problem" in the early part of the twentieth century—conflicts between workers and employers that often turned violent, as with the bombing of the *Los Angeles Times* office in 1910 by a member of the International Association of Bridge and Structural Iron Workers to protest the newspaper's vehemently antiunion stance under publisher Harrison Gray Otis. As for violence from the employer side, the Ludlow Massacre of 1914 helped create national awareness that the country had a "labor problem."[1] The first steps taken after events like these by the early scholars in our field involved careful empirical research into how labor and management officials in the clothing, mining, and other industries were dealing with the persistent conflicts between the two sides. Meanwhile, progressive thinkers and doers such as Louis Brandeis, who in 1916 became an associate justice on the U.S. Supreme Court, were also considering and speaking out about the related issues.

It is worth remembering these words of Brandeis: "Strong, responsible unions are essential to industrial fair play. Without them the labor bargain is wholly one-sided. The parties to the labor contract must be nearly equal in strength if justice is to be worked out, and this means that the workers must be organized and that their organizations must be recognized by employers as a condition precedent to industrial peace."[2]

Out of that work by the field's early scholars came the basic features of the New Deal legislation. As was noted in chapter 2, Harvard University professor Sumner Slichter helped lead a study group that Senator Robert Wagner drew from to draft the 1935 National Labor Relations Act (NLRA). The decades that followed saw a rise in union membership in the United States, as workers readily embraced unions as protectors of and advocates for their rights and aspirations as employees, empowered by the ability of union organizations to improve the lot of members and achieve their common goals thanks to the power of collective bargaining. This final chapter seems like the right place to take stock and address the big question that has gone largely unanswered in the accounts of my time at four educational institutions: Is management opposition to unions rational, and does it serve the best interests of the firm? Although I have described what constitutes the backstory to the question, I have not addressed an explanation of the steady and dramatic decline in union density over the past sixty years.

Unions: Past, Present, and Future

Those of us immersed in the field of industrial relations would quickly list strong and effective opposition by employers as one of the most important reasons for union decline. I would like to review examples mentioned in earlier chapters, and present some others in brief, through that prism.

Some of those tactics have little to do with labor-management issues directly. For instance, while observing an AFL-CIO convention in the late 1950s, during the height of the civil rights movement, when employers sought to exploit racial divisions to their advantage, I heard a delegate report on scurrilous tactics used by a company in the South. One of them involved James Carey, president of the International Union of Electrical Workers (IUE), and a whisper campaign about him dancing with a woman of color (who happened to be from Liberia). The IUE was involved in an organizing effort in the South at the time.

The Gardner Board and Carton Company employed the tactic of simply refusing to bargain (see chapter 2). The union had been recognized, and the company was under a duty-to-bargain obligation, but the company simply introduced its "final offer" at the start of negotiations. By behaving as though the only role for the union was to catch any errors management might have made in the offer, Gardner was essentially refusing to bargain.

During my time at the University of Chicago in the 1960s, the dramatic example of company opposition to unions emerged during the unsuccessful strikes by members of the American Federation of State, County, and Municipal Employees to organize workers at two health care institutions (see chapter 3). This was a time when unions and collective bargaining were very much in place in manufacturing—for example, the parties at International Harvester assumed unions would always be on the scene—but unionization had not yet reached the health care sector. In both instances, management hired replacement workers and refused to recognize the union. Indeed, it was not until 1987 that the National Labor Relations Board (NLRB) extended rule making to hospitals.

During the 1970s, while I was at Cornell University, there were clear signs of acceleration in the movement of manufacturing industries to the South. Textile companies that had been heavily based in New England and were extensively unionized were relocating to the South for lower wage rates, as well as taking advantage of the less-union-friendly "Southern culture." When the Amalgamated Clothing and Textile Workers Union attempted to organize J. P. Stevens (see chapter 4), it confronted a very different situation from what it had in the North. The company chose to act like other Southern employers and resisted efforts to be unionized.

When I attended the Labor Policy Association seminar with E. Robert Livernash, I caught a glimpse of the thinking of management from companies that had dealt with unions for many years.[3] Some two hundred pressmen working for the *Washington Post*, members of Local 6 of the Newspaper and Graphic Communications Union, were on strike at the time. The *Post* continued to produce newspapers using replacement workers. The situation served as a rallying point for the seminar, and the message was clear: union power needed to be confronted with assertive management policy and action. This approach was not to be construed as employer opposition to unions per se, but it certainly reflected employer opposition to the modus operandi of most unions.

The *Washington Post*, by the way, succeeded in busting its pressmen's union. The strike provoked publisher Katherine Graham to take her company public, largely beginning the era of "transformation of the daily newspaper in the United States from a family enterprise to a corporation with an obligation to its stockholders to 'maximize' profits"—with, of course, the attending pressure on newspaper unions across the board.[4]

By 1983, when Harry Katz, Thomas Kochan, and I were conducting fieldwork for the book *The Transformation of American Industrial Relations*, it had become clear that employer opposition to unionization was having a major impact in the U.S. manufacturing sector. In fact, we devoted an entire chapter to discussing examples of companies that were "double-breasting"— the practice of employing nonunion workers, often in a separate division, to supplement the work of union workers who are typically higher paid.[5] We were seeing more and more companies opening new plants and working hard to keep those new plants union free while "cooperating" or maintaining the "traditional" relationship with unions in plants already organized.

White-collar employment was another arena in which employers contested union organizing, especially in the manufacturing sector. I observed firsthand the aggressive approach Inland Steel took to prevent unions from representing workers in its warehouses. And Harvard, despite all its progressive attributes, worked very hard to resist its clerical and technical workers from winning a union representation election. (As I have described in chapter 5, the union ultimately prevailed, but only after filing appeals and orchestrating a very effective public relations campaign.)

So it is clear that employers do not want unions—or, put differently— resistance to "outside interference" and "unionization" is deeply ingrained as part of the behavior that goes with being an employer. Employers operating in the American culture of free enterprise and individualism simply do not want to be required to bargain with other parties.

In a static economy, employer opposition to union organizing would not explain a decline in union density. The organizing success unions experienced in the 1930s and 1940s in the private sector would persist, given that deunionization is rare. But in a dynamic economy, plants are continually being phased out and new ones opened. As it turns out, plants where unions have representation rights have been closed at a higher rate than unorganized plants. Those plants may have been legitimately obsolescent from a technical perspective, or it may have been because management chose to move to a lower-wage area—or both. What is also true is that the new plants tend not to become unionized—due in large part to concerted employer opposition to unions.

The automobile industry presents a dramatic picture of this phenomenon. When I began field research in the industry in the 1950s, the United Auto Workers represented almost every plant. By 2016, 40 percent of the auto industry workforce was in nonunion plants.

I also saw this in meatpacking. The large urban meatpacking plants, totally unionized by the Packinghouse Workers, were shut down, and operations were moved to new plants closer to the supply source. Many of the replacement operations remain unorganized.

The closing of the three plants in the Ithaca, New York, area that Robert Aronson and I studied in the 1970s (see chapter 4) similarly provided an opportunity to lower union density. And the deinstitutionalization of mental health facilities in New York State (also discussed in chapter 4) meant that unionized jobs in the state sector were being replaced by comparable jobs in hospitals and mental health institutions, often without union representation.

During my years at the MIT Sloan School of Management, I have seen several examples of operations shutting down with little chance for successor operations being unionized. The shutdown of the General Motors plant in Framingham meant a loss of jobs not only in Massachusetts but also in the United States; the company did not shift production and associated employment to other plants. Instead, auto jobs went to Japanese and German transplants, which largely remain unorganized.

The transportation industry provides a number of examples, too. JetBlue, a steadily growing airline that is largely unorganized (although flight attendants recently voted for unionization), flies many of the routes once handled by unionized Eastern Air Lines. The over-the-road trucking industry is now almost completely nonunion since the bankruptcy of PIE Nationwide (see chapter 5). And when the large international carrier DHL closed its Airborne Express division, it was not only employment that was lost but also union membership in the Teamsters.

Ease of entry in trucking is a key factor in explaining the shift toward nonunion employment. The surge in owner-operators stands in contrast to the difficulty in starting a new railroad; consequently, unionization in railroads has remained high—despite the Guilford Industries example (see chapter 5), where corporate ownership maneuvers and abrogation of labor agreements were employed in an effort to operate on a nonunion basis.

All of this, at least from my perspective, begs the big question: Is management opposition to unions rational, and does it serve the best interests of the firm? Although I do not have data with which to answer, I believe unions *can* add value.

Malcolm Lovell, who headed the Collective Bargaining Forum I introduced in chapter 5, argued that collective bargaining has the potential for adding value, and that management should see collective bargaining as serving the company's own economic interests.[6]

This brings us to the potential for management and unions to work together in creative ways to solve the pressing problems of both business and worker welfare. I have been very interested in these innovations, and many of them have been introduced in the preceding chapters. They fall into different categories. In some cases, the need for labor and management to work together arises as a result of the challenges of economic change. The Armour Automation Fund (see chapter 3) grappled with issues facing workers in the meatpacking industry as they were displaced through plant shutdowns in the urban areas of the Midwest. Drawing inspiration from that experience, the Continuity of Employment Committee, sponsored by New York State and the Civil Service Employees Association, created a process during the 1970s to help hundreds of workers regain their footing after being displaced as a result of the deinstitutionalization of mental health facilities (see chapter 4).

Other examples dealt with new methods for resolving conflict at the workplace. International Harvester's in-person handling of grievances meant that the extensive backlog could be substantially reduced. Airborne Express workers benefited from having their supervisors trained in how to practice more civil and respectful leadership. Bullying was no longer tolerated.

Some of the examples in earlier chapters dealt with new ways for conducting collective bargaining. The so-called Treaty of Detroit (see chapter 2), linking wage increases to productivity improvements, lasted as long as unions had power to impose the arrangement. Project agreements in the construction industry guaranteed that unions would not strike and employers would only hire union labor, and these arrangements continue in use presently.

The package of innovations included in the New Directions program (see chapter 5) introduced during the 1990s in the steel industry lasted for a decade, but never really engaged the workforce at the operating level. This program did place union-nominated directors on the boards of directors of major steel companies, and inaugurated forums for high-level discussion, but the partnership concept did not translate into changes on the ground.

The most frequently cited examples of labor management innovations deal with how work gets done. The Mechanization and Modernization Agreement signed in the West Coast longshore industry in the late 1940s (see chapter 3) dealt with the introduction of new technology and adjustments in crew size and work routines to match the automation taking place. The longwall method in coal mining (see chapter 4) made major contributions to productivity. Similarly, in automobile manufacturing, the modern operating agreement at Chrysler changed the way work was done. These innovations helped update work practices, but the cooperation that led to these programs has not been sustained.

The Scanlon Plan emphasized productivity improvement and the sharing of rewards (see chapter 5). Some companies, especially in the Grand Rapids, Michigan, area, are still using this gainsharing plan. Two other examples, of the automaker Saturn and the managed care organization Kaiser Permanente (both discussed in chapter 5), represent innovations that are comprehensive across strategic collective bargaining and operating levels. Although Saturn is no longer on the scene as of this writing, Kaiser is alive and well.

The development of interest-based bargaining has been a major development and has demonstrated its value in many relationships. Examples where innovations have had an impact and have exhibited staying power over a reasonably long period have been those that take into account the three levels of engagement: strategic, contract negotiations, and operations. At MIT, I often hear from Engineering School faculty of the importance of adopting a systems approach. So the integrated program at Kaiser Permanente, interest-based bargaining, the Scanlon Plan, and the health plan for Teamsters in St. Louis negotiated by Hal Gibbons as an extension of collective bargaining beyond the normal union agenda all have staying power because the parties put in place comprehensive, supportive systems. Saturn does not make the list. Although it had all the elements of a comprehensive system, key officials at the corporate level and UAW headquarters never supported it.

Still, the examples of the upside potential for unions and collective bargaining are impressive. Yet any genuine scorecard also carries examples that can be put on the negative side of an employer's ledger. Among those I've mentioned in earlier chapters, some have rather obvious business implications: the inability of the local union at Brockway Motors to envision the need for change (see chapter 4), and the resistance of public sector unions in Arlington,

Massachusetts, to joining the state health plan (chapter 5). Others are things companies may simply want to avoid getting mixed up in, such as the corruption investigation of the Teamsters Union (see chapter 2) and the exclusion of African Americans from the building trades in Chicago (see chapter 3).

I continue to believe that unions provide the best means for workers to exercise their voices, and that unions also provide the parties with opportunities to engage in creative collective bargaining. Industrial relations scholars in general believe the upside of unions outweighs the downside. In some cases, those of us in the field of industrial relations have helped foster important innovations. At the same time, we cannot ignore the reality of how management thinks about the posture it will take in the face of a union organizing campaign, and that most managers are risk averse and therefore work hard to remain union free. Still, though some managers are simply ideologically opposed to sharing power with unions, others might implicitly understand what Sandra Black and Lisa Lynch have documented in their research: that unions have both greater upside and downside potential for influencing productivity. For example, Black and Lynch found that in unionized manufacturing plants that had "transformed" labor-management practices—including with the use of teams, quality improvement processes, and highly engaged employees—achieved higher productivity than similarly structured nonunion plants. But they also found that unionized plants in which management was maintaining the traditional arm's-length relationship with the union performed worse than traditionally structured nonunion plants.[7]

My personal view is that it is indeed a hard sell to convince management to embrace the idea that their companies would be better were their employees represented by unions. Workers must have agency, and I am convinced that union representation is the best means to that end.

Over the past half century, the employer "must" (resistance to unions) has dominated the worker "ought" (desire to join unions). Will this dichotomy continue? Or will we see another major inflection—in the form of a surge in union growth—similar to that of the 1930s and 1940s for the private sector and the 1960s and 1970s for the public sector? Can unions rebuild their power within the existing structure of the labor movement? Or will some new forms of worker voice pave the way to a resurgence outside of that formal structure—such as the innovative examples of the National Domestic

Workers Alliance, the National Taxi Workers' Alliance, and Restaurant Opportunities Centers United?[8]

This is the subject of a worker voice project underway at MIT even as I write this book. It is clear that workers continue to want a voice at work so they can discuss a broad array of issues that affect their welfare. Early project data indicate a continuing gap between what workers feel they ought to have and what they experience. Moreover, an increasing number of workers would like to join some form of union but are not able to do so under the processes, organizing models, and employer strategies that undermine the concept of a level playing field for establishing collective bargaining relationships. Thus, some fundamental changes and innovations are required.

It may be time for Congress and the NLRB to allow for experimentation with new approaches on a trial basis. The 1935 NLRA limited other forms of engagement when it endorsed collective bargaining as the appropriate way to structure labor management relations—done largely to eliminate so-called company unions at the local plant level that employers in many industries had established to avoid independent organizations. Could cooperatives that seek to advance worker interests and create value through shared ownership and governance arrangements be tested? How about unions that represent less than a majority of employees in an enterprise, or works councils similar to those that function well in Germany and other European countries? This was contemplated when Volkswagen established an auto manufacturing plant in Tennessee.

In a September 1, 2017, op-ed piece in the *Wall Street Journal* titled "American Workers Need a New Kind of Labor Union," Oren Cass—a senior fellow at the Manhattan Institute who had served as the domestic policy director for Mitt Romney's 2012 presidential campaign—advocated the creation of worker co-ops and works councils as their representatives in collective bargaining. What Cass calls a "labor co-operative" would be "controlled by dues-paying members to advance employment and create value, not merely reallocate it."

Would workers join such organizations? The number might be high for organizations not carrying the formal label of "trade union." But what about employers? How would they react? German and Japanese companies with plants in the United States might accept these arrangements that are similar to the institutions in place in their home countries—works councils in

Germany and company unions in Japan.[9] And other employers might embrace co-ops. In fact, in earlier days in the United States, employee representation plans and company unions were quite popular with management.

It seems shortsighted to remain stuck with an outmoded law that prevents management and workers from benefiting from arrangements that might, if designed to ensure that workers have a real rather than a management-controlled voice, help break the long-standing logjam over labor policy and usher in a new era of worker voice and representation.[10] It is a tall political order, but perhaps a time will come when the political stars realign to open up these and other possibilities. And for the time being, the Supreme Court decision in *Janus v. American Federation of State, County, and Municipal Employees, Council 31* outlawing union dues checkoff in the public sector (see chapter 5) takes us farther away from a reordering of policies governing the employment relationship.

As the search for new approaches to ensuring workers have a voice moves forward, it is important to note again that unions continue to remain strong in several sectors, including transportation, utilities, the public sector, and some parts of manufacturing. My experience with the airline, trucking, and railroad industries suggests there will continue to be a wide range of union-management relationships, some of which seem to be frozen in time and not ready to change practices, while others are on the cutting edge of innovation and change. I am thinking of the effort to eliminate bullying behavior by supervisors at the now defunct Airborne Express; the labor-management partnership at Western Airlines, which unfortunately disappeared when Delta Airlines acquired the company; and agreements to modify work rules in the railroad industry.

Whatever lies ahead for unions, the deep social and economic divisions currently facing the United States demand of us that we figure out how to adapt what we have learned from years of negotiations, dispute resolution, and conflict management to help close these divides and begin what will inevitably be a long healing process.

Richard Walton and I drew on the pioneering work of Mary Parker Follett—known as the Mother of Modern Management for her contributions to classical management theory—in developing the concept of integrative bargaining.[11] There is a rich body of advanced research and practice that has built on Follett's core idea: that common ground can best be found between two opposing parties when they identify some shared interests and respect each other's different points of view. We have an opportunity to put to work this insight and the advances in negotiations theory and practice that have come along in recent years.

I have tried my hand at this a bit in working to bridge the divides between police and minority groups in my own community and a neighboring community. One lesson I learned is that although at first glance there may not appear to be any shared interests when a police officer questions a young person, especially someone from a minority group, they are often from the same community. When police interact regularly with high school students, both on location as well as in the broader community, there can be a basis for some rapport, even if only to share comments about recent sporting events.

Others have developed tools to facilitate dialogue and multiparty negotiations over issues people feel deeply about. Joel Cutcher-Gershenfeld and the Stakeholder Alignment Collaborative have developed visual tools for mapping alignment or differences in interests among multiple participants in complex and often controversial issues.[12] Tools of this sort, when used by impartial facilitators, might offer ways to break down barriers and get people talking about shared as well as conflicting interests.

New Wage-Setting Norms

There is no single silver bullet that can solve the thirty-year problem of growing income inequality and the gap that has developed between productivity growth and wage growth. Indeed, as some of my colleagues suggest, we will need an entirely new social contract at work to reverse these two trends.[13] One thing is clear: there is little hope of returning to the heyday of strong unions in the postwar era, when collective bargaining could take wages out of competition and spread wage increases by the threat of a strike or use of formal or informal pattern bargaining. We can learn some things from the Scanlon Plan and the productivity bargaining experiments in Great Britain (see chapter 3). Some adapted or modern forms of gainsharing, profit sharing, or employee ownership could be part of a path forward. The bottom line for the economy is that new ways need to be found to foster increases in productivity and the sharing of rewards.

More generally, we need some new consensus on appropriate norms for setting wages. Once upon a time, the War Labor Board was instrumental in legitimizing and institutionalizing wage norms and practices of cost-of-living adjustments, as well as careful comparison across firms employing similar workers and competing in similar product markets. Now every firm seems to operate "on its own bottom."

Can we foresee a time when the public and leaders of public- and private-sector organizations come together to agree on a set of broad principles to guide wage adjustments? I don't know whether this is likely or even possible, but I do know that the current situation is unsustainable. The search for new wage norms and the institutions and policies to enforce and spread them will continue to be a worthy focus of research in the years to come.

The Future of the Corporation

In a capitalist system with a strong market focus, the economic "must" to lower costs dominates the human "ought" to address the consequences for workers. As a result, among stakeholders, workers are treated as far less than equal and, at best, are always playing catch-up. At worst, their interests are totally ignored in capital allocation decisions. Such was the situation that produced the battles at Eastern Air Lines and Guilford railroads and the ones I encountered as a union-nominated director at PIE Nationwide (see chapter 5). My experience and that of other colleagues serving as union-nominated directors suggests the difficulty in changing these priorities, given the operating principles of the free enterprise system.

But there is a growing recognition that change is needed. Perhaps the era of maximizing shareholder value over everything else—a largely post-1980s development—has run its course. It clearly has no shortage of critics.

In the years following World War II, the strength of unions, and perhaps the ethos of executives who grew up in the Depression and experienced the trauma of the war produced a more balanced approach to the responsibilities of executives and the corporations they led. What goes around may indeed come around, but probably only if the academic community does a better job of documenting and publicizing the costs of attending primarily to shareholders and minimizing responsibility to workers and communities that have a stake in corporate enterprises.

In 2018, cities around the country, including Boston, competed to lure Amazon to locate its "second headquarters" (ultimately, the company chose

Long Island City, New York, and Arlington, Virginia). Each prepared a package of incentives to win the prize. Examples of this sort abound in our cities and states; Wisconsin, for example, offered the Chinese electronics firm Foxconn $3 billion in tax incentives to build a plant in the state. What if instead of competing over how much they can offer, cities and states got together and told Amazon, Foxconn, and others that they want to hold them accountable for returning dividends to the region by providing good-quality jobs and contributing to the welfare of the community? It might take that type of collective reframing of the relationship between communities and corporations and their mutual responsibilities to turn what has become a race to the bottom into a positive sum opportunity for all stakeholders. At a minimum, researchers and policymakers would do well to develop a method for calculating the rate of return on these investments.

Would worker representation in corporate governance make any difference in changing this exclusive attention to shareholder value? If my experience and that of others who have sat on corporate boards as worker- or union-nominated directors are any indication, this can be a step in a positive direction—but it is far from sufficient. Our primary contribution has been to speak up and take actions to avoid bad decisions/actions that may have crossed ethical or even legal lines. But aside from playing a watchdog role, one or two board members cannot change a culture that reinforces the view that employees are, at best, secondary stakeholders. Something more powerful will be needed. Figuring out what that something might be would be a worthy and promising direction for future research in our field.

The Adjustment Disconnect Union Leaders Face

In some cases, the terms of the collective bargaining agreement and associated practices have set the stage for disruptive changes initiated by management. In other cases, changes in market conditions or new technological developments have rendered current practices obsolete. Rank-and-file union members want to protect what they see as hard-won wages and work rules, while management teams wrestle with uncertainties in the marketplace for their companies' products and services. Labor leaders find themselves in the middle, and though they know the future will require major adjustments they often support the status quo for political reasons. The stories about Brockway Motors and Bethlehem Steel's plant in Lackawanna, New York, are examples of such "legacy" effects overpowering economic realism (see chapter 4). Even if union leaders are well informed about the environment facing the employer with which they are negotiating, and even if they are sympathetic to the need to institute some adjustments, it is more than likely that their members view the situation quite differently.

In my experience, when workers are asked to accept concessions—for example, teachers being asked to take on more work by extending the school day, or any worker being asked to shell out substantially more to cover health care costs—the inevitable response from most of them is the same: "I've worked here for a long time, and for most of those years I've given more than I've received." Public-sector workers have an added, and even more specific, complaint: "I've accepted being *paid less* than jobs in the private sector in exchange for excellent fringe benefits. To reduce those benefits now violates *everything.*"

So, it is not surprising to find managers and worker representatives talking past each other. Management feels compelled to discuss increasing competition, the challenges of delivering exciting new products on schedule, and the need to reduce costs. Meanwhile, union leaders point to the rising cost of living and increasing quality and productivity pressures on workers. The result is something we might call an "adjustment disconnect." But the challenge of addressing this disconnect can lead to negotiating new forms of adjustment, as discussed in the case of the Armour Automation Fund.

The key lies in expanding the agenda by asking what sorts of adjustments might compensate workers for absorbing the costs of needed changes. New training, retirement incentives, opportunities to work together to solve tough competitive problems, or new ways of organizing work that are both more efficient and perhaps more satisfying all need to be explored. This is where the creativity and mutual goodwill of management and labor are put to the test. Negotiating, facilitating, and managing through such disconnects is one of the critical challenges in labor relations.

Working with Parties through Arbitration

Arbitration has long been an active component of industrial relations, and I would be overlooking a good chunk of my own activity in the field if I did not share some thoughts on it. In the arbitrator role, I have followed in the footsteps of an earlier generation of academics. James Healy of Harvard Business School probably devoted at least half his time to the practice. Early members of the Industrial Relations Section at MIT, such as Douglass Brown and Charles Myers and, limited their involvement to one a day a week, following the customary allowance for remunerative work. I heard my own first case when I was at the University of Chicago. Since then I have conducted approximately a half dozen hearings annually.

The history of arbitration comprises several major periods. The first began in the 1940s and continued for a decade or two, during which the leading practitioners of our art were mediators first and arbitrators second. They embodied the activism of George Taylor, a professor at the Wharton School of the University of Pennsylvania. Given that arbitration is inevitably an event in an *ongoing* relationship, it is important to allow the parties to make intelligence choices about the conduct of arbitration. The process must be one that places the parties in charge. To paraphrase Taylor, the procedures of arbitration, to have continuing usefulness, must themselves be a subject of agreement by the parties.[14]

Gradually, successive generations of arbitrators increasingly limited themselves to interpreting the contract and deciding specific grievances. This legalistic approach made sense during the decades when everything was largely stable. However, with the dramatic changes in the environment we began to see unfolding in the early 1980s, a more relevant conception is needed for our role as arbitrators.

Over the years some important changes have taken place in what is the final step of the grievance procedure. The first change is that having a case docketed for arbitration does not mean a hearing will take place. Statistics from the American Arbitration Association suggest that more than half of scheduled cases are either withdrawn or postponed indefinitely. Alex Colvin, a faculty member at the ILR School, studied 3,945 arbitration cases and found that only 1,213 were decided by an award after a hearing.[15]

So it would seem that we arbitrators are serving as focal points for the parties to engage in settlement discussions in order to *avoid* arbitration ("better the devil you know than the devil you don't"). This suggests that perhaps options for settling the grievance should have been explored more fully before filing for arbitration. I have no problem with this development because it is important for cases to be settled whenever they can, with the parties taking ownership of the outcomes. But it should be acknowledged that arbitrators are increasingly playing a different role from one of hearing cases; we are serving as scheduling reminders for the parties, and especially for their lawyers, to focus on reaching agreements.

Lawyers have become involved more because, for the most part, the actual decision makers aren't involved in arbitration hearings. Instead—especially on the management side, but also on the union side—the advocates tend to be lawyers, and this makes the hearings unnecessarily formal; it also brings difficulty in engaging decision makers. The parties use lawyers more frequently now than in the past because the cases have become more complex and often involve legal issues beyond what arises out of the collective bargaining agreement

Another change concerns the subject matter of cases brought to arbitration. The majority of cases now involve some form of discipline. Management has the responsibility for imposing discipline if it believes employees have broken rules or behaved improperly, and unions have the legal responsibility to represent its members in the grievance and arbitration process. But there may be cases in which the union is reluctant to expend its resources for a case an arbitrator is most likely to decide for the employer. Because of the union's potential liability to a suit on the part of a disgruntled grievant (threatening to sue on the grounds that the union has failed in its duty to provide fair representation), many cases get appealed to arbitration where the merits of the case are truly quite weak. Many refer to this as making the process, for arbitrators, akin to efforts to achieve the elusive goal of "full employment."

I have heard discharge cases in which management might be willing to reinstate the grievant worker—perhaps on a probationary basis—if only the union representative would allow the grievant to make an apology and present evidence about changed behavior. But the union advocate does not pursue this possibility of compromise, arguing instead that the action of management is unjustified.

Another reason arbitrators do not venture into the more informal, conciliatory type of arbitration and follow the advice of George Taylor is that it is easy to run afoul of the interests of one side or the other, thereby losing acceptability. There's also a more questionable reason: by allowing the case to proceed through the full hearing process, complete with post-hearing briefs, advocates are able to book several additional days of compensation.

Speaking of acceptability, I am reminded of an unusual arbitration hearing among the several conducted in the mid-1960s by Doug Brown, who had been invited by George Shultz to spend a sabbatical year at the University of Chicago. I had expressed interest in such hearings, and Brown invited me to join him. To my surprise, about an hour into the hearing and after the lawyer for the union had been carrying on in a very aggressive, vituperative fashion, Brown announced, "I'm not here to listen to this diatribe, and I am returning this case to the American Arbitration Association for reassignment to another arbitrator."

I was stunned. I admired Doug for taking the high road without worrying whether he'd get any cases from that union in the future. To this day, I have never walked out on a case, nor have I heard of a colleague doing the same (although some have told me they have threatened to do so). It would be refreshing to have this happen from time to time.

Although I have not resigned from a case, I have been involved in cases where one or both sides have attempted to use the arbitration hearing to "get even" with the other side. In such situations I allow some "therapeutic venting" but set limits to prevent an escalation of antagonisms.

Arbitrators do get "fired," and sometimes we only know this when we stop getting appointments from the employer or union. That was made very explicit for me after I sustained the disciplining of a telephone worker who had verbally challenged management after being assigned to work on Christmas Day. I made the mistake of allowing a member of management to speak to me off the record; he told me that his authority was on the line and that sustaining the discipline was needed to validate his leadership. The union was convinced that the one-week suspension I sustained was excessive, and I was delisted from this panel. Had I not been influenced by that private conversation, I probably would have reduced the length of the suspension.

Acceptability, especially if one is a full-time arbitrator, is a reality that comes with the territory. Although arbitrators may worry about their continuing acceptability, surviving is beyond their control. And the parties usually are realistic about the outcomes of their cases. If arbitrators seek to alter decisions to fashion something they anticipate would be more acceptable to both, the greater risk is that if fashioned to a contrived outcome, arbitrators' decisions will be a surprise to both parties and, indeed, raise questions of whether arbitrators really decided cases on their merits or maneuvered them to keep their jobs.

"Style" has become a favorite discussion topic at annual meetings of the National Academy of Arbitrators. Should arbitration be a more formal court-room type of proceeding, with the arbitrator playing a judge-like role and relying on the contract, as advocated by J. Noble Braden, or should we continue with the more informal style, as practiced by George Taylor?[16]

I think arbitrators should play the role of a "pilot" who is hired to perform a specific function and uses imagination and creativity as unforeseen circumstances are encountered. Another model is that of the process consultant. The distinguishing feature of labor arbitration (compared to other quasi-legal procedures) is that the parties own the process. And the outsider brought into the relationship would be remiss not to point out opportunities for the parties to improve their process. When the "pilot" wants to alter the process, he or she can get the advocates into the hall and seek to persuade them of the benefits of an adjustment. Then, if this is not possible—even with threats—and everyone will be stuck with the more formal procedures, at least the parties have been warned.

In my own arbitration work, opportunities arise rather regularly to help the parties shape a more effective arbitration process, not to mention the quality of the larger labor-management relationship. These typically occur at particular junctures in the proceeding. For instance, it sometimes becomes clear that the employer has not proven the case for discharge and the grievant should be returned to work. However, it is also clear that reinstatement to the original position will create considerable turmoil. At such a juncture there is an opportunity to suggest to the parties that they negotiate the specific job assignment for reinstatement.

Another opportunity occurs when, even without waiting for posthearing briefs, it is clear to me that I am hearing an "open and shut case" with an obvious decision at the end. The logical step is to ask the parties whether they would be willing to receive a summary judgment. A third opportunity occurs when one or both of the advocates are new to the case, and/or the issue has been ineptly formulated. It is prudent to allow time for the parties to get up to speed and even to suggest a better formulation of the real issue at hand.

Putting on my research hat, we could go back to the parties to conduct a postmortem evaluation—that is, to inquire how the arbitration decision affected other issues and the labor-management relationship. The concept of the learning organization is very much in vogue; it would be interesting for all of us to find ways to revisit some of our cases in such a way. It might also affect our thinking when we encounter similar issues in the future.

Some arbitrators make conscious efforts to help resolve disputes before or at the early stages of a hearing through what is often called med-arb—that is, if the mediation effort is unsuccessful, the parties proceed to arbitration. Stephen Goldberg developed a variant of this approach in which the parties agree to take the case to a process that first involves mediation complete with an advisory opinion (in an effort to reach settlement) and, if still unresolved, the third party issues a binding decision.[17] I participated in this program for a number of years and deem the approach very effective.

Others reverse the process, using arb-med. Arnold Zack, a former president of the National Academy of Arbitrators, favors this approach, in which the neutral hears the case and reaches a decision but does not reveal it to the parties, and then asks permission to mediate.[18] Arnold points out that posthearing mediation is much faster, more informed by the parties' arguments, and more focused on the core issues. If there is no agreement after some fixed time of mediation (an hour, say, or three hours, or even a day), the neutral's decision is imposed on the parties. If there is an agreement, the earlier written decision is destroyed without the parties learning what it had been. A major benefit of arb-med is that more of the facts are in evidence—in contrast to med-arb, in which there is a tendency for the parties to hold back during the mediation phase to protect their interests going into arbitration.

The desire to remain neutral (to ensure acceptability) often conflicts with actions we should take outside of arbitration sessions, especially on matters of public policy. After all, who is better informed about collective bargaining than labor arbitrators? We should not be reluctant to take a position when restrictive legislation is being considered—in Wisconsin, for example, where there has been an emasculation of collective bargaining in the public sector.[19] Wisconsin was the first state to give public employees bargaining right back in 1959.

I sent a letter to the president of the National Academy of Arbitrators urging the organization to take a position in opposition to legislation under consideration in a number of states that restricts collective bargaining following the Wisconsin model. I argued that, as arbitrators with substantial knowledge about the workplace, we understand that for collective bargaining to be a valid process for resolving disputes and shaping solutions to the myriad issues inherent in the employment relationship, unions need to be strong, and the intent of the legislation making the rounds of a number of state legislatures has been to weaken public sector unions substantially. The academy declined to take a position, however—either because its leaders did not feel it appropriate to enter into the political arena or because such a position might affect the acceptability of our members conducting hearings in the future when agencies of the states being criticized would be parties to arbitration.

We do not have to accept the narrow role of the Bradenistic style of arbitration, of only conducting a quasi-legal proceeding. Given that arbitration is an event in an ongoing relationship, we can be attentive to the interplay of the hearing and this larger process. I am not advocating freewheeling intervention that might have been appropriate in the early days of collective bargaining but an approach that enables the parties to make intelligent choices about the conduct of arbitration. I am advocating a process that leaves the *parties* in charge, not the contract.

I am urging arbitrators to do more process management—which means presenting options. In a relationship, someone has to take the initiative, and more frequently that ought to be arbitrators, if only to stop the clock for a process check. Of course, more often than not the advocates will respond, "Let's stick to the book." But I cannot think of any disadvantages in arbitrators serving up new options for the parties.

On balance, do we as arbitrators add value to the field of industrial relations? My answer is a qualified yes, though certainly not as much value as decades ago, when arbitrators were helping parties learn how to work together in new relationships. Present arbitration mirrors the routinization of collective bargaining. In rare instances, we do craft creative settlements and help the parties move beyond individual grievances to fashion solutions to ongoing problems.

Given the magnitude of the challenges facing labor and management, it might be time for arbitrators to reconsider the advice of George Taylor and put their problem-solving hats back on whenever they can.

A Tribute to Union Leaders

The dilemmas facing union leaders are fertile ground for researchers. They may just offer an opportunity to discover how the current and next generation of union leaders will build on the legacy of some of the earlier leaders mentioned in this book. Among them, most notably, are Lynn Williams, the United Steelworkers president who envisioned a labor movement that championed a broad role for unions in corporate governance, and Jack Sheinkman of the Amalgamated Clothing and Textile Workers Union, who recognized that his union had to adapt to a world of expanding imports by working with high-fashion menswear producers. Similarly, the twenty-first century's union leaders facing the "disruption" of completely new ways of working and getting things done could learn from the experience of Don Ephlin, the visionary UAW leader who helped conceive Saturn as a "different kind of company" with a broad role for the union in managing the enterprise. Then there is Kris Rondeau, founder of the Harvard Union of Clerical and Technical Workers, who invented her own community relationship building strategy for organizing and leading a truly modern labor organization. Somehow these leaders were able to manage the expectations of their members, who often favored the status quo, as well as the environment and their management counterparts—all the while making convincing cases for change.

These leaders did not develop their ideas or vision in a vacuum; each of them engaged the parties with different points of view: labor, management, academics, and other groups. Many of us who were lucky enough to interact with them learned firsthand about the challenges they faced in navigating between the economic imperative to change and the political pressure to maintain the status quo. In my experience, engaging with leaders struggling with these dilemmas can have the satisfying side benefit of building friendships that last a lifetime, and I hope this aspect of our field carries on long into the future.

The Fragile Nature of Joint Labor-Management Initiatives

Scholars have always been interested in studying (and, in some cases, fostering) labor-management cooperation and the programs that have resulted. These initiatives have been successful only when significant opportunities for making a difference existed and the parties took ownership of the process. Among examples on the positive side of the ledger I've presented in this book are the Armour Automation Fund, the Continuity of Employment Committee, and the partnership between Kaiser Permanente and the coalition of its unions. On the negative side, there is the example of the Nassau County, New York, project that served the U.S. Department of Labor's need for a demonstration and one political leader's entrepreneurial ambitions (see chapter 4).

But even positive cooperative and partnership relationships that have emerged in response to critical problems have been difficult to sustain over extended periods. Understanding why is a question for researchers and a challenge to future labor and management practitioners. Does the mixed motive nature of labor-management relations dictate that cooperation will almost always be temporary? Or can robust partnerships be sustained through the periodic conflicts that seem inevitable as time goes on? Can new tools of multiparty negotiations and change management be developed to help leaders navigate through these pivotal events?

Progress in helping to understand and strengthen the sustainability of cooperative relationships would go a long way toward cementing a strong role for the study and practice of work and employment relations.

A Tribute to Mentors and Colleagues

By now you have surely noted a theme that carries through each of the chapters of this book: the importance of mentors and colleagues. As I look back on my experiences over sixty years, the most lasting memories are about the people who played those roles. At Harvard, Ben Selekman and Bob Livernash introduced me to industrial relations as a field of study, opened doors to practitioners, and instilled a deep appreciation for getting off campus and into the field to see labor-management relations firsthand. At the University of Chicago, George Shultz demonstrated how to stand up for a junior faculty member in the face of criticism and threats to the Graduate School of Business—an action that served as a model for me when I found myself in the position of dean. Albert Rees, also at GSB, helped all of us think about our roles in a balanced, analytical way, whether we had a proclivity to support unions (as I did) or we were one of the economists with an inclination to oppose them. At Cornell University, Lois Gray guided me through New

York State's complicated union politics. And at MIT, Charles Myers, Abraham Siegel, and Phyllis Wallace welcomed me and allowed me to step in and lead a very talented group of faculty and PhD students through a period of fundamental change.

I could go on and name many more people, but the point here is less to recount how they helped me and more to encourage this tradition of mentoring, community building, and collegial support that has been a hallmark of my experience and, indeed, of our profession. Perhaps it is a by-product of dealing with conflict, negotiations, and other tense situations in our work that binds us together more than what I see in other faculty groups. Whatever it is, it is an asset worth preserving and carrying forward in the years to come.

From Industrial Relations to Work and Employment Relations

The field of industrial relations (now often referred to more appropriately as work and employment relations) has seen its ups and downs over the sixty years reflected in this book. To some extent, its rise and decline paralleled the rise and decline of unions. Some faculty and programs that seem to have faded were too tied to the problems and institutional arrangements they grew up studying or practicing. In some cases, the strong attachment to labor-management relations that was so invigorating when those issues were front page news and intellectually challenging became blinders. But in other cases the field has redefined itself, and some academic programs that broadened and are now training new generations of students to address the changing problems in the world of work continue to thrive. That should serve as fair warning; it is important not to let our values and beliefs in institutions, policies, or practices suppress our willingness to study the subject objectively and critically.

Setting these worries aside, the future of work and employment as a field of study is wide open. Perhaps it is even poised to take center stage in the social sciences and everyday practice and policy, where industrial relations was once situated. The future of work is a major concern given the potential impacts of technological innovations in robotics, digital manufacturing, artificial intelligence, machine learning, and untold inventions yet to come. Sorting out how society copes with these changes and how workers fit into the equation of technological change will occupy scholars from multiple disciplines for the foreseeable future. Those trained in the field of work and employment relations can play prominent roles in the unfolding debates—not so much by predicting the future directions of technological change but by bringing their grounded understanding of work design, training systems, and employee engagement and negotiations into the processes for managing technological change. It will be rewarding to engage and watch this play out.

One final question is worth pondering: Where within university structures will the study of work and employment flourish in the years ahead?

Chicago, Cornell, Harvard, and MIT—the institutions discussed in this book—all once had dedicated faculty in the industrial relations field of study and made distinctive contributions to the field at different points in time. At the start of the twenty-first century, however, the business schools at Chicago and Harvard have no substantial programs or faculty doing research in this area. Meanwhile, Cornell and MIT continue to have strong programs, with dedicated faculty and students contributing in major ways. I believe the differences are related to the earlier point about broadening. The Chicago and Harvard programs did not broaden to deal effectively with the changing nature of work and employment relations, while Cornell and MIT embraced the changes and adapted accordingly.

Perhaps the lesson here is that it is less about where a work and employment relations program is situated—that is, whether it's in a business school, more broadly within a university, or even structured in some other way—than about the ability and willingness to take up new issues and challenges as they arise. Programs that do that well—and especially programs that listen to and support the graduate students and junior faculty members who are the sources of fresh ideas, methods, and issues—will lead the way to the future for our field and for the world of work.

Fortunately, we have been able to expand our agenda at the Sloan School with full support from the administration. Being part of an institution that emphasizes solving problems (the engineer's motto) has provided a culture that fosters innovation. For me that is best illustrated with the subject that has been my passion. Because theory, research, and practice in negotiations has been such a big part of my own work over the years, I will end with a perspective on where things stand now with that topic and where I hope it will go in the years ahead.

Since the 1990s, the field of negotiations and conflict management has shown robust development. This is reflected in an explosion of courses, the creation of research and program centers, the launching of journals, and the formation of professional organizations. Can we say that the field is ready to rest on its laurels? Not yet. There is still much more work needed to understand and manage conflict.

There are a number of agenda items as we look ahead. Organizations have become more complex; achieving consensus across interests and boundaries has become elusive. Even though most managers know the gist of interest-based bargaining, the number of those who use it effectively is not large. But beyond the specific work and employment relations arena, negotiations and conflict management as a field of study offers much to our society. For instance, we live in a polarized political system characterized by fixed-sum behavior. How can we bring more of a problem-solving approach to the political arena? And with race still a deeply adversarial issue—as illustrated by the issues around police-community relations—how can we help there? Then there are all sorts of other places that negotiation theory might inform solutions to pressing societal problems, from the problem of torture in interrogations (see chapter 5), to the "tribal" galvanization of political and cultural positions exacerbated by the use of social media, to the challenges women face in the workplace.

The list could be expanded. My point is that society and our civil order are in desperate need of new ideas. We need savvy individuals who can help opposing parties find integrative outcomes in a mixed-motive world that has become intensely distributive. The field is ripe for research to understand better the barriers and forces that have left so many sectors locked into dysfunctional processes that produce poor outcomes.

We can do so much better as individuals, organizations, communities, and as a society. As it did leading up to the New Deal, industrial relations and its "offspring," work and employment relations, has much to offer, as do negotiation and conflict management.

NOTES

1. An Industrial Relations Journey

1. Slichter, Healy, and Livernash, *The Impact of Collective Bargaining on Management*.

2. Founded in 1905, the Industrial Workers of the World—whose members were often referred to as the Wobblies—was a self-described advocate of "revolutionary industrial unionism" that famously organized all workers in an industry into one big union regardless of specific trade or skill level; this was in sharp contrast to the prevailing craft unions of the time. William D. "Big Bill" Haywood was a founder of the IWW and the central leader of major strikes throughout the United States in the first two decades of the twentieth century. Elizabeth Gurley Flynn played a leading role in many of the IWW's strikes; she was also a founding member of the American Civil Liberties Union and left the IWW to join the Communist Party USA.

3. See Commons, *Institutional Economics*; and Webb and Webb, *Industrial Democracy*.

4. Two standard references that chronicle these basic insights are Kochan, *Collective Bargaining and Industrial Relations*, 1–23; and Kaufman, *The Origins and Evolution of the Field of Industrial Relations in the United States*, 3–18.

5. See Weil, *The Fissured Workplace*.

2. Apprenticeship

1. Slichter, *Union Policies and Industrial Management*.
2. Slichter, Healy, and Livernash, *The Impact of Collective Bargaining*.
3. Slichter, Healy, and Livernash, 6.
4. Avins, Larcom, and Weissbourd, "Why MBAs Haven't Got a Clue about Front-Line Workers."
5. Selekman, Selekman, and Fuller, *Problems in Labor Relations*.
6. Selekman and Selekman, *Power and Morality in a Business Society*.
7. Walton and McKersie, *A Behavioral Theory of Labor Negotiations*.
8. Ironically, the labor-management relationship at Brown & Sharpe changed dramatically. After a period of fruitless negotiations, the IAM accused the company of refusing to bargain in good faith when the company withdrew all clauses in the contract, thereby forcing the union into a strike. At one point during a 1982 strike, police violently attacked a mass picket of eight hundred strikers and sympathizers, which led to a public apology by the Rhode Island governor. Ultimately, the National Labor Relations Board charged Brown & Sharpe with entering into negotiations with the purpose of not reaching agreement with the union—in effect, seeking to break the union so it could operate as an open shop. The Brown & Sharpe story illustrates the cycle that many labor management relationships have followed over the last fifty years: labor management cooperation is not sustained, the competitive position of the company weakens, and new management takes over and institutes radical changes.
9. The former headquarters of Lever Brothers is now part of the MIT Sloan School of Management. A once adjoining soap plant is just a memory.
10. The IUE existed only because its predecessor, the United Electrical, Radio and Machine Workers of America, had been essentially driven out of the CIO because of its alleged ties to the Communist Party. Since then, it has merged with the Communications Workers of America and is now the IUE-CWA.
11. Mechanical engineer Frederick Winslow Taylor, the father of so-called scientific management, pioneered the time study, through which—using a timekeeping device—a task is observed continuously and then broken down into its component parts, which can then be rearranged for maximum efficiency. The time study quickly became associated with what unions called speed-up and characterized as management's effort to intensify the rate of production without any commensurate increase in pay.
12. See, for example, Levy and Temin, "Inequality and Institutions in 20th Century America." For the purpose of historical correctness, it should be noted that this was actually the *third* pact to be known as the Treaty of Detroit. The first, in 1807, was between the United States and four Native American nations: the Chippewa, Ottawa, Potawatomi, and Wyandot. The second was between the U.S. government and the Chippewa and Ottawa.
13. This postwar social contract grew out of legislation during the New Deal that established a minimum wage, other wage and hour regulations, and labor laws that allowed workers to unionize and thus establish the bargaining power with which they could enforce wage determination norms and principles in negotiating with employers.
14. For a review of this history, see Kochan and Dyer, *Shaping the Future of Work*.

15. Livernash, *Comparable Worth.*
16. Foulkes, *Personnel Policies in Large Nonunion Companies.*
17. Dunlop, *Industrial Relations Systems.*

3. Becoming a Journeyman

1. Gordon and Howell, *Higher Education for Business.*
2. Shultz, quoted in Kaufman, *The Origins and Evolution,* 106.
3. See Seidman, *American Labor from Defense to Reconversion;* Seidman, *The Needle Trades;* Seidman, *Union Rights and Union Duties;* and Seidman, *The Yellow Dog Contract.*
4. Reeves, *Freedom and the Foundation.*
5. Formally the Labor Management Reporting and Disclosure Act of 1959, the Landrum-Griffin Act (named for its two sponsors in the U.S. House of Representatives, Democrat Phil Landrum of Georgia and Republican Robert P. Griffin of Michigan) requires that unions hold secret elections, guarantees certain rights of members, barred members of the Communist Party from holding union office (which was ruled unconstitutional in 1965), requires that unions submit annual financial reports to the U.S. Department of Labor, and establishes other rules among its provisions.
6. Lipset, Trow, and Coleman, *Union Democracy.*
7. The IRRA was founded in 1947 and currently is known as the Labor and Employment Relations Association. It includes professionals in academic research and education, compensation and benefits, human resources, labor and employment law, labor and management resources, labor markets, economics, public policy, training and development, and union administration and organizing.
8. Lewis, "Union Relative Wage Effects."
9. Rees and Shultz, *Workers and Wages.*
10. Rees, *The Economics of Trade Unions,* 194–95.
11. Rees and Shultz, *Workers and Wages.*
12. McKersie and Shropshire, "Avoiding Written Grievances."
13. McKersie, "Structural Factors and Negotiations in the International Harvester Company," 302.
14. The UAW was successful, but only after several years of grassroots organizing and winning certification elections. The CIO threw the Farm Equipment Workers Union out of the house of labor in 1949, and this action certainly helped the UAW in its campaign to represent all International Harvester workers. Seymour and the UAW were committed to an ideology that supported the capitalist system.
15. Independent Study Group, *The Public Interest and National Labor Policy.*
16. Slichter, Healy, and Livernash, *The Impact of Collective Bargaining.*
17. Shultz and Aliber, *Guidelines, Informal Controls, and the Marketplace.*
18. Shultz and Weber, *Strategies for the Displaced Worker.*
19. Myers, "The Impact of Computers on Knowledge Industries."
20. Walton and McKersie, *A Behavioral Theory of Labor Negotiations.*
21. Northrup, "Book Review."

22. Hartman, *Collective Bargaining and Productivity.*

23. McKersie and Hunter, *Pay, Productivity, and Collective Bargaining.*

24. McKersie and Brown, "Nonprofessional Hospital Workers."

25. In 1919 the Washburne Elementary School in Chicago was renamed and repurposed as the Washburne Trade and Continuance School, where—with the sponsorship of numerous unions—students of high school age could begin training for various vocational careers. It began with carpentry and electrical engineering, and soon was rapidly expanding its programs.

26. McKersie, "Vitalize Black Enterprise."

27. McKersie, "The Civil Rights Movement and Employment."

28. McKersie, *A Decisive Decade.*

29. Mississippi Power & Light Co. v. Mississippi ex rel. Moore, 487 U.S. 354, No. 86-1970, 1988.

4. Managing a Shop

1. In addition to funds from the state, the ILR School relied on funds from tuition and other locally generated revenue.

2. "Mini-mill" steelmakers use electric arc furnaces to melt scrap metal, as opposed to blast furnaces to melt iron as in the traditional steelmaking process.

3. William Nordhaus, "Retrospective on the 1970s Productivity Slowdown."

4. U.S. GAO, *The Federal Role in Improving Productivity.*

5. Ives, "The New York State School of Industrial and Labor Relations," 40–42.

6. Personal correspondence with the author, 2017.

7. One of those business agents was the father of my MIT colleague Arnie Barnett. He spoke with considerable pride about his son going to college and now teaching at MIT. Arnie Weber, a colleague at the University of Chicago, was also the son of a Local 3 business agent and had studied at the University of Illinois. Both had some of their college expenses covered by a special scholarship that Local 3 established for the children of its members. The fund had an annual budget of approximately $300,000.

8. Shortly thereafter, Jack led a successful effort to merge his union with the International Ladies' Garment Workers Union with a new (and easy-to-remember) name: UNITE, the Union of Needle Trades, Industrial, and Textile Employees.

9. Wirtz, "The Challenge to Free Collective Bargaining," 303.

10. Kochan, Lipsky, Newhart, and Benson, "The Long Haul Effects of Interest Arbitration."

11. Howlett, "Arbitration in the Public Sector."

12. Herbert, "Jerome Lefkowitz."

13. Barr, "Robert D. Helsby."

14. ILR School, "Remembering Harold Newman."

15. Thomas Kochan, interview with the author, Cambridge, Massachusetts, September 12, 2017.

16. Aronson and McKersie, *Economic Consequences of Plant Shutdowns in New York State.*

17. McKersie and McKersie, *Plant Closings*.

18. Ehrenberg, *The Regulatory Process and Labor Earnings*.

19. McKersie, "ILR Dean Robert B. McKersie Discusses Affirmative Action."

5. Returning to the Bench

1. For an example of his work, see MacGregor, *The Human Side of Enterprise*.

2. For examples of these scholars' work, see Lipsky, "The Labor Market Experience of Workers Displaced and Relocated by Plant Shutdowns"; Mitchell, *Essays on Labor and International Trade*; and Sayles and Strauss, *The Local Union*.

3. For examples of Myers's work, see Harbison and Myers, *Management in the Industrial World*; and Myers and Shultz, *The Dynamics of a Labor Market*.

4. For examples of his work, see Piore, *Birds of Passage*; and Piore and Doeringer, *Internal Labor Markets and Manpower Analysis*.

5. The replacement workers organized a new union, the National Air Traffic Controllers Association, in 1987; it had no connection with PATCO. President Clinton lifted the civil service ban on all PATCO strike participants in 1993.

6. Ray Rogers is largely responsible for developing the corporate campaign strategy used by labor unions (and some movements for social change) in their fights with employers. The goal is to force a company to change its behavior not through strike action but by using the results of specialized research and analysis of the company's corporate, financial, and political ties to develop tactics that will put public economic and political pressure on executives, directors, shareholders, and associated institutions. The corporate campaign approach frequently employs boycotts as well. Rogers was instrumental in developing the boycott against J. P. Stevens discussed in chapter 4.

7. Hormel workers at the meatpacking company's headquarters in Austin, Minnesota—represented by Local P-9 of the United Food and Commercial Workers Union—went on strike in August 1985 after management demanded a 23 percent pay cut. The strike, which lasted ten months, garnered considerable national attention. In 1992 the UAW waged a five-month strike against construction equipment maker Caterpillar; the company responded with a threat to replace its entire unionized workforce. Then, in 1994, more than ten thousand UAW members struck again for seventeen months; part of the company's strategy at the time was to move as much production as possible to new, smaller plants in so-called right-to-work states in the South where unions were largely nonexistent. A. E. Staley, a corn-processing company in Decatur, Illinois, decided in July 1993, after a decade of labor disputes, to lock out its workers represented by the Allied Industrial Workers of America. That precipitated a series of events that culminated in Decatur becoming a "war zone" of union battles—with street fighting of the sort that hadn't been seen in the United States since the 1930s—as Caterpillar workers in the same city struck, along with workers at a Firestone tire plant, joining the Staley workers in picketing and public protests.

8. Kochan, Katz, and McKersie, *The Transformation of American Industrial Relations*.

9. Leavitt, "The Old Days, Hot Spots, and Managers' Lib."

10. Cappelli, "Central Government Influence on Public Sector Pay."

11. Verma, "Union and Nonunion Industrial Relations at the Plant Level."

12. Ichniowski, "How Do Labor Relations Matter?"

13. For a review of the high-performance work research, see Appelbaum, Gittell, and Leana, *High Performance Work Practices and Sustainable Economic Growth.*

14. Slichter, *Union Policies and Industrial Management.*

15. Slichter, Healy, and Livernash, *The Impact of Collective Bargaining on Management.*

16. Commons, "American Shoemakers, 1648–1895."

17. Dunlop, *Industrial Relations Systems.*

18. Katz, *Shifting Gears.*

19. Wever, "Power, Weakness and Membership Support in Four U.S. Airline Unions."

20. Cappelli, "Competitive Pressures and Labor Relations in the Airline Industry."

21. Belobaba, Odoni, and Barnhart, *The Global Airline Industry.*

22. Charles E. Wilson, in his confirmation hearing before the U.S. Senate Armed Services Committee, 1952. Quoted in Safire, *Safire's Political Dictionary.* Wilson was responding to a question regarding conflicts of interests and actually said, "For years I thought that what was good for our country was good for General Motors, and vice versa."

23. Unpublished personal report given by the author to the then-dean of the Sloan School; private papers of the author.

24. Rubinstein and Kochan, *Learning from Saturn.*

25. Lovell et al., *Making It Together.*

26. Gomes-Casseres, "Nummi."

27. Katz, *Shifting Gears.*

28. MacDuffie and Krafcik, "Integrating Technology and Human Resources."

29. Metaphorically speaking, *distributive bargaining* can be thought of as the approach to negotiation used when there is a pie to divide, and *integrative bargaining* is about trying to make a bigger pie.

30. See, for example, Bazerman and Neale, *Negotiating Rationally.*

31. Rowe, "Negotiation and Conflict Management."

32. Figuring out how to give more attention to internal negotiations of interacting parties is a very important teaching challenge going forward. Some negotiations courses have taken the plunge.

33. McKersie, "Agency in the Context of Labor Negotiations."

34. Walton, Cutcher-Gershenfeld, and McKersie, *Strategic Negotiations.*

35. In 1998 Guilford purchased the name, colors, and logo of the defunct Pan American World Airways and in 2006 rebranded its rail carrier as Pan Am Railways. At the time of this writing in 2018, the traditional railroad craft unions are back representing the company's workers. Notably, Pan Am Railways, and Guilford before it, are widely regarded as perhaps the worst-managed railroad ever and the worst to work for—with special disdain held out for the private owner, the Mellon family.

36. Fisher, Ury, and Patton, *Getting to Yes.*

37. Cutcher-Gershenfeld et al., "Collective Bargaining in the Twenty-First Century; Cutcher-Gershenfeld and Kochan, "Taking Stock"; Cutcher-Gershenfeld, Kochan, and Wells, "In Whose Interest?"

38. San Juan Unified School District and San Juan Teachers Association, *Collective Bargaining Contract.*

39. Fonstad, "Report of Findings."

40. Shultz and McKersie, "Participation–Achievement–Reward Systems"; Shultz and McKersie, "Stimulating Productivity."

41. See, for example, Bennis, *On Becoming a Leader.*

42. Lesieur, *The Scanlon Plan.*

43. The Scanlon Plan is still in place in several companies in Grand Rapids, Michigan. The National Center for Employee Ownership is a leading proponent of these plans.

44. Kochan et al., *Healing Together.*

45. McKersie et al., "Bargaining Theory Meets Interest-Based Negotiations."

46. A crucial decision that sealed CBF's fate took place at a 2003 meeting when labor members vetoed a proposal to merge with the Aspen Institute, an international think tank founded in 1950. The unionists felt their influence would be diminished in a larger organization.

47. The CBF eventually issued a report of its discussions. See Collective Bargaining Forum, *New Directions for Labor and Management.*

48. Truman, "Address at the Opening Session of the Labor-Management Conference." It should be noted that two years later Congress passed—and then overrode Truman's veto of—the Taft-Hartley Act, which restricted sharply the activities and power of labor unions. Despite that veto, Truman ended up using Taft-Hartley a dozen times during his presidency to combat striking unions.

49. The Intelligence Science Board was chartered in 2002 to advise the Office of the Director of National Intelligence on emerging scientific and technical issues of special importance to the intelligence community, using outside expert advice and, as its mission stated, "unconventional thinking." The DNI disbanded the board in 2010.

50. The case was notable because of Soufan's reported approach. A Lebanese American former FBI agent, Soufan spoke fluent Arabic and worked hard to develop a rapport with sources. After the September 11, 2001, attacks in New York City, for instance, when he was the only FBI agent in New York City who spoke Arabic, he reportedly sat on the floor with suspects, sharing tea and engaging in friendly arguments over politics and religion while educing intelligence.

51. Kolb, *The Mediators.*

52. In 2004 the Union of Needle Trades, Industrial, and Textile Employees (UNITE) and the Hotel Employees and Restaurant Employees International Union (HERE) effected an unusual merger of unions representing workers in largely unrelated industries, bringing together nearly a half million members and solving two problems: HERE had significant organizing opportunities but little cash to pursue them, and UNITE was wealthy, by labor union standards, but losing significant numbers of members as its primary economic sector moved out of the United States. The union today is known as UNITE HERE.

53. At the time I did not wonder about having the receptionist on an upper floor of a building of only three stories. But given the violence that has often swirled around the Teamsters union in general and Local 25 in particular, I came to realize that having the

first floor as a buffer where husky Teamsters could be stationed was a wise security measure.

54. PIE comes from the company's original name, Pacific Intermountain Express.

55. Jay Siegel, correspondence with the author, undated.

56. In a defined *benefit* pension plan, the employer promises a specific pension payment upon retirement that is predetermined, based on a formula that accounts for the employee's earnings history, length of service, age, and other factors. In a defined *contribution* plan, more commonly known as a retirement saving plan, employer and employee contributions are defined in advance but the benefit to be paid out upon retirement is not known in advance.

57. The saga of these multiemployer funds continued. When United Parcel Service pulled out of the Central States Fund in 2007, that fund was soon in trouble. The obligations were substantial given the large number of retirees and, given that payments into the fund were based on per-capita assessments, the contributions were inadequate because of the declining number of workers employed by the remaining companies

58. William M. Vaughn III, from a roundup of written reflections in the personal papers of the author, undated.

59. Hoerr, "Solidaritas at Harvard."

60. Mena, "Layoffs Due to Recession Stopped after June."

61. Nelson, "MIT Endowment Decreased."

62. When budget cuts became necessary at the ILR School in the 1970s, we developed a plan for layoffs that did not stage the reductions. This allowed us to say to the organization, "We have taken a hit, but there will be no further reductions in the foreseeable future. So let's get back to normal as quickly as we can."

63. Thurow, quoted in MIT, "Phyllis A. Wallace."

64. Piore and Doeringer, *Internal Labor Markets.*

65. Kochan and Dyer, *Shaping the Future of Work.*

66. For some examples of Osterman's work, see Osterman, *Who Will Care For Us?*; Osterman et al., *Working in America*; and Osterman and Shulman, *Good Jobs America.*

67. For examples of these scholars' work, see Abraham and Houseman, *Job Security in America*; Black and Lynch, "How to Compete"; Black and Lynch, "What's Driving the New Economy?"; and Landers, Rebitzer, and Taylor, "Rat Race Redux."

6. Taking Stock and Looking Ahead

1. This was an attack on miners by the National Guard and a private police force working for the Colorado Fuel and Iron Company, whose chief owner was John D. Rockefeller. Perhaps this history is what motivated the Rockefeller Foundation decades later to provide funds for the creation of the Industrial Relations Sections at MIT and Princeton University.

2. Brandeis, *The Curse of Bigness.*

3. The now-defunct Labor Policy Association enrolled firms interested in supporting legal measures to constrain the role of unions. For example, in 1994 testimony before the federal Commission on the Future of Labor-Management Relations, Steven Darien

of the pharmaceutical giant Merck—speaking on behalf of the Association—endorsed an "option" in the commission's *Fact Finding Report* regarding how to deal with "employee involvement" at its member companies. The option took direct aim at unions: the National Labor Relations Act "should no longer limit the freedom of nonunion employers to establish procedures by which its employees will 'deal with' (as opposed to 'collectively bargain' about) conditions of employment." See Darien, "Statement of the Labor Policy Association."

4. Bagdikian, "Laboring under Illusions."

5. Kochan, Katz, and McKersie, *The Transformation of American Industrial Relations.*

6. Lovell, "Principles for New Employment Relationships."

7. Black and Lynch, "How to Compete."

8. The National Domestic Workers Alliance, founded in 2007, is a confederation of over sixty organizations and chapters comprising more than twenty-thousand housekeepers, nannies, and eldercare providers in thirty-six U.S. cities and seventeen states. The National Taxi Workers' Alliance began in New York City and in 2011 became an AFL-CIO affiliate—the first group of independent, non-hourly-wage contractors in the oldest U.S. labor federation. The Restaurant Opportunities Center United works to improve wages and working people for fourteen million Americans in the restaurant industry.

9. Whereas "company unions"—worker organizations in which employers played a dominant role—were outlawed in the United States in 1935 as part of the NLRA and deemed contrary to international labor law by Convention 98 of the International Labour Organization (because they were not "independent" trade unions), such unions are common in Japan. Loyalty to one's employer has long been a mainstay of Japanese culture, and the lack of independence of company unions is thus not considered detrimental in Japanese society. Nevertheless, there are some independent unions in the country.

10. In many cases management dominated the process of establishing a structure for workers' voices and free collective bargaining did not exist. That was why the NLRA prohibited collective bargaining unless the organization on the side of the table was an independent organization representing worker interests—which, in most cases, meant a trade union. It was with that history in mind that the AFL-CIO so vigorously opposed the 1995 Teamwork for Employees and Managers (TEAM) Act and other efforts to create structures that do not adhere to the principle of free trade unions. The TEAM Act, vetoed by President Bill Clinton, was designed to weaken the NLRA and make it possible for employers to displace independent unions that bargained freely on behalf of workers.

11. Follett was a pioneer in the fields of organizational theory and organizational behavior. Her work was informed by her early career as a social worker in the Roxbury neighborhood of Boston, where she developed her theories in group dynamics. It was Follett's work that led to the concept of matrix-style organizations. She is also credited with making significant contributions to the idea of "reciprocal relationships," advocating what she called integration based on her concept of "power with" rather than "power over." She also coined the term "win-win" to describe her work with groups.

12. See, for example, Stakeholder Alignment Collaborative, "Five Ways Consortia Can Catalyze Open Science."

13. Kochan and Dyer, *Shaping the Future of Work*.

14. Taylor, "Effectuation of Arbitration by Collective Bargaining."

15. Colvin, "An Empirical Study of Employment Arbitration."

16. Braden, "Problems in Labor Arbitration."

17. Goldberg, "Mediation of Grievances under a Collective Bargaining Contract."

18. Zack, "The Quest for Finality in Airline Disputes."

19. In 2011 the Wisconsin legislature passed Act 10, also known as the Wisconsin Budget Repair Bill, ostensibly to address a projected state budget deficit of $3.6 billion. But Republican governor Scott Walker had made little effort to conceal the fact that a major impetus of the bill was to attack Wisconsin's strong public-sector unions. The effort provoked a massive occupation of the Wisconsin state capitol building by unionists and their supporters. Ultimately upheld by the Wisconsin Supreme Court, the act limits collective bargaining for most public employees to wages and sets a cap for wage increases unless approved by referendum. Further, it limits contract terms to one year and freezes wages if a contract expires before a new contract is settled. Going well beyond "budget repair," the act requires that collective bargaining units take annual votes to maintain certification as a union, eliminates the requirement that members of those units pay dues, and prohibits employers from collecting dues on a union's behalf.

Bibliography

Abraham, Katherine G., and Susan N. Houseman. *Job Security in America: Lessons from Germany*. Washington, DC: Brookings Institution Press, 2010.

Appelbaum, Eileen, Jody Hoffer Gittell, and Carrie Leana. *High Performance Work Practices and Sustainable Economic Growth*. Washington, DC: Center for Economic and Policy Research, 2011.

Aronson, Robert Louis, and Robert B. McKersie. *Economic Consequences of Plant Shutdowns in New York State*. Ithaca, NY: New York State School of Industrial and Labor Relations, Cornell University, 1980.

Avins, Jeremy, Megan Larcom, and Jenny Weissbourd. "Why MBAs Haven't Got a Clue about Front-Line Workers." *Boston Globe*, April 26, 2018.

Bagdikian, Ben H. "Laboring under Illusions: Maximizing Profits at the *Washington Post*." *Washington Monthly*, January 1976, 26–35.

Barr, Martin L. "Robert D. Helsby." New York State Public Employment Relations Board. http://www.perb.ny.gov/wp-content/uploads/2018/04/Helsby.pdf.

Bazerman, Max H., and Margaret A. Neale. *Negotiating Rationally*. New York: Free Press, 1992.

Belobaba, Peter, Amedeo Odoni, and Cynthia Barnhart, eds. *The Global Airline Industry*. New York: Wiley, 2009.

Bennis, Warren. *On Becoming a Leader*. New York: Basic Books, 1989.

Black, Sandra E., and Lisa M. Lynch. "How to Compete: The Impact of Workplace Practices and Information Technology on Productivity." *Review of Economics and Statistics* 83, no. 3 (2001): 434–45.

——. "What's Driving the New Economy? The Benefits of Workplace Innovation." *Economic Journal* 114, no. 493 (2004): F97–F116.

Braden, J. Noble. "Problems in Labor Arbitration." *Monthly Labor Review* 13 (1948): 143–69.

Brandeis, Louis D. *The Curse of Bigness: Miscellaneous Papers of Louis D. Brandeis.* Edited by Clarence M. Lewis. New York: Viking, 1934.

Cappelli, Peter. "Central Government Influence on Public Sector Pay." DPhil diss., University of Oxford, Nuffield College, 1984.

——. "Competitive Pressures and Labor Relations in the Airline Industry." *Industrial Relations: A Journal of Economy and Society* 24, no. 3 (1985): 316–38.

Collective Bargaining Forum. *New Directions for Labor and Management.* Washington, DC: U.S. Department of Labor, 1987.

Colvin, Alexander J. S. "An Empirical Study of Employment Arbitration: Case Outcomes and Processes." *Journal of Empirical Legal Studies* 8, no. 1 (2011): 1–23.

Commons, John R. "American Shoemakers, 1648–1895: A Sketch of Industrial Evolution." *Quarterly Journal of Economics* 24, no. 1 (1909): 39–84.

——. *Institutional Economics.* New York: Macmillan, 1934.

Cutcher-Gershenfeld, Joel, and Thomas A. Kochan. "Taking Stock: Collective Bargaining at the Turn of the Century." *Industrial and Labor Relations Review* 58, no. 1 (2004): 3–26.

Cutcher-Gershenfeld, Joel, Thomas A. Kochan, John-Paul Ferguson, and Betty Barrett. "Collective Bargaining in the Twenty-First Century: A Negotiations Institution at Risk." *Negotiation Journal* 23, no. 3 (2007): 249–65.

Cutcher-Gershenfeld, Joel, Thomas A. Kochan, and John Calhoun Wells. "In Whose Interest? A First Look at National Survey Data on Interest-Based Bargaining in Labor Relations." *Industrial Relations* 40, no. 1 (2001): 1–21.

Darien, Steven M. *Statement of the Labor Policy Association before the Commission on the Future of Worker-Management Relations.* August 1994. Cornell University ILR School Digital Commons. https://digitalcommons.ilr.cornell.edu/cgi/viewcontent.cgi?article=1339&context=key_workplace.

Dunlop, John Thomas. *Industrial Relations Systems.* New York: Holt, 1958.

Ehrenberg, Ronald G. *The Regulatory Process and Labor Earnings.* New York: Academic Press, 1979.

Fisher, Roger, William L. Ury, and Bruce Patton. *Getting to Yes: Negotiating Agreement without Giving In,* 2nd ed. New York: Penguin, 1991.

Fonstad, Nils. "Report of Findings from the Pilot Study Examining the Role of a Two-Day Seminar on Interest-Based Bargaining in the Negotiation Practices of Participants." Working Paper 99-5, Harvard Law School, Program on Negotiation, Cambridge, MA, 1999.

Foulkes, Fred K. *Personnel Policies in Large Nonunion Companies.* Englewood Cliffs, NJ: Prentice Hall, 1980.

Goldberg, Stephen B. "Mediation of Grievances under a Collective Bargaining Contract: An Alternative to Arbitration." *Northwestern University Law Review* 77 (1982): 270–315.

Gomes-Casseres, Ben. "Nummi: What Toyota Learned and GM Didn't." *Harvard Business Review*, September 1, 2009, 73.

Gordon, Robert A., and James E. Howell. *Higher Education for Business*. New York: Columbia University Press, 1959.

Harbison, Frederick Harris, and Charles Andrew Myers. *Management in the Industrial World: An International Analysis*. New York: McGraw-Hill, 1959.

Hartman, Paul T. *Collective Bargaining and Productivity: The Mechanization and Modernization Agreement*. Berkeley: University of California Press, 1969.

Herbert, William A. "Jerome Lefkowitz: A Pragmatic Intellect and Major Figure in Taylor Law History." New York State Public Employment Relations Board. http://www.perb.ny.gov/wp-content/uploads/2018/04/lefkowitz.pdf.

Hoerr, John. "Solidaritas at Harvard." *American Prospect* 14 (1993): 67–82.

Howlett, Robert. "Arbitration in the Public Sector." In *Proceedings of the 15th Annual Institute on Labor Law, the Southwestern Legal Foundation*, edited by Virginia Shook Cameron, 234. New York: Bender, 1969.

Ichniowski, Bernard E. "How Do Labor Relations Matter? A Study of Productivity in Eleven Manufacturing Plants." PhD diss., Massachusetts Institute of Technology, Alfred P. Sloan School of Management, 1983.

Independent Study Group of the Committee for Economic Development. *The Public Interest and National Labor Policy*. Washington, DC: Committee for Economic Development, 1961.

Ives, Irving M. "The New York State School of Industrial and Labor Relations—A New Venture in Education." *Journal of Educational Sociology* 19, no. 1 (1945): 40–42.

Katz, Harry C. *Shifting Gears: Changing Labor Relations in the U.S. Automobile Industry*. Cambridge, MA: MIT Press, 1985.

Kaufman, Bruce E. *The Origins and Evolution of the Field of Industrial Relations in the United States*. Ithaca, NY: ILR Press, 1993.

Kochan, Thomas A. *Collective Bargaining and Industrial Relations: From Theory to Policy and Practice*. Homewood, IL: Irwin, 1980.

Kochan, Thomas A., and Lee Dyer. *Shaping the Future of Work: A Handbook for Action and a New Social Contract*. Cambridge, MA: MIT Press, 2017.

Kochan, Thomas A., Adrienne E. Eaton, Robert B. McKersie, and Paul S. Adler. *Healing Together: The Labor-Management Partnership at Kaiser Permanente*. Ithaca, NY: ILR Press, 2009.

Kochan, Thomas A., Harry Charles Katz, and Robert B. McKersie. *The Transformation of American Industrial Relations*. Ithaca, NY: ILR Press, 1986. Reprint, New York: Basic Books, 1989.

Kochan, Thomas A., David B. Lipsky, Mary Newhart, and Alan Benson. "The Long Haul Effects of Interest Arbitration: The Case of New York State's Taylor Law." *ILR Review* 63, no. 4 (2010): 565–84.

Kolb, Deborah M. *The Mediators*. Cambridge, MA: MIT Press, 1983.

Landers, Renee M., James B. Rebitzer, and Lowell J. Taylor. "Rat Race Redux: Adverse Selection in the Determination of Work Hours in Law Firms." *American Economic Review* 86, no. 3 (1996), 329–48.

Leavitt, Theodore. "The Old Days, Hot Spots, and Managers' Lib." *Administrative Science Quarterly* 41, no. 2 (1996): 288–300.

Lesieur, Frederick G. *The Scanlon Plan: A Frontier in Labor-Management Cooperation.* Vol. 1. Cambridge, MA: MIT Press, 1968.

Levy, Frank, and Peter Temin. "Inequality and Institutions in 20th Century America." NBER Working Paper 13106, National Bureau of Economic Research, Cambridge, MA, May 2007.

Lewis, H. Gregg. "Union Relative Wage Effects." In *Handbook of Labor Economics*, vol. 2, edited by Orley C. Ashenfelter and Richard Layard, 1139–81. Amsterdam: Elsevier, 1986.

Lipset, Seymour Martin, Martin Trow, and James Coleman. *Union Democracy: The Internal Politics of the International Typographical Union.* New York: Free Press, 1956.

Lipsky, David. "The Labor Market Experience of Workers Displaced and Relocated by Plant Shutdowns: The General Foods Case." PhD diss., Massachusetts Institute of Technology, 1967.

Livernash, E. Robert, ed. *Comparable Worth: Issues and Alternatives.* Washington, DC: Equal Employment Advisory Council, 1980.

Lovell, Malcolm R. "Principles for New Employment Relationships: A Report of the Collective Bargaining Forum." *Perspectives on Work* 3, no. 1 (1999): 32–39.

Lovell, Malcolm R., Susan Goldberg, Larry W. Hunter, Thomas A. Kochan, John Paul MacDuffie, Andrew Martin, and Robert McKersie. *Making It Together: The Chrysler-UAW Modern Operating Agreement.* Washington, DC: U.S. Department of Labor, 1991.

MacDuffie, John P., and John Krafcik. "Integrating Technology and Human Resources for High-Performance Manufacturing: Evidence from the International Auto Industry." In *Transforming Organizations*, edited by Thomas A. Kochan and Michael Useem, 209–26. New York: Oxford University Press, 1992.

MacGregor, Douglas. *The Human Side of Enterprise.* New York: McGraw-Hill, 1960.

Massachusetts Institute of Technology. "Phyllis A. Wallace" (obituary). *The Tech* 112, no. 65 (1993): 1, 10.

McKersie, Robert B. "Agency in the Context of Labor Negotiations." In *Negotiating on Behalf of Others: Advice to Lawyers, Business Executives, Sports Agents, Diplomats, Politicians, and Everybody Else*, vol. 1, edited by Robert H. Mnookin and Lawrence E. Susskind, 181–85. Thousand Oaks, CA: Sage, 1999.

——. "The Civil Rights Movement and Employment." *Industrial Relations* 3, no. 3 (May 1964): 1–21.

——. *A Decisive Decade: An Insider's View of the Chicago Civil Rights Movement during the 1960s.* Carbondale: Southern Illinois University Press, 2013.

——"ILR Dean Robert B. McKersie Discusses Affirmative Action." *Cornell Chronicle*, March 2, 1972, 6.

——. "Structural Factors and Negotiations in the International Harvester Company." In *Structure of Collective Bargaining*, edited by Arnold R. Weber, 279–303. Glencoe, IL: Free Press of Glencoe, 1961.

——. "Vitalize Black Enterprise." *Harvard Business Review*, September–October 1968, 88–99.

McKersie, Robert B., and Monte Brown. "Nonprofessional Hospital Workers and a Union Organizing Drive." *Quarterly Journal of Economics* 77, no. 3 (1963): 372–404.

McKersie, Robert B., and Laurence Colvin Hunter. *Pay, Productivity, and Collective Bargaining*. New York: Macmillan, 1973.

McKersie, Robert B., and William S. McKersie. *Plant Closings: What Can Be Learned from Best Practice*. Washington, DC: U.S. Department of Labor, 1982.

McKersie, Robert B., Teresa Sharpe, Thomas A. Kochan, Adrienne E. Eaton, George Strauss, and Marty Morgenstern. "Bargaining Theory Meets Interest-Based Negotiations: A Case Study." *Industrial Relations: A Journal of Economy and Society* 47, no. 1 (2008): 66–96.

McKersie, Robert B., and William W. Shropshire. "Avoiding Written Grievances: A Successful Program." *Journal of Business* 35, no. 2 (1962): 135–52.

Mena, Elijah L. "Layoffs Due to Recession Stopped after June." *The Tech* 130, no. 3 (2010): 1, 6.

Mitchell, Daniel J. B. *Essays on Labor and International Trade*. Los Angeles: Institute of Industrial Relations, University of California, 1970.

Myers, Charles Andrew. "The Impact of Computers on Knowledge Industries, Part II." Working Paper, Massachusetts Institute of Technology, Alfred P. Sloan School of Management, Cambridge, MA, 1969.

Myers, Charles Andrew, and George P. Shultz. *The Dynamics of a Labor Market: A Study of the Impact of Employment Changes on Labor Mobility, Job Satisfactions, and Company and Union Policies*. New York: Prentice Hall, 1951.

Nelson, Meghan. "MIT Endowment Decreased by 20 Percent Last Fiscal Year, Ending 7 Years of Growth." *The Tech* 129, no. 3 (2009): 1, 13.

New York State School of Industrial and Labor Relations at Cornell University. "Remembering Harold Newman: Mentor and ILR Friend Honored by Scheinman Institute." July 24, 2008. https://www.ilr.cornell.edu/news/remembering-harold-newman.

Nordhaus, William. "Retrospective on the 1970s Productivity Slowdown." NBER Working Paper No. 10950, National Bureau of Economic Research, Cambridge, MA, 2004.

Northrup, Herbert R. "Book Review: Organizational Behavior: A Behavioral Theory of Labor Negotiations." *ILR Review* 19, no. 3 (1966): 459–60.

Osterman, Paul. *Who Will Care For Us? Long-Term Care and the Long-Term Workforce*. New York: Russell Sage Foundation, 2017.

Osterman, Paul, Thomas A. Kochan, Richard M. Locke, and Michael J. Piore. *Working in America: A Blueprint for the New Labor Market*. Cambridge, MA: MIT Press, 2011.

Osterman, Paul, and Beth Shulman. *Good Jobs America*. New York: Russell Sage Foundation, 2011.

Piore, Michael J. *Birds of Passage: Migrant Labor and Industrial Societies*. Cambridge: Cambridge University Press, 1979.

Piore, Michael J., and Peter B. Doeringer. *Internal Labor Markets and Manpower Analysis*. Lexington, MA: Heath Lexington, 1976.

Rees, Albert. *The Economics of Trade Unions*. Chicago: University of Chicago Press, 1962.

Rees, Albert, and George P. Shultz. *Workers and Wages in an Urban Labor Market.* Chicago: University of Chicago Press, 1962.

Reeves, Thomas C. *Freedom and the Foundation: The Fund for the Republic in the Era of McCarthyism.* New York: Knopf, 1969.

Reuther, Elisabeth Dickmeyer. *Putting the World Together: My Father Walter Reuther, the Liberal Warrior.* Lake Orion, MI: LivingFocre, 2004, 350–51.

Rowe, Mary. "Negotiation and Conflict Management." Course No. 15.667, Massachusetts Institute of Technology, Sloan School of Management, Spring 2001. https://ocw.mit.edu/courses/sloan-school-of-management/15-667-negotiation-and-conflict-management-spring-2001/.

Rubinstein, Saul A., and Thomas A. Kochan. *Learning from Saturn: Possibilities for Corporate Governance and Employee Relations.* Ithaca, NY: ILR Press, 2000.

Safire, William. *Safire's Political Dictionary.* New York: Oxford University Press, 2008.

San Juan Unified School District and San Juan Teachers Association. *Collective Bargaining Contract between San Juan Unified School District and San Juan Teachers Association.* July 1, 2017. https://www.sanjuan.edu/cms/lib/CA01902727/Centricity/Domain/4377/SJTA%20COLLECTIVE%20BARGAINING%20CONTRACT_1618_Revised%20July%201%202017.pdf.

Sayles, Leonard R., and George Strauss. *The Local Union: Its Place in the Industrial Plant.* New York: Harper, 1953.

Seidman, Joel I. *American Labor from Defense to Reconversion.* Chicago: University of Chicago Press, 1953.

——. *The Needle Trades.* New York: Farrar & Rinehart, 1942.

——. *Union Rights and Union Duties.* New York: Harcourt, Brace, 1943.

——. *The Yellow Dog Contract.* Baltimore: Johns Hopkins University Press, 1932.

Selekman, Benjamin M., Sylvia Kopald Selekman, and Stephen H. Fuller. *Problems in Labor Relations.* New York: McGraw-Hill, 1950.

Selekman, Sylvia Kopald, and Benjamin M. Selekman. *Power and Morality in a Business Society.* New York: McGraw-Hill, 1956.

Sharone, Ofer. *Flawed System/Flawed Self: Job Searching and Unemployment Experiences.* Chicago: University of Chicago Press, 2013.

Shultz, George P., and Robert Z. Aliber. *Guidelines, Informal Controls, and the Marketplace.* Chicago: University of Chicago Press, 1966.

Shultz, George P., and Robert B. McKersie. "Participation–Achievement–Reward Systems (PAR)." *Journal of Management Studies* 10, no. 2 (1973): 141–61.

——. "Stimulating Productivity: Choices, Problems and Shares." *British Journal of Industrial Relations* 5, no. 1 (1967): 1–18.

Shultz, George P., and Arnold R. Weber. *Strategies for the Displaced Worker: Confronting Economic Change.* New York: Harper, 1966.

Slichter, Sumner H. *Union Policies and Industrial Management.* Washington, DC: Brookings Institution, 1941.

Slichter, Sumner H., James J. Healy, and E. Robert Livernash. *The Impact of Collective Bargaining on Management.* Washington, DC: Brookings Institution, 1960.

Stakeholder Alignment Collaborative. "Five Ways Consortia Can Catalyze Open Science." *Nature* 543: 615–18.

Taylor, George W. "Effectuation of Arbitration by Collective Bargaining." In *Critical Issues in Labor Arbitration: Proceedings of the Tenth Annual Meeting, National Academy of Arbitrators*, edited by Jean T. McKelvey. Washington, DC: BNA, 1957.

Truman, Harry S. "Address at the Opening Session of the Labor-Management Conference," November 5, 1945. American Presidency Project. https://www.presidency.ucsb.edu/node/230498.

U.S. General Accounting Office. *The Federal Role in Improving Productivity: Is the National Center for Productivity and Quality of Working Life the Proper Mechanism?* Washington, DC: U.S. General Accounting Office, 1978.

Verma, Anil. "Union and Nonunion Industrial Relations at the Plant Level." PhD diss., Massachusetts Institute of Technology, Alfred P. Sloan School of Management, 1983.

Walton, Richard E., Joel Cutcher-Gershenfeld, and Robert B. McKersie. *Strategic Negotiations: A Theory of Change in Labor-Management Relations*. Cambridge, MA: Harvard Business Review Press, 1994. Reprint, Ithaca, NY: ILR Press, 2000.

Walton, Richard E., and Robert B. McKersie. *A Behavioral Theory of Labor Negotiations: An Analysis of a Social Interaction*. New York: McGraw-Hill, 1965. Reprint, Ithaca, NY: ILR Press, 1991.

Webb, Sydney, and Beatrice Webb. *Industrial Democracy*. London: Longmans, 1897.

Weil, David. *The Fissured Workplace: Why Work Became So Bad for So Many and What Can Be Done to Improve It*. Cambridge, MA: Harvard University Press, 2014.

Wever, Kirsten R. "Power, Weakness and Membership Support in Four U.S. Airline Unions." PhD diss., Massachusetts Institute of Technology, Department of Political Science, 1987.

Wirtz, W. Willard. "The Challenge to Free Collective Bargaining." In National Academy of Arbitrators, *Proceedings of the Sixteenth Annual Meeting*, 1963.

Zack, Arnold M. "The Quest for Finality in Airline Disputes: A Case for Arb-Med." In American Arbitration Association, *American Arbitration Association Handbook on Labor Arbitration & ADR*, 3rd ed., 317–325. Huntington, NY: Juris, 2016.

INDEX

Note: Italicized page numbers with a *G* indicate photographs in the gallery located after page 66.

CPSIA information can be obtained
at www.ICGtesting.com
Printed in the USA
LVHW090359180319
610822LV00033B/18/P